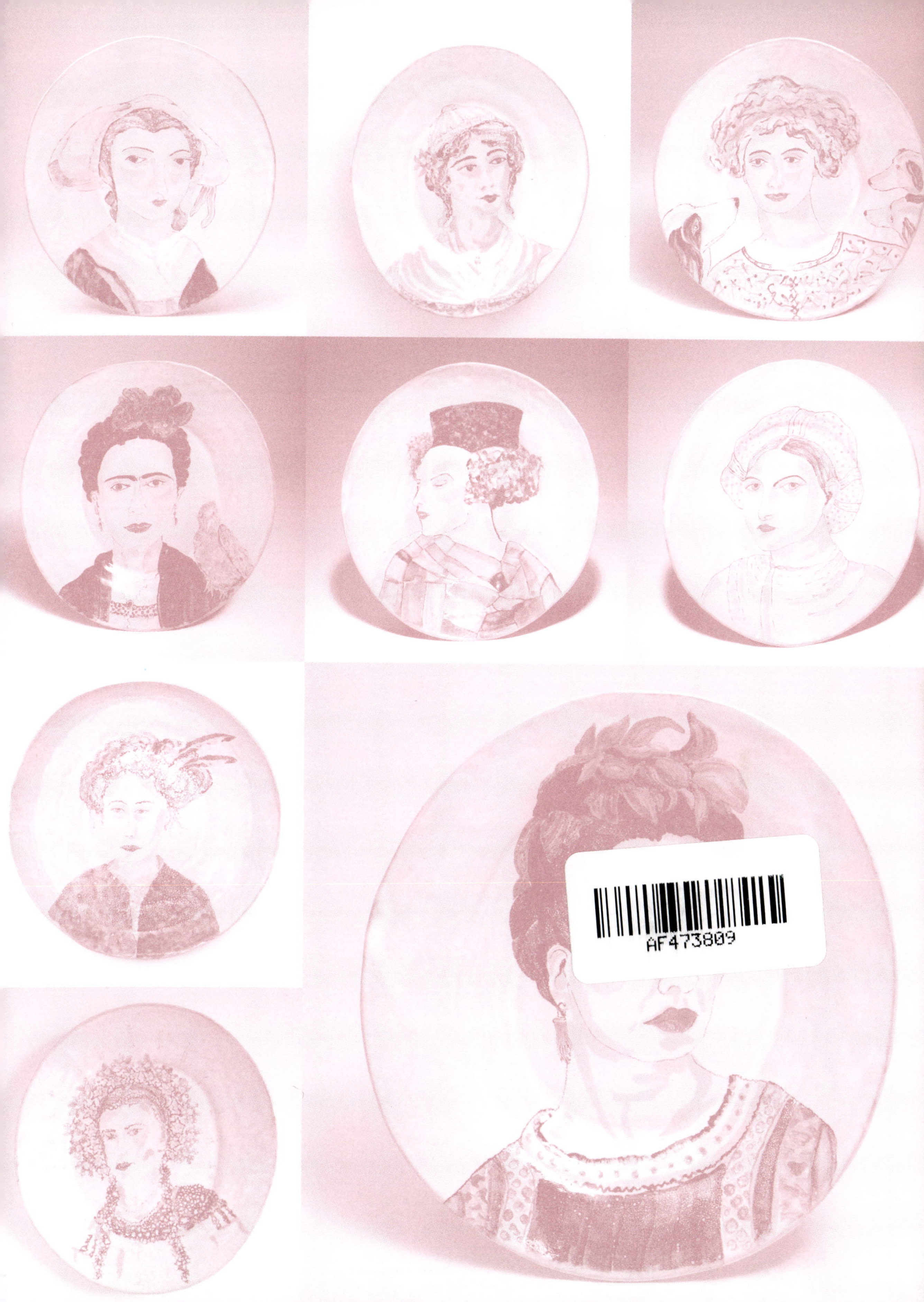

A Journey Painted in Clay

Agalis Manessi

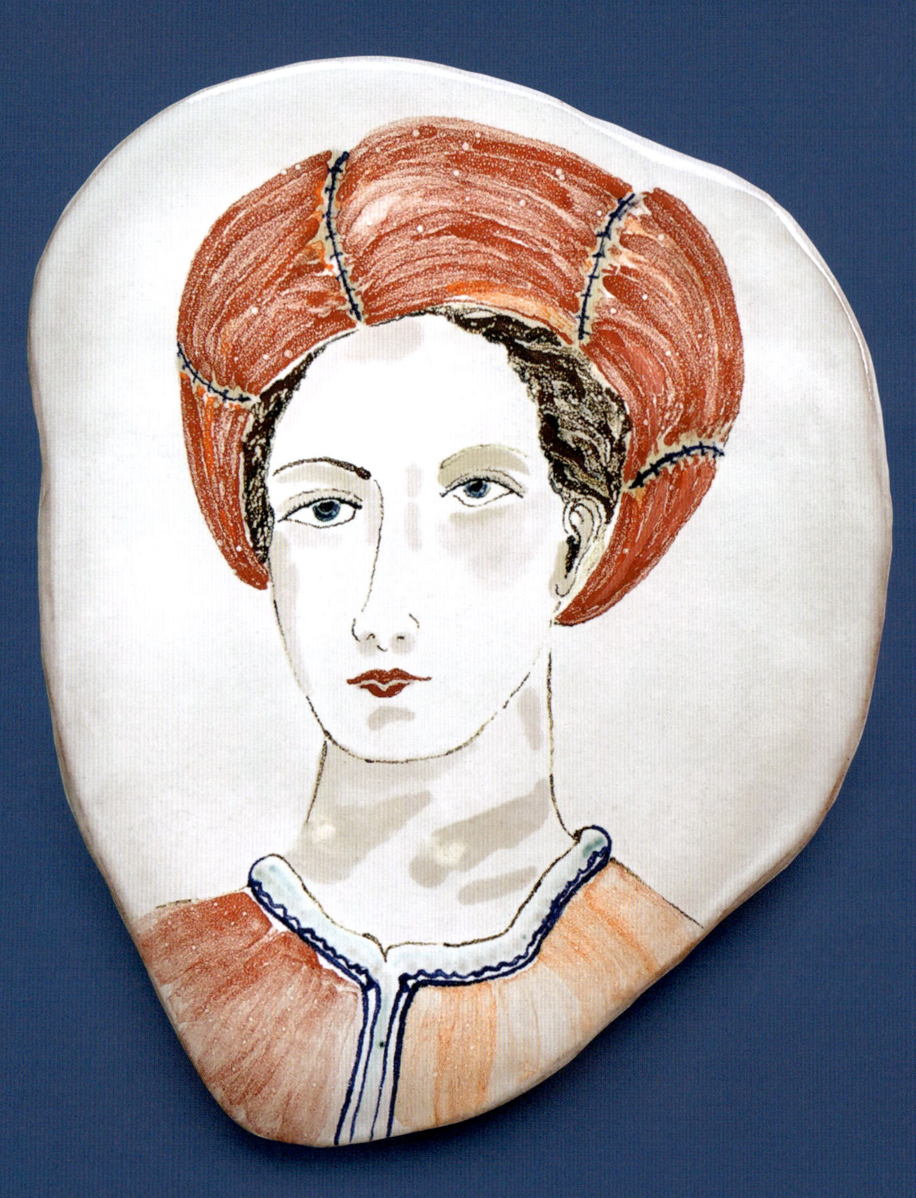

A Journey Painted in Clay

Agalis Manessi

UNICORN

'To those who tax me with my writing and drawing, I say that I have done what I can and am not obliged to do more. If they bring the wording, the writing and the drawing to greater perfection, I shall be obliged to them; then what I hope will happen to the art of the potter will also happen to this labour of mine – seen by many and by many handled, it will arrive at its perfection'.

–Cipriano Piccolpasso
The Three Books of the Potter's Art, 1556

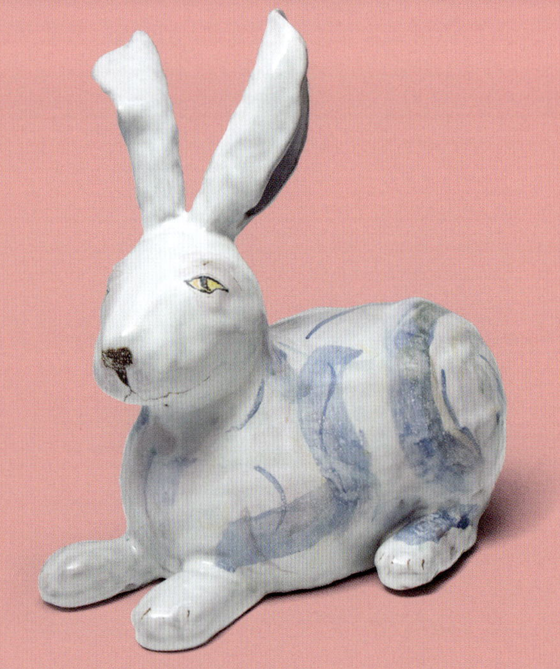

Published in 2023 by Unicorn an imprint of
Unicorn Publishing Group
Charleston Studio
Meadow Business Centre
Lewes BN8 5RW
www.unicornpublishing.org

All images Rob Kesseler and Agalis Manessi unless otherwise stated below:

p.11 Petro Manessi; p.23 Museum of the Home, London; p.40 Kind permission of the V&A; p.60 (top) The Courtauld, London; p.66 (bottom) National Portrait Gallery; p.68 the British Museum; p.72 The Charleston Trust © The Estates of Duncan Grant and Vanessa Bell, DACS 2021; p.65 © Musée d'Orsay, Dist. RMN-Grand Palais / Patrice Schmidt; p.122, p.123 Kind permission of the Archaeological Museum, Corfu, Greece; p.127 Marco Kesseler

ISBN 978 1 91139 757 1

10 9 8 7 6 5 4 3 2 1

Designed by Matthew Wilson
Printed by Finetone Ltd

agalismanessi.com

Contents

Foreword

Jenni Lomax

Amongst the ethereal light, heavenly colour and emotional intensity of Giotto's cycle of paintings for the Scrovegni Chapel lies a love of simple, earthly things. Domestic objects, working people and the animals that are a part of daily life are painted with as much love and care as persons of noble birth, saints or angels. This hallowed space in the Italian city of Padua is a far cry from Agalis Manessi's basement studio in Kennington, south London. However, time spent with Manessi alongside her raw clays and glazes, works in progress and finished pieces, soon reveals a close affinity with Giotto's way of recognising the objects and creatures that fundamentally sustain and enhance life as well as bearing witness to it.

Growing up on the Greek Island of Corfu, Manessi (b. 1952) had little or no experience of seeing art in museums or galleries. She met with the iconic forms of classical Greek sculpture only in reproduction or in gift-shop interpretations. Despite this limited knowledge of art history, her love of making and drawing – and of observing the world she lived in – impelled her towards becoming an artist. When she moved to London in the early 1970s to study art she already knew she wanted to work with clay and ceramics, even though her only experience with the material was through playing with mud

Fresco Figure in Cobalt, 19 × 18cm, 2023.

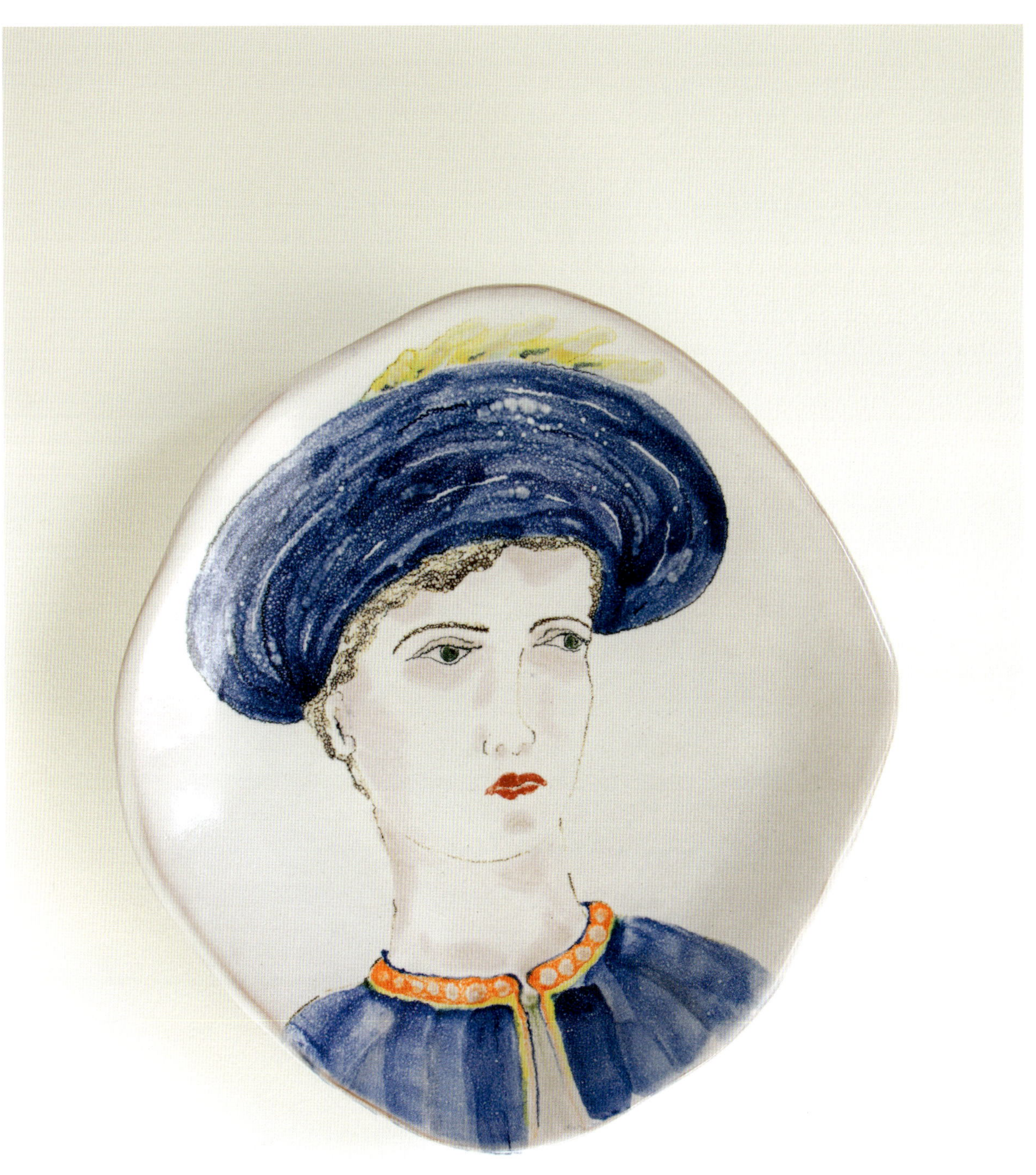

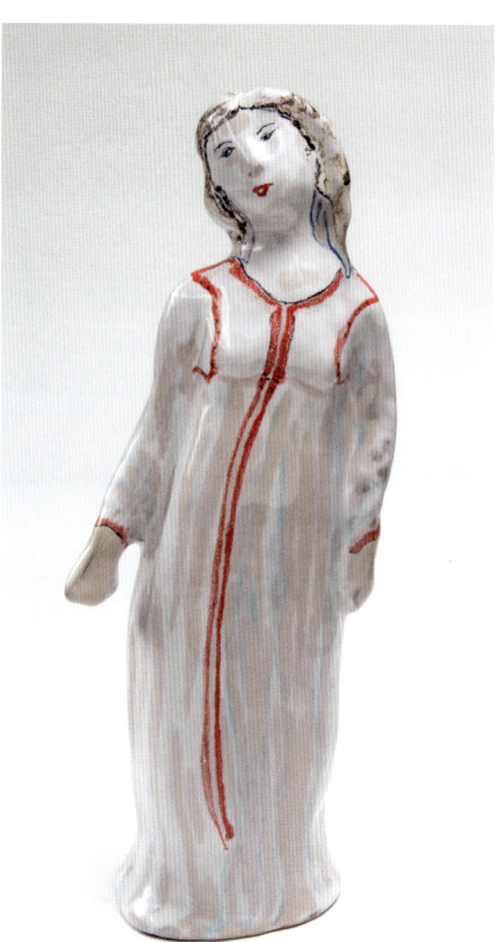

and wet sand and watching the local potters on the edge of town making their traditional earthenware cooking pots.

Agalis Manessi's sculptural objects and vessels are hand-modelled and painted forms, created either by coiling or by intuitively squeezing a lump of clay until an expressive shape emerges. Coiling and hand-modelling are techniques that are slower and offer a deeper connection with the clay than with throwing or slab-building. Her chosen methods of manipulating clay are those that are most physically intimate and responsive to touch. She talks about being able to pinch, flatten and feel her way around the shape that is forming. On her frequent forays into museums, Manessi not only gathered her library of creatures and personalities but was able to learn the traditions of ceramics; the different kinds of clays and glazes; and the varied symbolic meanings, use and hierarchies of sculptures and pottery from across continents and time.

Fresco Woman from Tolentino, 24 × 7 × 5 cm, 2011.

Understanding the history and properties of her materials, Manessi first chose to work with porcelain, enjoying its delicate, powdery whiteness. Later she turned to red earthenware clay, realising that, as with Renaissance ceramic statues and reliefs, terracotta allows a more nuanced and lively use of colour, especially when applied with an opaque white surface of tin-oxide glaze. This historic ceramic process, maiolica, is one that requires confidence and dexterity. Applying colour in brushstrokes on to an unfired glazed surface is a risky activity, needing clear intention and a painter's touch. After bringing into being her animal forms, figures, platters and vessels, it

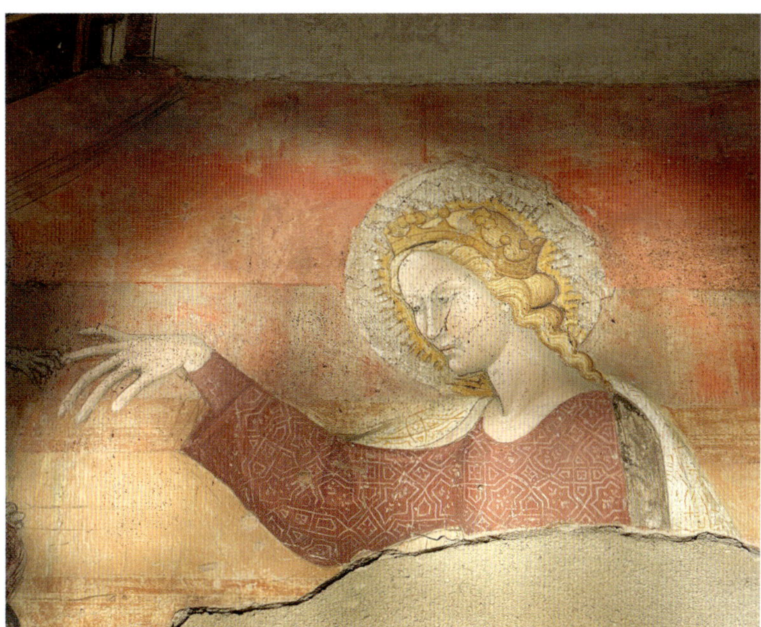

Fresco detail. Giovanni d'Agnolo di Balduccio, Basilica di San Domenico Arezzo, Italy.

is Manessi's fluency with colour and line that imbues each clay object with its characterful soul. Earthly angels are clothed in delicately painted dresses with beautifully drawn hats and hair adornments, patterns and colours all keenly observed and taken from all manner of history paintings. Gentle, resting hounds have been transposed from landscapes and hunting scenes along with lively, quick-witted hares. Manessi's plates, shallow bowls and vessels are supports for painted portraits of people of differing status and calling – mostly of women, sometimes men (and often of cats). These heads or full-body portraits are usually of people who have been recorded in paintings, though at times she has created an image from a snapshot or from life. Her portrait works have a celebratory quality, informed by the painted earthenware chargers of Victorian times that celebrated kings and queens, weddings and christenings or notable achievements.

The following sections of this book expand on the multiple facets of Agalis Manessi's work and her very individual approach to making it. Her skills as both potter and painter are well described and its pages are illustrated with wonderful examples of her painted clay objects, all of which embody the artist's deep understanding and love of her chosen material and of the provenance of her subjects. Her carefully rendered animals, angels and people, like those painted by Giotto, are kind and watchful, seemingly sharing the burden of life while each being in possession of a compelling presence all of its own.

A Journey Painted in Clay

Agalis Manessi

It is a vivid memory; I am eight years old when my father takes me for a walk, past the old port, and leads me to the back of some bombed-out buildings, saying with a twinkle in his eyes, 'έλα, θέλω να σου δείξω κάτι' ('I want to show you something'). A dark room in a long brick building with an earthen floor and a low ceiling is a welcome break after our walk in the hot summer sun. Two men in woollen vests, trousers rolled up, smiling at us but silent, are sitting on potter's wheels, dipping their hands in water, and pushing lumps of clay on them whilst kicking with one leg, and as if by magic they are producing tall flowerpots!

This is my first encounter with clay. The brothers, both of whom are unable to talk or hear since birth, as my father explains later, are utterly absorbed in their task; there is a serenity and calmness on their faces whilst throwing which is captivating even to a child. This is in Corfu where I was born, grew up and went to school, at a time when there was no art at school, so my experience of creativity and culture was more in reading and imagining, looking at pictures, playing with natural materials – stones, twigs, leaves and flowers creating patterns from the wealth of nature abundant all around me; looking and absorbing colour, playing with earth and sand.

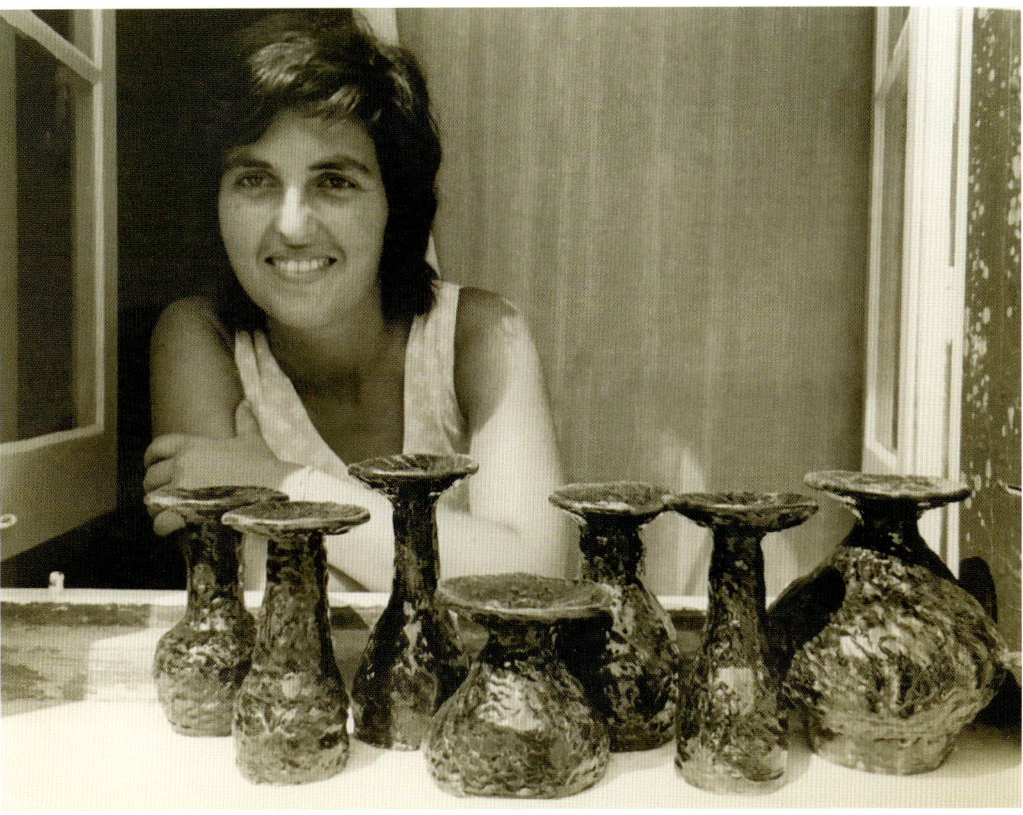

Agalis Manessi, Corfu 1973.

Twelve years later I find myself in London, accepted and enrolled at an Arts Foundation Course at Hammersmith College of Art, a beautiful Arts & Crafts building that seems to buzz with an atmosphere of creativity. There is a lot of drawing, 3D work using wood, paper, wire, breeze-blocks and clay. There seems to be much emphasis on textiles, making things out of fabrics, painting on fabrics, dyeing fabrics. There is a lot to adjust to after a much more structured and formal education at home in Greece; staff and students are on friendly first-name terms; language and concepts at times seem hard to understand, I am feeling my way, a little in the dark. Most of my fellow students seem sophisticated in their approach to work, with a clear direction as to where and what they will be studying next. Painting, printmaking, illustration and textiles seem to be popular choices. Above all we spend time drawing with a tutor's guidance, helping us to understand form and volumes and encouraged to be bold and not afraid to make mistakes. We are making marks using pens, pencils, brushes, colours. The choice seems endless. There is Art History taught too, putting things in context. My knowledge is

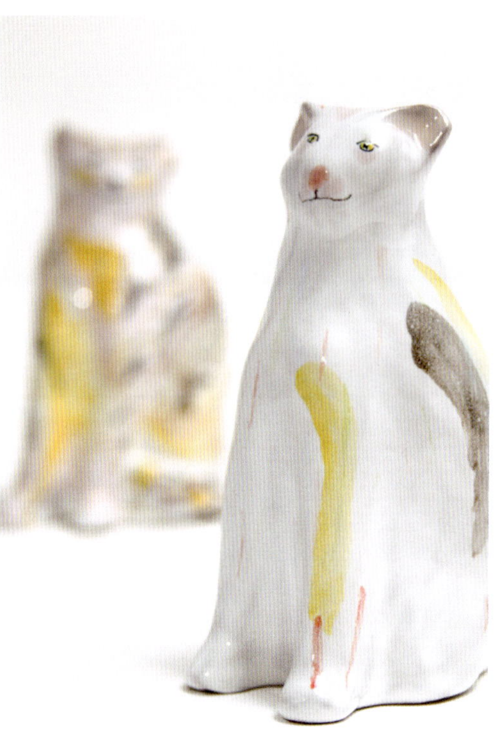

Bow Belle Cat,
14 × 9 × 8 cm, 2013.

very poor as art was never a subject or part of our curriculum at school in Greece. We are working towards an Art History A-Level. I try hard to learn how to write essays, to remember artists' names, dates and their movements. I manage to get an O-Level!

There are no ceramics as such at the college, so no kilns, techniques or glazes and the knowledge that goes with all of that, but nevertheless I am thinking of applying to study ceramics. It seems a more down-to-earth art subject, the material is soft, I can manipulate it, perhaps I do not have to be hugely talented to make something. I am drawn to this idea: I like the feel of the clay when we attempt to sculpt a bust – it has a flexibility, a natural softness, and makes me think of movement and dance, my first love for the arts. My tutor, an ex-member of the Bonzo Dog Doo-Dah Band, suggests I make cut-out silhouettes of pots from card which we stand on an old wind-up gramophone. Spinning at 78 rpm, the cut-outs appear as solid forms, and I start to understand the idiosyncratic, creative possibilities within British art education.

After considering where to apply next I decide that my first choice will be the Central School of Art and Design. After all, coming from a small island in the Ionian Sea, I want to be in the big city and all it has to offer:

museums, exhibitions, music, theatres, all within close proximity, and in particular the British Museum, with what seems like endless corridors and collections of ancient Greek ceramics. Having grown up amidst shops selling cheap touristic replica souvenirs, it is a revelation to see the magnificent Attic-ware vases with their sensual paintings depicting mythological narratives. The irony of having to leave home to experience the artefacts of my own plundered culture as well as those of others like the museum's treasure trove of Chinese ceramics only becomes apparent to me later. Decolonising museum collections aside, it nevertheless plays an important role in gradually widening my understanding and knowledge of the place of ceramics in the evolution of society since the dawn of civilisation. The experience sows the seeds of enquiry, encouraging me to look and look again, a journey of discovery and fulfilment.

My application at the Central School of Art & Design is successful and so my 'journey painting in clay' begins.

During the summer break before my first year as a full student of ceramics, I am back in Corfu. I approach Mr Apostolides, a local potter, and ask if I can work with him to familiarise myself with the material and the whole process: making, firing, glazing, re-firing. He kindly agrees to let me work in his workshop for two months. I have to be there at 7.30am before the heat of the day kicks in and we work until 2.30pm, Monday to Saturday. His workshop takes me back to my first encounter as an eight-year-old: an earthen floor, a cool dark space with only two incandescent light bulbs, his throwing wheel to one side. He is the Master, a tall, middle-aged man in clay-covered shorts, sandals, and a vest. He handles the clay with great dexterity, force and ease and, despite his large hands, with delicacy and accuracy. His helper and assistant, Annetta, emerges from the shadows at the back of the studio, a petite, slightly built middle-aged woman whose bird-like stature exudes a sinuous strength and

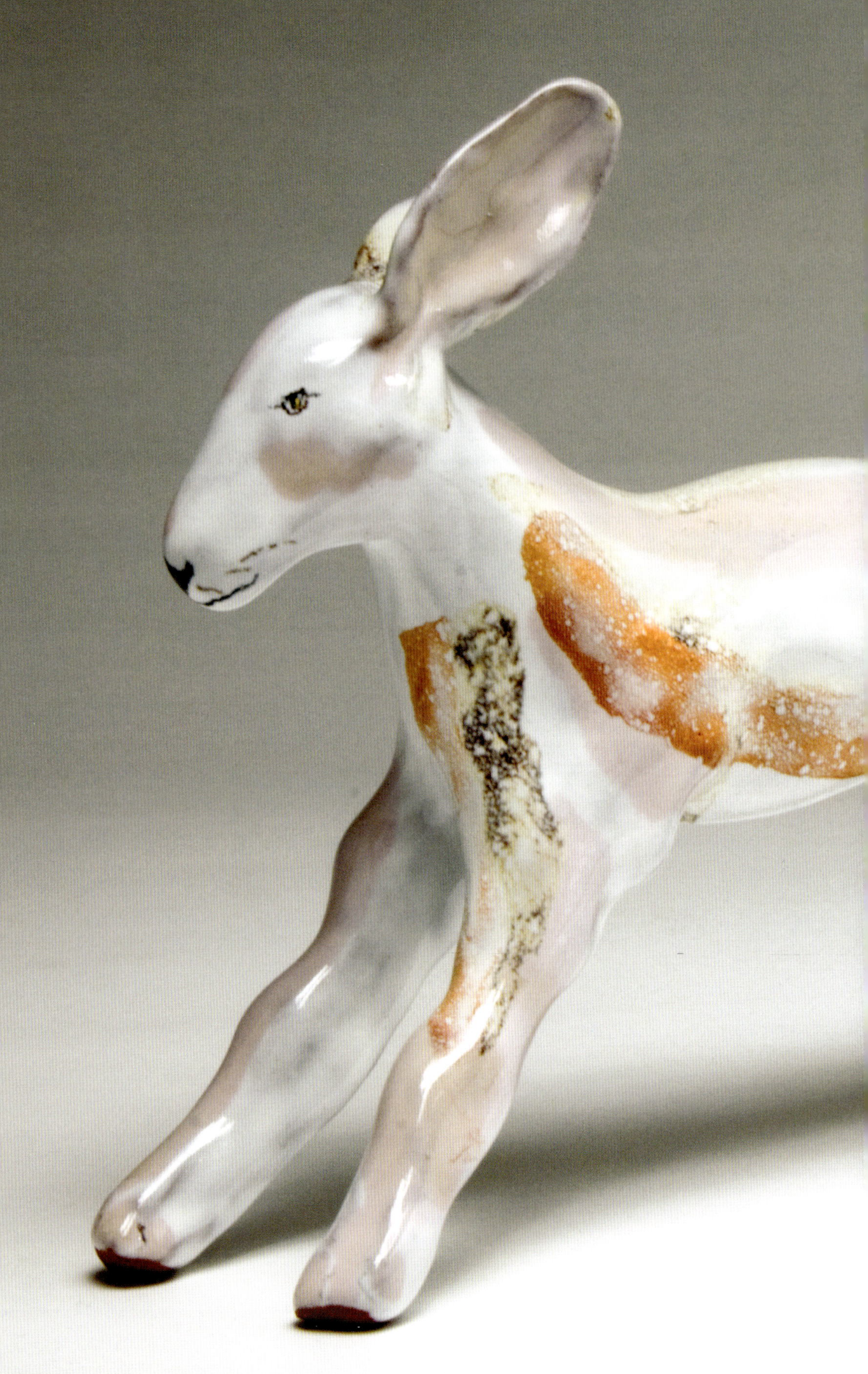

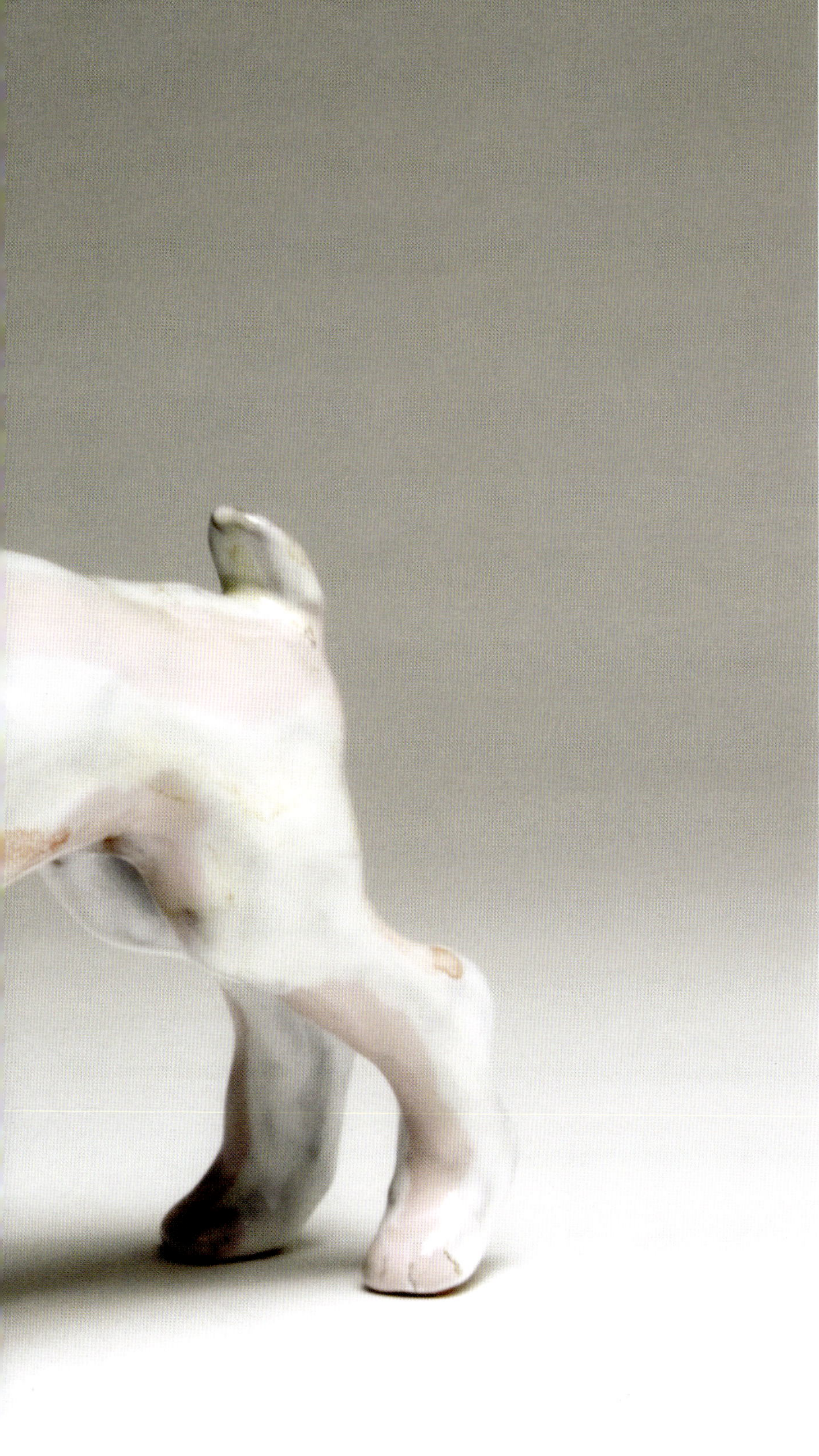

Running Hare with Orange Streak, 14 × 19 × 7 cm, 2012.

energy. He tells her what his plan is for the day, 60 mugs and 20 small amphorae! She prepares all his clay, wedging it and cutting it into exact portions for the task, patting them into balls from which he throws piece after piece – all in equal size, dimension and height, his wet hands manipulating the clay in a kind of repetitive dance. It is mesmerising. As soon as one is finished it is cut off the wheel, placed on a plank, which when full, with about 16 pieces, is carried by Annetta outside into the sunshine. They are a great team.

He gives me my instructions, a small book with black and white photos and drawings of vessels from which he chooses what I must attempt to make through coiling. He can be both critical and encouraging and so through touch and manipulation of the material I start to develop the haptic sensibility needed to transform the inert material into physical form.

We fall into a pattern of working side by side; it is all-absorbing. By early afternoon the sun has done its work and his pieces are ready for turning, refining the shapes to be left on shelves in the workshop to dry for firing. I am given a small shelf for what he calls my 'artwork'. And so we continue. At the end of the third week, we have enough work ready for firing. This is truly exciting; the kiln is situated around the corner from the workshop. It is dug into the earth, and looks like a mound with a brick chimney. I have to carry the dry work carefully to it and Annetta enters the kiln chamber, stacking the work to the roof, climbing up a small wooden stepladder to achieve this. Once the chamber is tightly packed, she seals the opening with bricks and wet clay. The kiln is woodfired and is continuously fed till late at night to reach an earthenware temperature of around 1080°C, which is judged by colour of heat and years of experience. The following day is a day of rest!

There is excitement and anticipation in the air when we prise the door apart to discover that all the work nestled inside has changed colour from pale grey to a warm buff. When it comes to glazing all the domestic ware, mugs, jugs, vases are dipped in a big dustbin filled with what looks like a huge quantity of milk, which is in fact a clear glaze, and then the bases are sponged clean so they will not stick to the shelves during the second firing. The amphorae are left unglazed to be passed to the Master's son, who has studied decorative techniques in Italy and will be painting them with patterns inspired by ancient Attic wares using household paint before they are delivered to various souvenir shops for tourists. In my case, for my 'artworks' I am given a glaze containing manganese oxide, which will give it something special! And so my pottery summer continues.[1]

The journey begins in earnest 50 years ago in 1973 on a Monday morning at the Central School. The first-year group starts its programme with hand-building and our teacher is the artist Gordon Baldwin. I feel uncertain of what he is asking of us as he talks about concepts, proportions, balance – it all seems a bit beyond me in terms of understanding how this can be put into practice, but his enthusiasm, eloquence and energy are infectious and so it is a very positive start. We are immersed in the subject. There is throwing, of course, to be mastered as well as all hand-building techniques, also mould-making, slip-casting, glaze technology. Drawing, decorative techniques, screen-printing and contextual studies make up each intensive and stimulating week.

This is truly a golden era for art colleges, and the Central School and we are privileged to have so many wonderful teachers to guide us, all of them significant makers and practising artists or designers in their own right.

The painter Geoffrey Rogers' introduction to colour theory is captivating; he shows us the work of Josef Albers and how colours interdepend and react with each other; this is a real journey of discovery. Eileen Nisbet's own sculptural ceramics are created with such attention to detail, where colour, translucency, innovation and fine finish leave one in awe of how they may have been created by hand, they are so utterly perfect. Her gentle manner and quietly positive attitude are so very encouraging. Dan Arbeid's attitude to clay seems the exact opposite: the material is used in a rough way, pushed and pulled together with energy and bravado, and he manages to retain that in the finished pieces. There is a playfulness in his work, referencing ancient Greek forms, architecture and medieval ware. Throwing is taught by John Chipperfield: his work is refined and perfect shapes with tall narrow necks and perfectly fitted lids emerge quickly out of the amorphous lump of clay, he throws with ease and dexterity. There is a different approach from Walter Keeler when he is teaching us throwing. Once the basic shape is thrown, we are encouraged and invited to interfere with its perfection whilst the clay is still moist, pressing and manipulating the shape, adding decorative elements to it. We work with many different clays, each one with unique properties; Gillian Lowndes draws on her unique approach to materiality, encouraging us to push and handle clay differently, every stage monitored to take advantage of things going wrong and using them to advantage. Glaze technology, a fascinating and alchemical part of ceramics, which remains to this day something of a mystery to me, concludes the week. It entails mixing materials which through the firing process become a layer of glass covering the ceramic object, adding and mixing metal oxides and stains with the glaze, creating a palette of colours of subtlety and vibrancy that makes your heart sing.

Around the corner we meet at the British Museum for sketching and drawing upon historical references for inspiration: the fixing of a handle, the curve of a spout, the marks left by the maker's

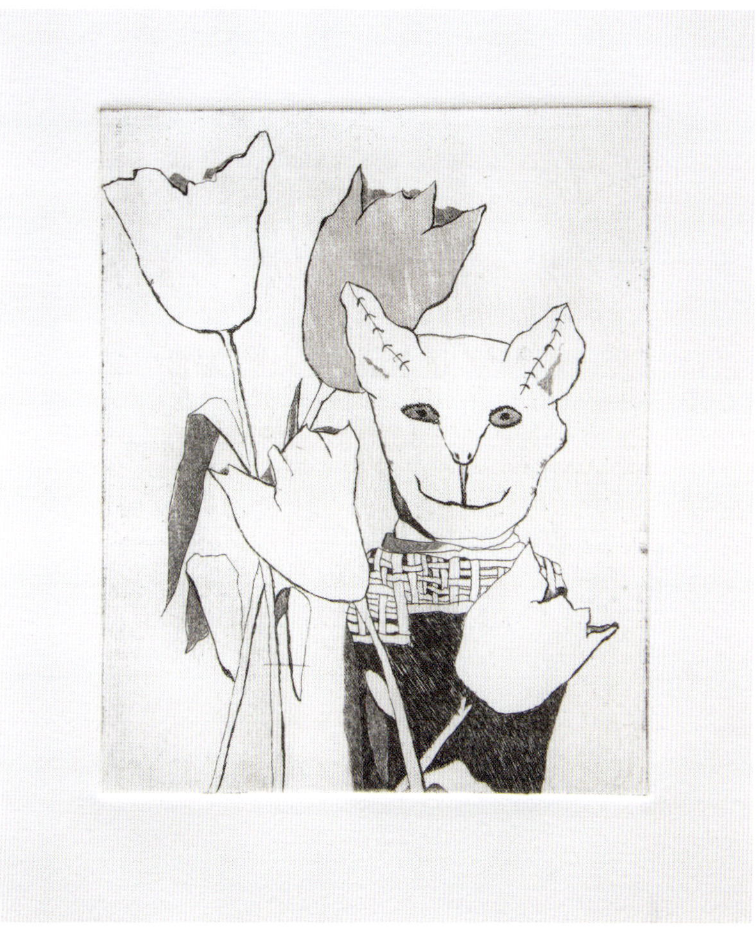

Cat Amongst the Tulips. Etching, 24 × 20 cm, 1980.

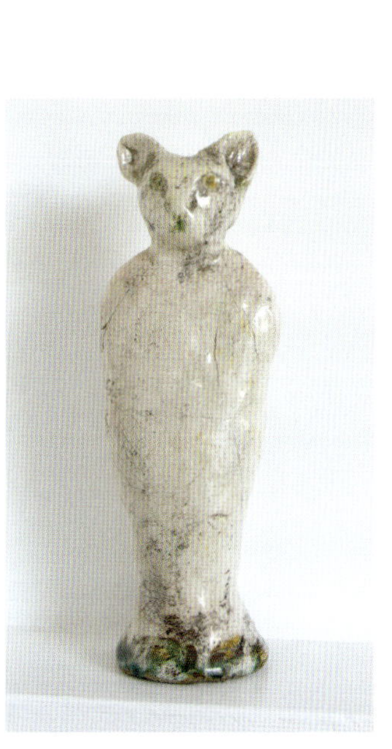

Mummified Cat, Raku, 20 × 7 × 5 cm, 1981.

hand. Looking at the Egyptian section I see the mummified cats. Wrapped in cloth, they seem to be gently smiling at me and I scribble some drawings. The way the linen swaddling wraps around them gives them a statuesque solidity that makes me think of coiled forms and starts to feed into my ceramic pieces both as modelled figurines and drawings directly on the clay.

Three years pass quickly and I know that clay is what I want to continue with. Setting up a studio in Hackney means making choices as to what materials I am going to use. Narrowing things down, I decide to work with porcelain, and hand-building is my preferred way of working. I find that the haptic qualities and slower pace of slab-building and coiling give me the opportunity to play and experiment with forms in a more organic way. The vessels are inscribed with fine tools, the meandering lines then infilled with metal oxides as colouring agents. I enjoy creating a fluid narrative using plants and animals around the curved surfaces. My work starts to be shown in some galleries and it is good to see the response from new audiences.

Working in the studio is a solitary activity. I am fortunate, though, to be offered a post teaching ceramics part-time in Further Education, Special Needs and Mental Health Centres as part of an Occupational Therapy team. I discover the different benefits this humble material has through my students' work, how it seems to ground people, enabling them to discover their creativity and helping them to focus and relax and how much they value their short time making for just a few hours a week.[2]

Within my own work I feel restricted by the limited palette achieved at high stoneware temperatures and I am seeking a change in order to work with a greater and more vibrant colour response. Yellow seems to be the colour that eludes me working in porcelain and my preferred glaze turns it to the palest of browns or pink. Again, it is a museum collection from which I draw new impetus, this time the Victoria and Albert Museum. A treasure-trove of applied and decorative arts, its cabinets are filled with the finest examples of the potter's art from around the world: it is a mesmerising spectacle. I spend a whole day looking and admiring pieces, amongst which a large plate with a portrait in the centre stares out at me. A brilliant touch of yellow calls for my attention. The plate made in Montelupo, Italy, around 1470 is maiolica, tin-glazed earthenware. The colours are fresh, painted with loose brushstrokes. The enigmatic figure draws me in. I am instantly drawn to the vibrant colours of maiolica and the immediate freshness of these painterly wares. My decision is taken; I will step back from porcelain and stoneware glazes and investigate maiolica and earthenware clays. This will become my new form of expression, and I paint my first portrait plate.

To begin with I use a buff clay but quickly switch to red terracotta as it gives a cooler, brighter response. Tin-glaze painting is a

Woman with Blue Irises, (rear view). Inlaid and painted porcelain, 32 × 19 × 15 cm, 1983

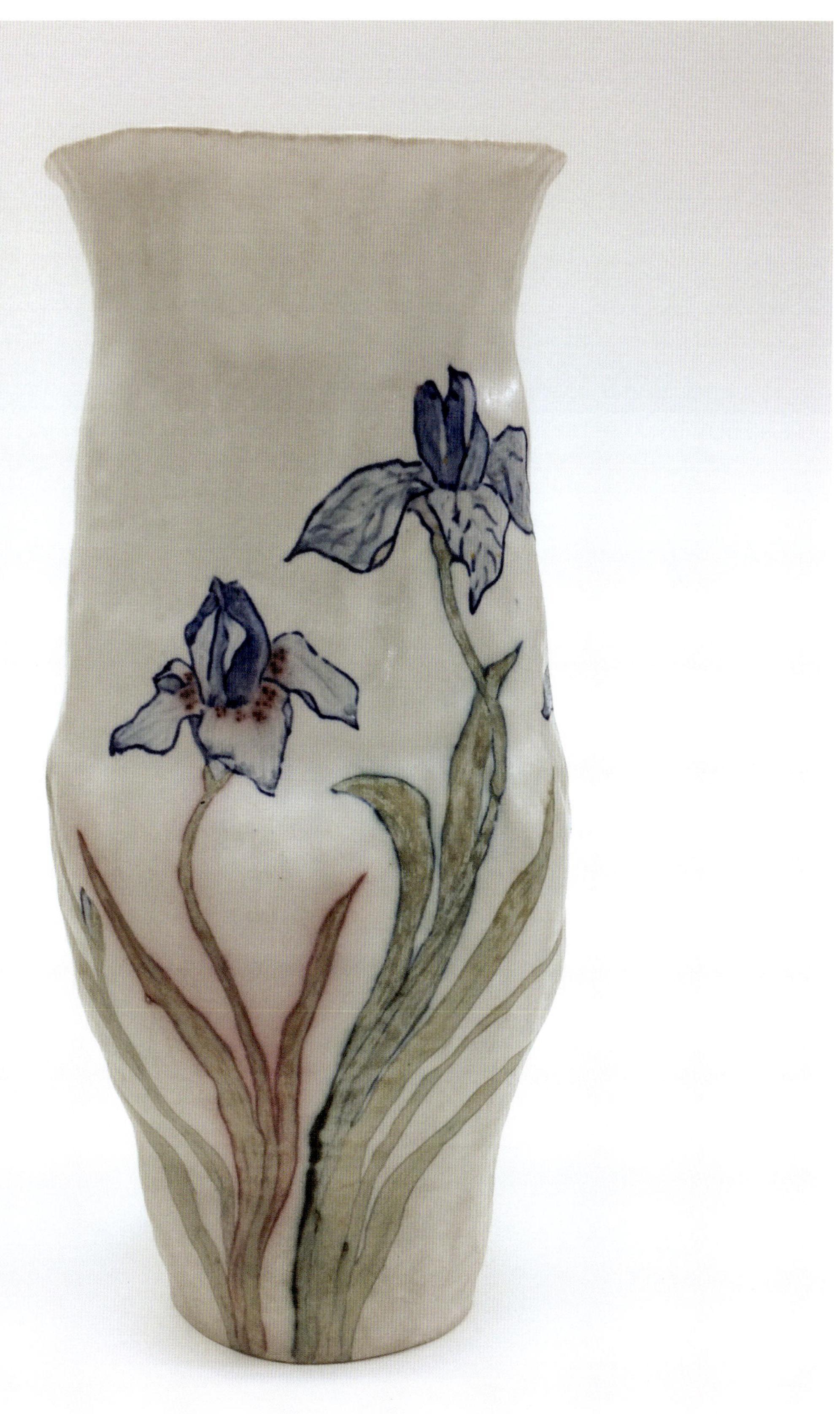

From Memory.
30 × 28 cm, 1984.

rewarding yet deceptively unforgiving process. I am now painting directly on the raw glaze, which in itself is a more risky and challenging technique with greater potential for things to go wrong, but when it works it has the freshness of watercolour painting, hopefully capturing something poetic within its narrative. I think of it as maiolica magic. Dishes become canvases for still-life subjects; vessels are painted with the flowers they are destined to contain.

Influences and images collide as memories of the Egyptian cats fuse into vessels, becoming catamorphic vases, like characters in

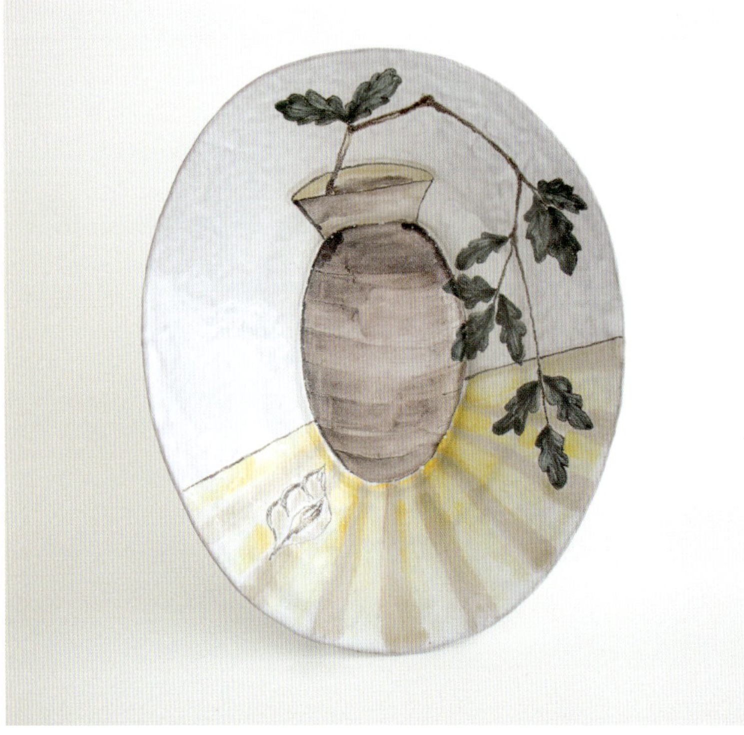

Still Life with Oak Leaves, 31 × 26 cm, 1987.

a story. Feline faces emerge around the tops, casting wry sideways glances. Looking at paintings as well as objects in museums and galleries continues to be a great source of inspiration. As I am walking through the Museum of the Home, another maiolica dish catches the eye. This is also a Montelupo plate of the same period as the portrait one, but this time it is covered in an intricate, intertwined pattern. There is something about the pattern and its complexity that stays in my mind. A catamorphic vessel is ready and waiting to be adorned and the pattern starts to envelop it like a lacy cloak.

Montelupo Dish. Tin-glazed earthenware plate. c.1560–1580. Montelupo maiolica plate from Museum of the Home's collection.

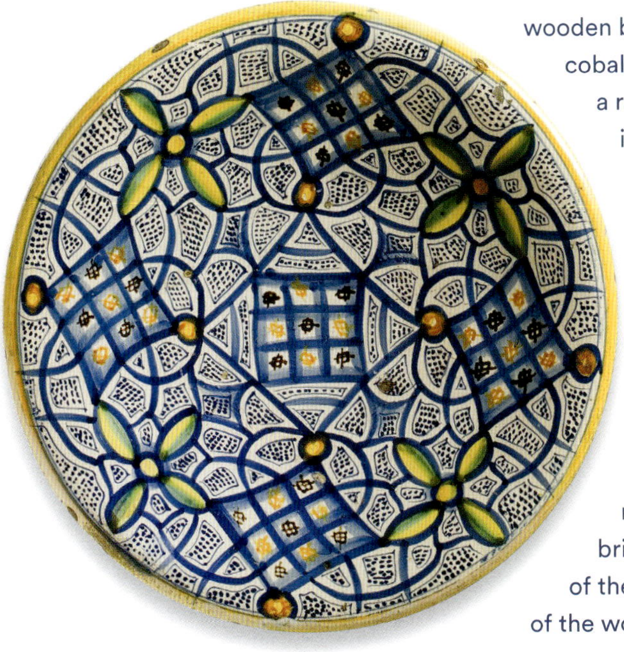

Early willow-pattern ware is also on display. It is hand-painted with cobalt oxide on a white background. Focusing on these objects I realise that small brushstrokes and marks are brought together to create the scene of weeping willows over a stream, a wooden bridge and a pagoda in the background. The cobalt blue is very seductive, and I start 'dressing' a range of catamorphic vessels by using the inventive marks as reference, producing a kind of garment on their dimpled surface. A number of 'Willows' emerge, some smiling, some sleeping, some looking knowingly and directly at the viewer.

Modelling figures continues to offer new opportunities for expression. Hounds and figures are formed by manipulating a solid piece of clay, trying to discover the 'animal' within, not over-modelling, thus allowing the painting to bring out the full character and personality of the piece in the second firing. An exhibition of the work of the artist Antonio di Puccio Pisanello

(1395–1455) at the National Gallery in 2001 acts as another catalyst; I am struck by the animals present in *The Vision of Saint Eustace* (1438–42), a forest hunting scene, dogs standing, a hunting hound and a hare running, St Eustace looking in disbelief at the vision of a stag with a crucifix between his antlers. It is a painting full of mystery and I am drawn mostly to the hound and the running hare: their elegant forms stand out and sing to me. I start to model a number of hares, some standing, some running or leaping, some sitting. Hunting hounds as well begin to emerge and once I start looking around, they seem to be featured in a great number of paintings; some are nestled under a table, some next to their owner's feet, at other times resting at the edge of a painting, seeming to observe the scene; occasionally they are centre-stage. In everyday life too dogs are all around: I see them in the parks, in the Tube, in the street. They vary in shape, size and colouring, but what draws me most of all is their expression and arresting, communicative eyes.

Looking at Pisanello's meticulous drawings of animals leads me in other directions, to other sources, to Expressionist paintings where animal forms are simplified within a few lines, with loose brushstrokes evoking the character of the animal. Expressionism's refreshing directness is appropriate for the soft modelling of clay, inviting the creation of a more abstract interpretation.

I am drawn to Franz Marc (1880–1916), the German Expressionist artist who painted many animals using vibrant colours and energetic brushstrokes. His own dog, Rossi, is depicted lying in the snow with a calm, well-observed facial expression. I love his slightly angular, faceted body and the use of colour, so I embark on a long relationship with Rossi. The shapes and the sizes vary: the dogs can be smiling, sleeping, resting; the colours too can be warmer or colder, softer or stronger, jubilant. I empathise with his feelings towards animals when in 1915 Marc wrote,

Geffrye's Cloak,
34 × 20 × 15 cm, 2016.

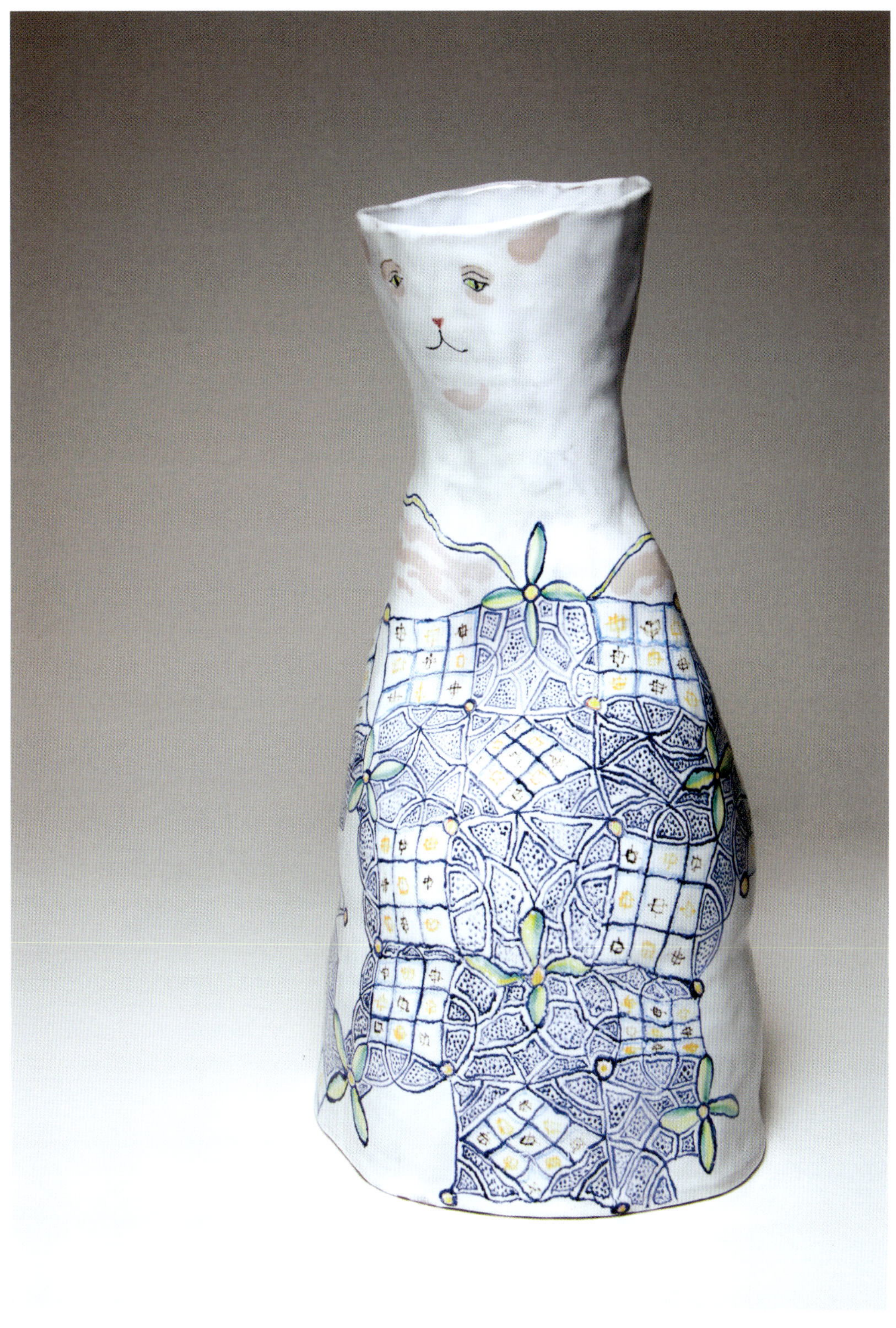

'People with their lack of piety, especially men, never touched my true feelings ... but animals with their virginal sense of life awakened all that is good in me.'

Cats are another story; I make no excuse for my obsession with cats! Independent creatures, they are self-contained, both wonderfully entertaining and aloof, admired and revered since ancient times. They pose to be drawn, to be modelled and to be stroked. I admire their agility and ability to pounce and climb. I love to watch the way they move. I am a cat-lover who never tires of observing them. I am not alone in this obsession; they have inspired many others before me and have been written about extensively. The subject of Christopher Smart's (1722–71) poem about his cat, 'For I

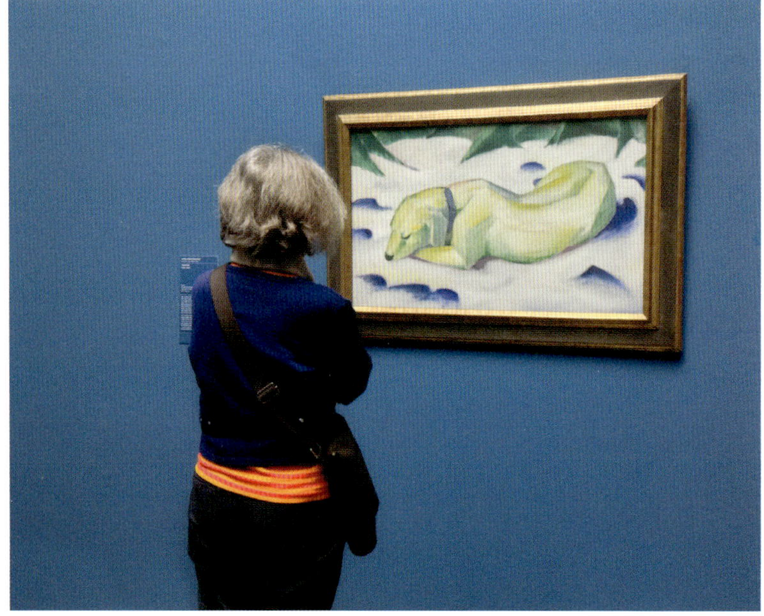

AM in front of *Dog Lying in the Snow*. Franz Marc 1911. Städel Museum, Frankfurt.

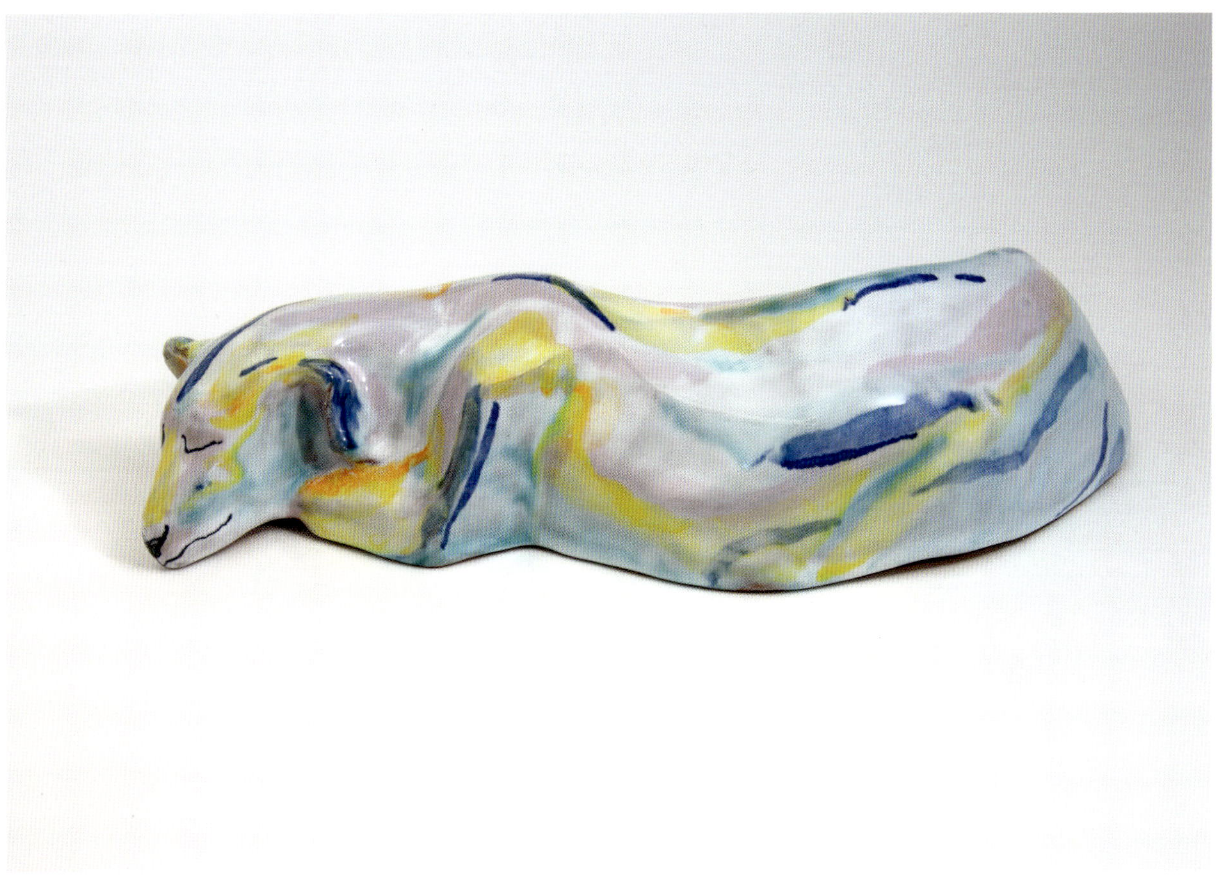

Copper Dog for Franz Marc, 26 × 7 × 17 cm, 2017.

will consider my Cat Jeoffry…', is considered by Hilary Mantel to be 'the greatest cat in the English language'. The poem is profoundly observant of the daily movements and behaviour of this enigmatic creature and I return to it again and again.

Cats have been made in clay through the ages as children's toys, decorative objects, statuettes, or sacred objects. Seriality is both a natural progression for the artist as themes are pursued, as well as in the industrial production of ceramics. At the Potteries Museum and Art Gallery in Stoke-on-Trent the Keiller collection of 667 cow cream jugs is herded into a glass cabinet. Their repeated forms are made unique through the application of splattered oxides on the glaze. As my cats start to emerge, small ones, big ones, decorative ones, florid ones, ginger and tortoiseshells start to crowd the shelves in my studio, I discover that the collective name is a clowder of cats. My clowder is made up of simple cat forms, each one developing its own character. A chance encounter with a watercolour painting of a Kalighat Indian cat with a fish in its mouth in the V&A spawns a new series. Others acquire passengers on their backs, a friendly owl, a swallow, a second cat leaning in for comfort.

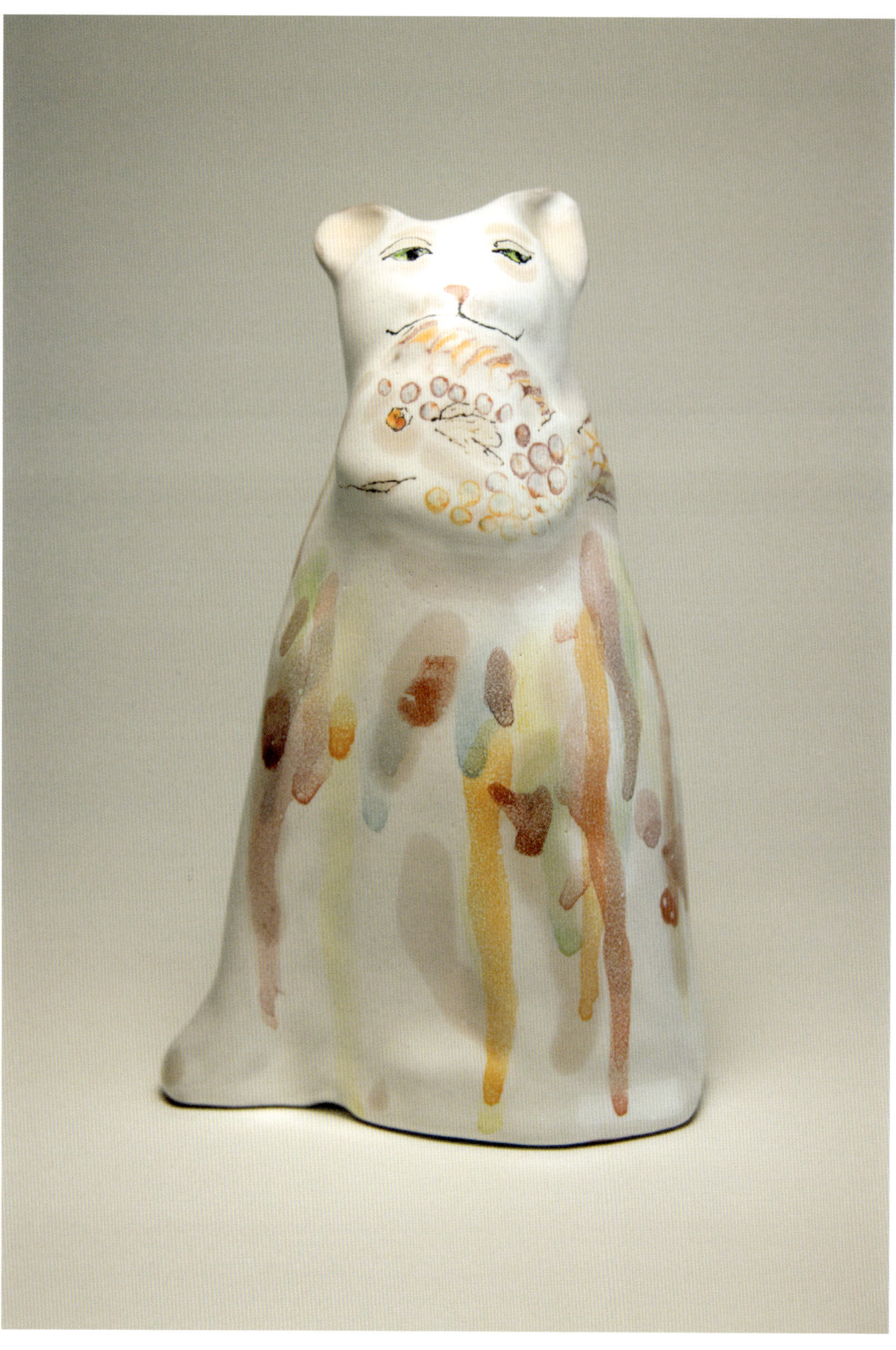

A Big Mouthful,
18 × 8 × 12 cm, 2017.

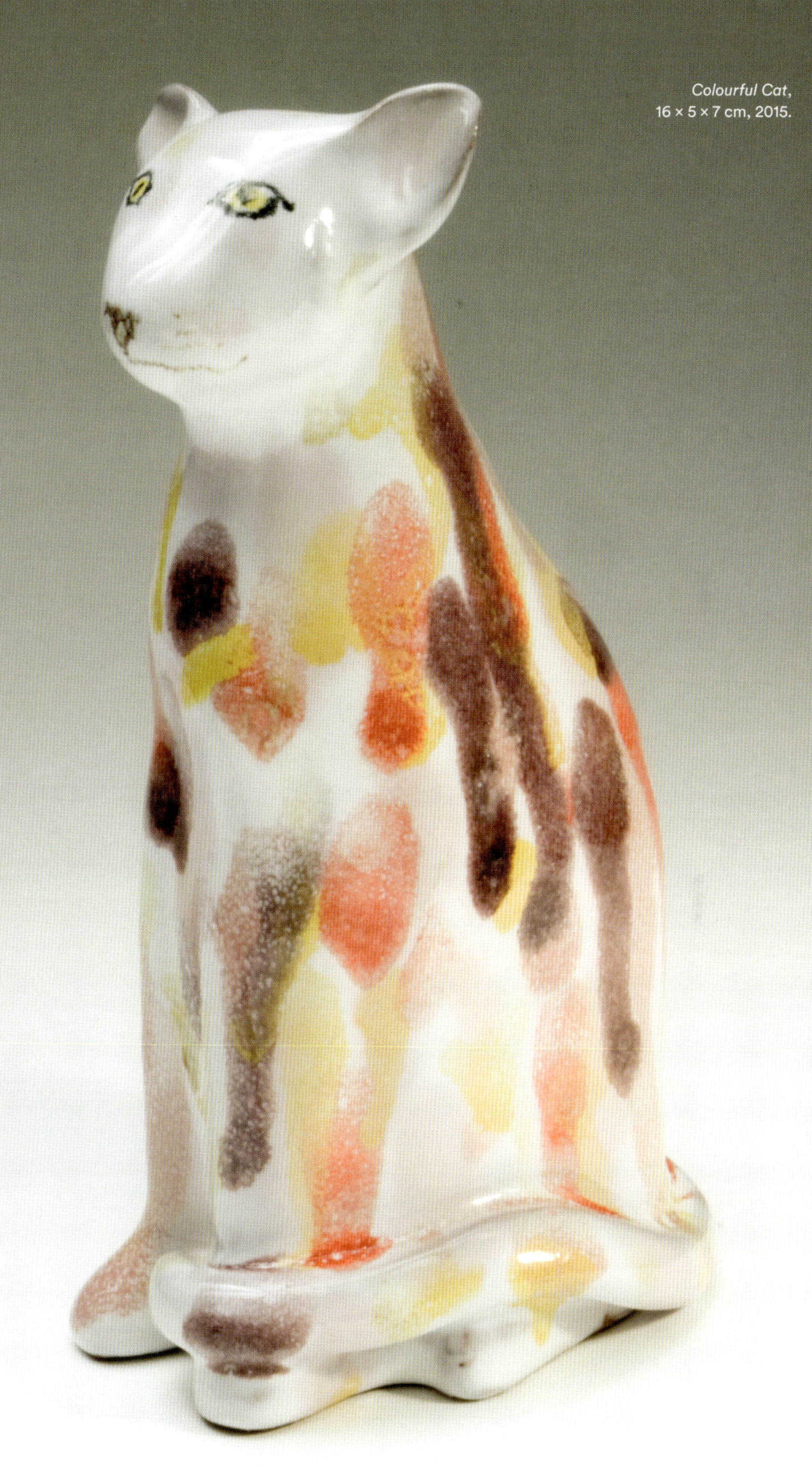

Colourful Cat,
16 × 5 × 7 cm, 2015.

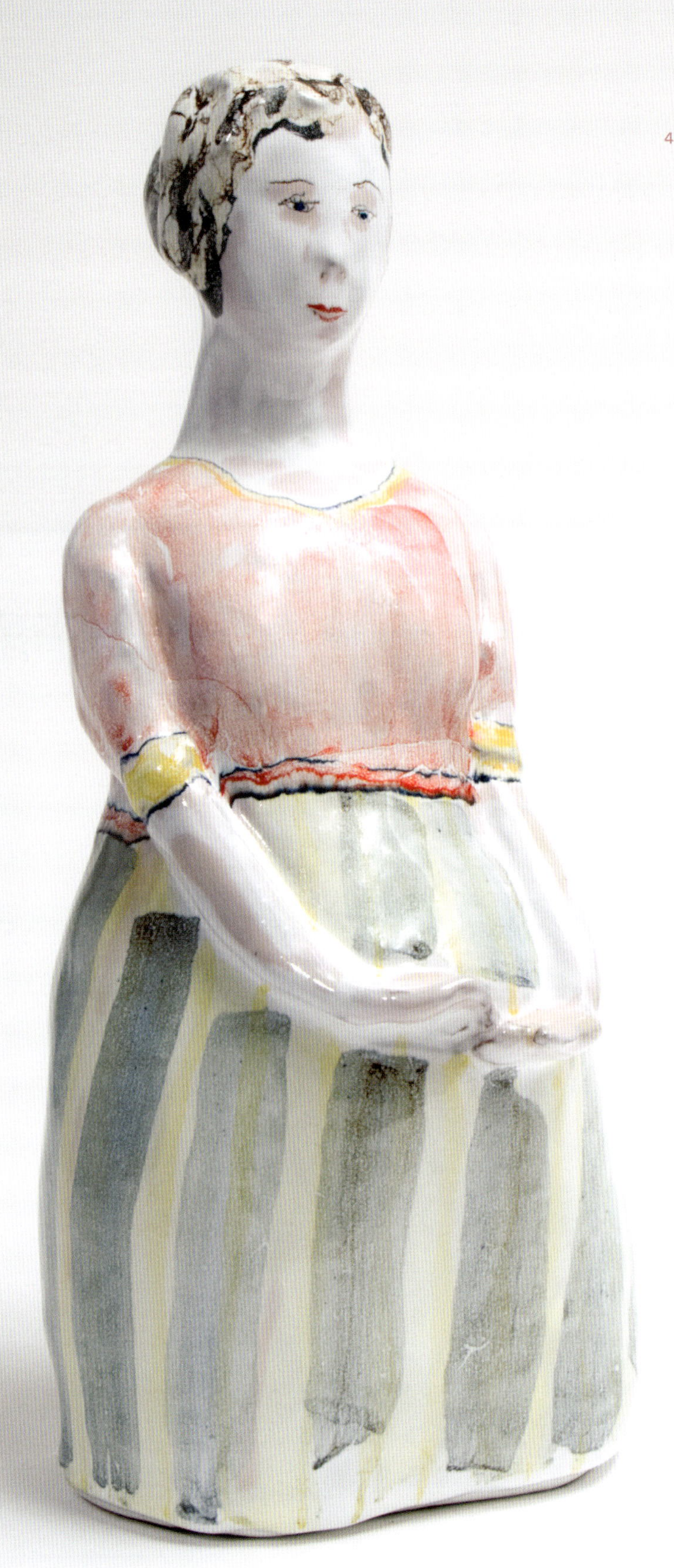

Shepherdess,
45 × 20 × 17 cm, 2013.

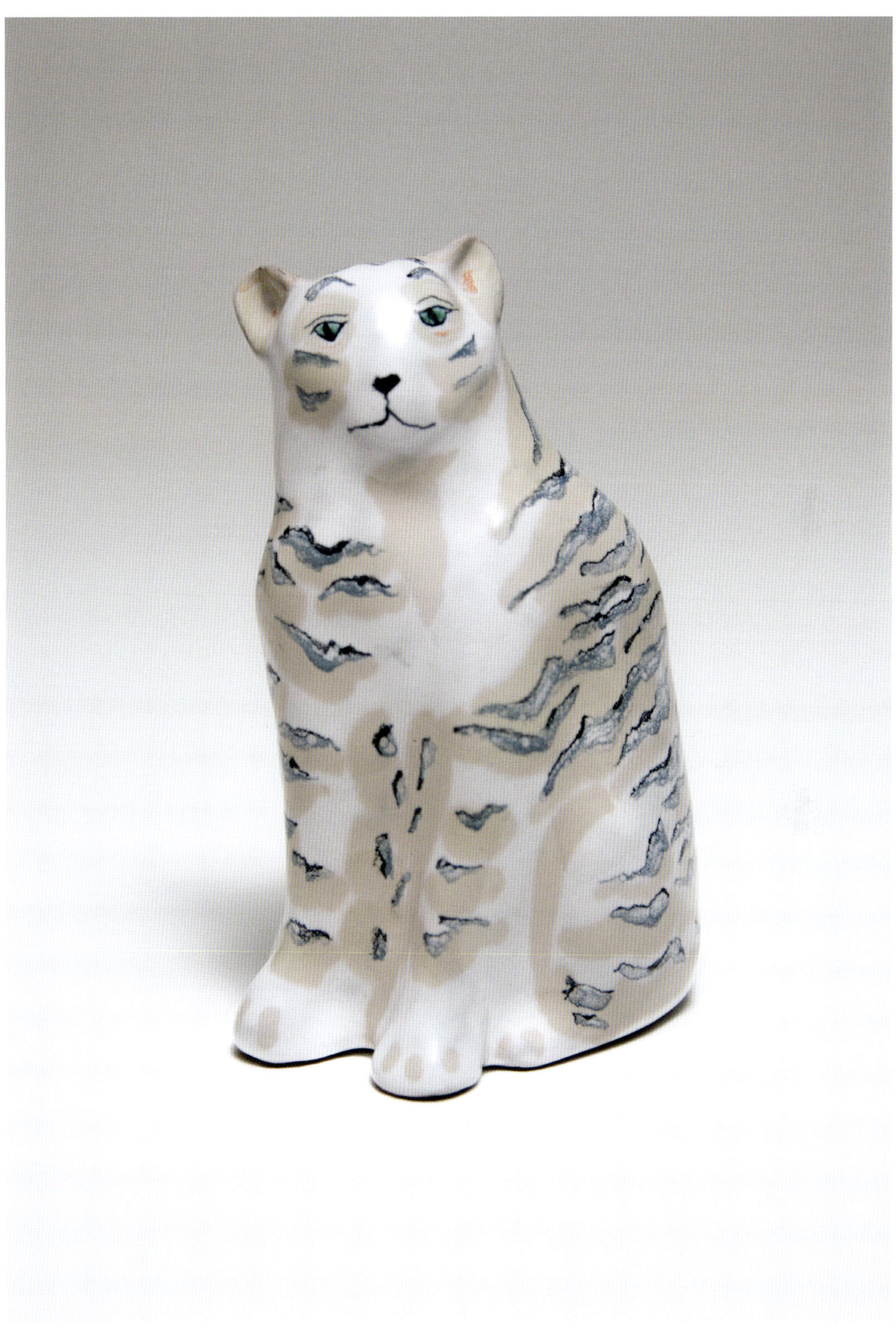

Serious Cat in Grey,
11 × 8 × 7 cm, 2016.

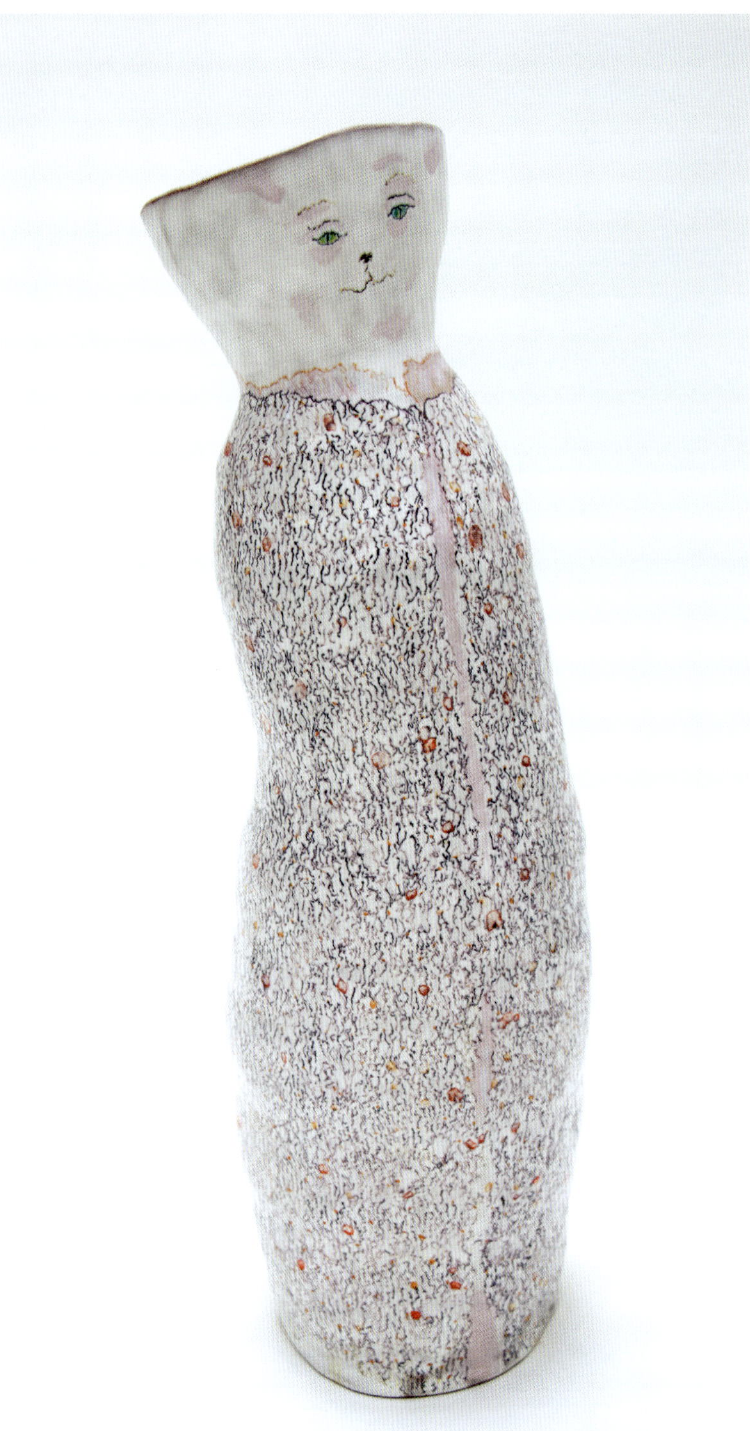

In a Meadow,
46 × 14 × 14 cm, 2022.

Menagerie with Owl,
40 × 13 × 13 cm, 2015.

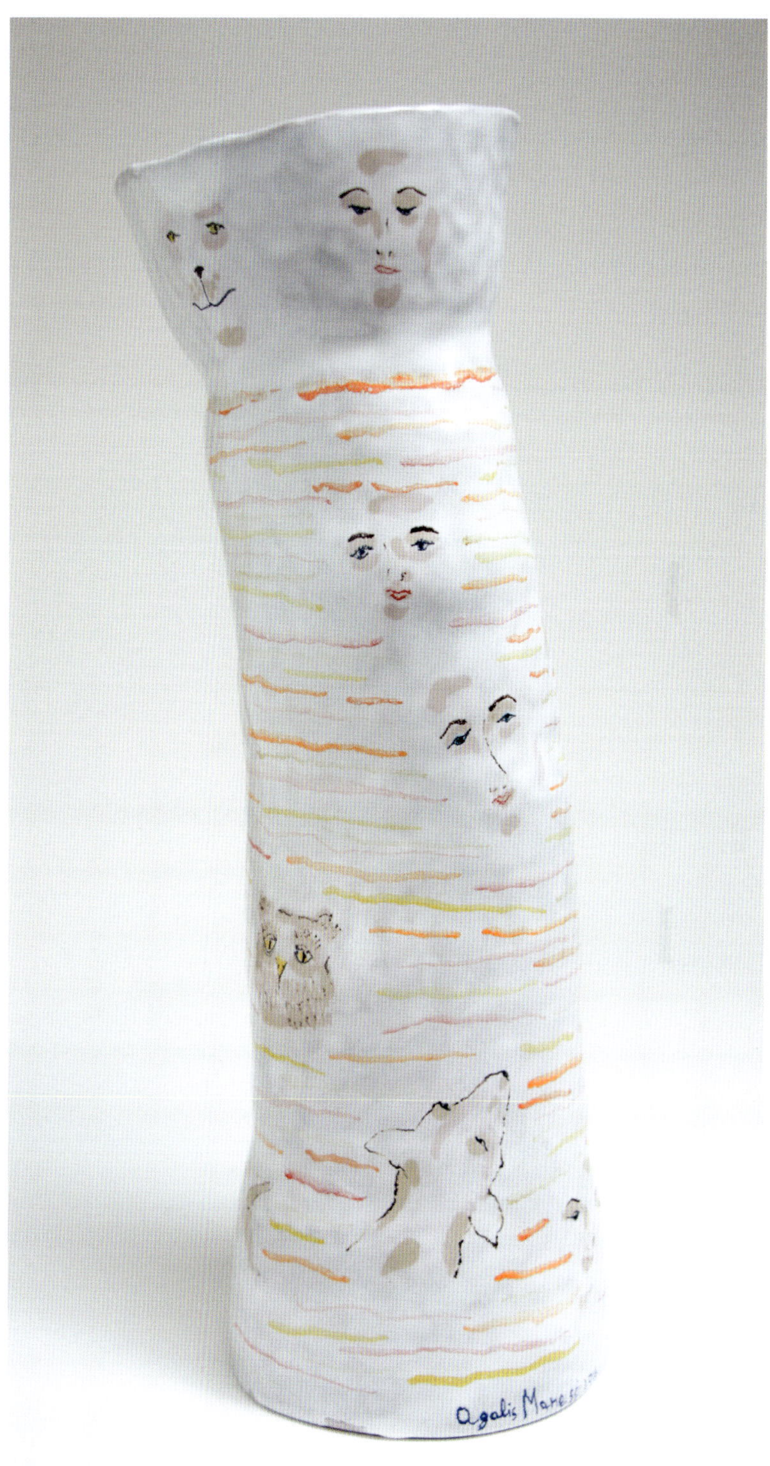

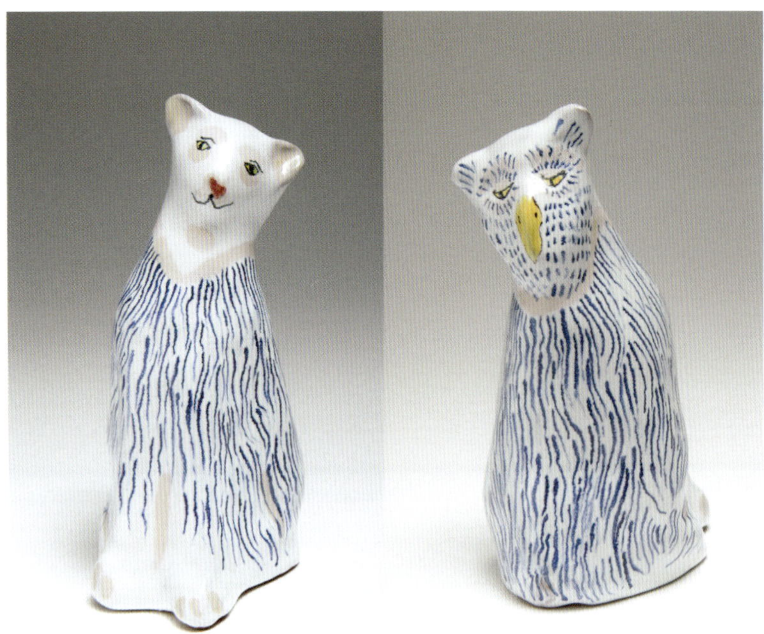

Cobalt Blue Owl Cat, (front and rear view), 12 × 8 × 6 cm, 2016.

From cats to figures seems to be a natural progression and again I return to my Greek roots and become fascinated with the Tanagra figurines from about 300 BCE, with their flowing garments supporting the small statues. Chinese Ming Dynasty figures of musicians and court attendants too with their lush green copper glazes and softly modelled forms catch my eye. Modelled from a solid lump, the soft clay can be bent gently to show movement in the figure, the head pushed to gaze up, down or sideways.

Each year on my journeys travelling overland back and forth to Greece I take time to explore frescoes in churches and museums. I revel in Giotto's deep blue skies and the arresting facial expressions on the faces of Piero della Francesca's subjects. Angels, religious scenes, Bible stories, crowded gatherings of elegant and colourful forms with expressive faces and elaborate

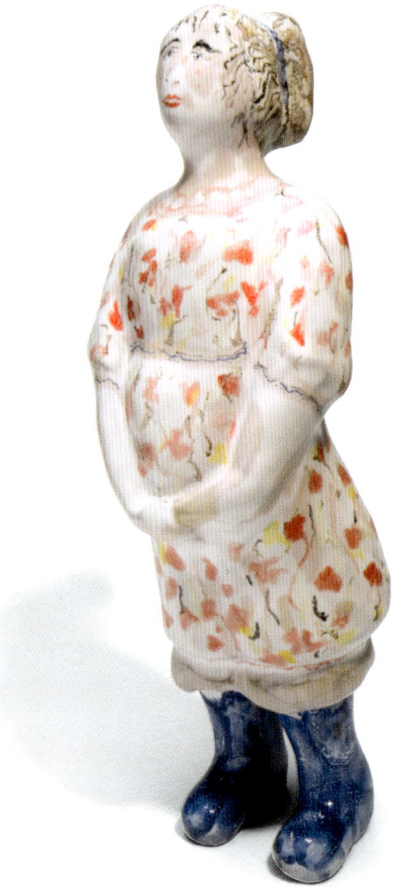

Rosie in the Garden, 24 × 9 × 7, 2010. After *Rosie in the Garden*, Olwyn Bowey.

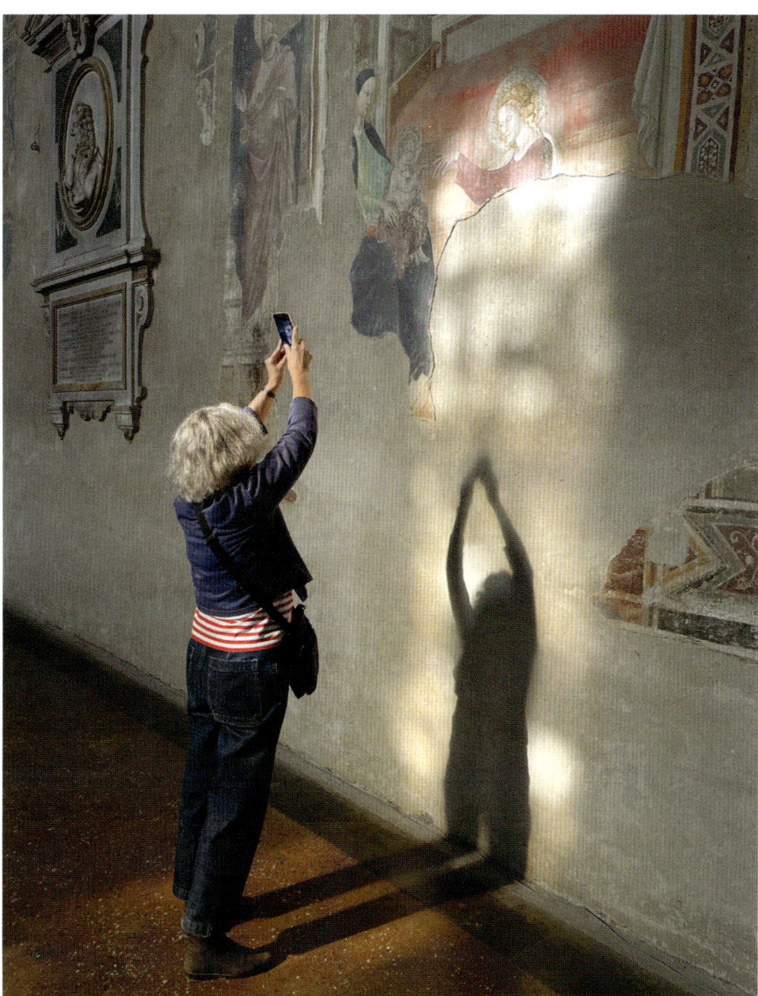
AM in Basilca di San Domenico, Arezzo.

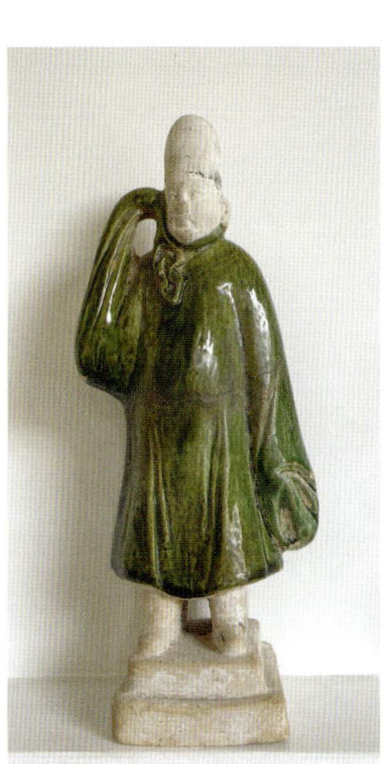
Ming Dynasty figure, Glazed earthenware. Collection AM.

headgear look either directly or beyond the viewer, a wealth of human emotion depicted within these scenes. The warmth in the richly depicted pleated garments, the golden yellows, subtle pinks, warm oranges, topped with vibrant red hats, stays with me. I know that I will have to try and bring them to life in my maiolica painting.

By now books and postcards are reminders for a wealth of images to draw from and they have become part of my toolbox. Inevitably, technology offers other means of recording and the mobile phone becomes the tool of choice to capture details and faces for reference once back in the studio. These photos serve as a reminder of colour combinations and features which occasionally progress into watercolour sketches, an opportunity to practice brushwork before they take shape in clay. The watercolour painting,

Memory from Brancacci.
Watercolour on paper,
41 × 30 cm, 2019.

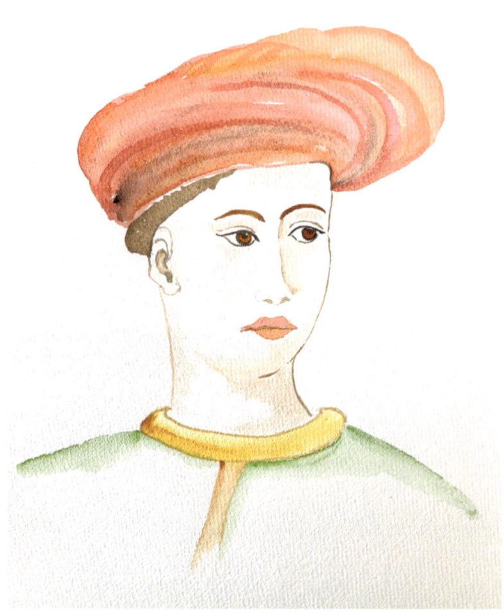

its fluid transparency, the mixing of colours as I go along, being able to see instantly the result and how colours relate to each other, is refreshing for me. Within a few minutes a character appears on the paper. I am able to judge ways of approaching a portrait using a variety of brushes, large Japanese ones as well as fine sable ones. I can see how features like the shape of the mouth, the colour of the eyes, as well as the direction in which they are looking, can change the whole personality of the subject.

Coiled larger plates become my canvases, their size and shape having a portrait in mind. It is a long process, and when things go wrong there is no going back. Making some smaller plaquettes gives me the opportunity to produce some of the portraits in a sketchy, and freer way and helps me to try painting and drawing more experimentally. I look at paintings, drawings and photographs of women artists, musicians, writers: there is a fascination in discovering life details and faces of the creators of works which enrich my own life.

And so the journey continues ...

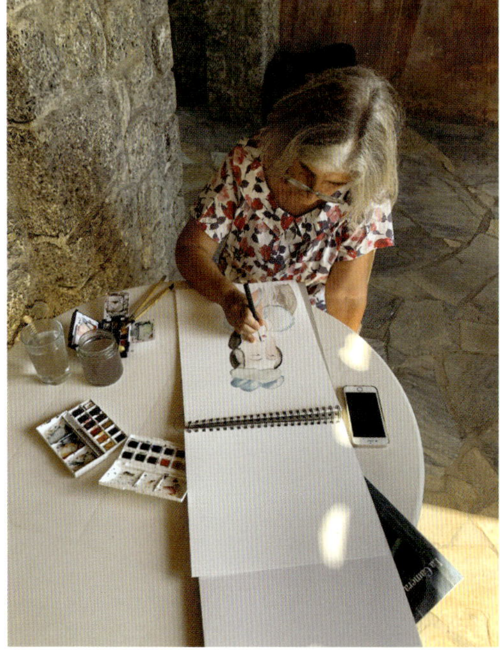

Study from a Chinese Vase.
Watercolour on paper,
41 × 30 cm, 2019

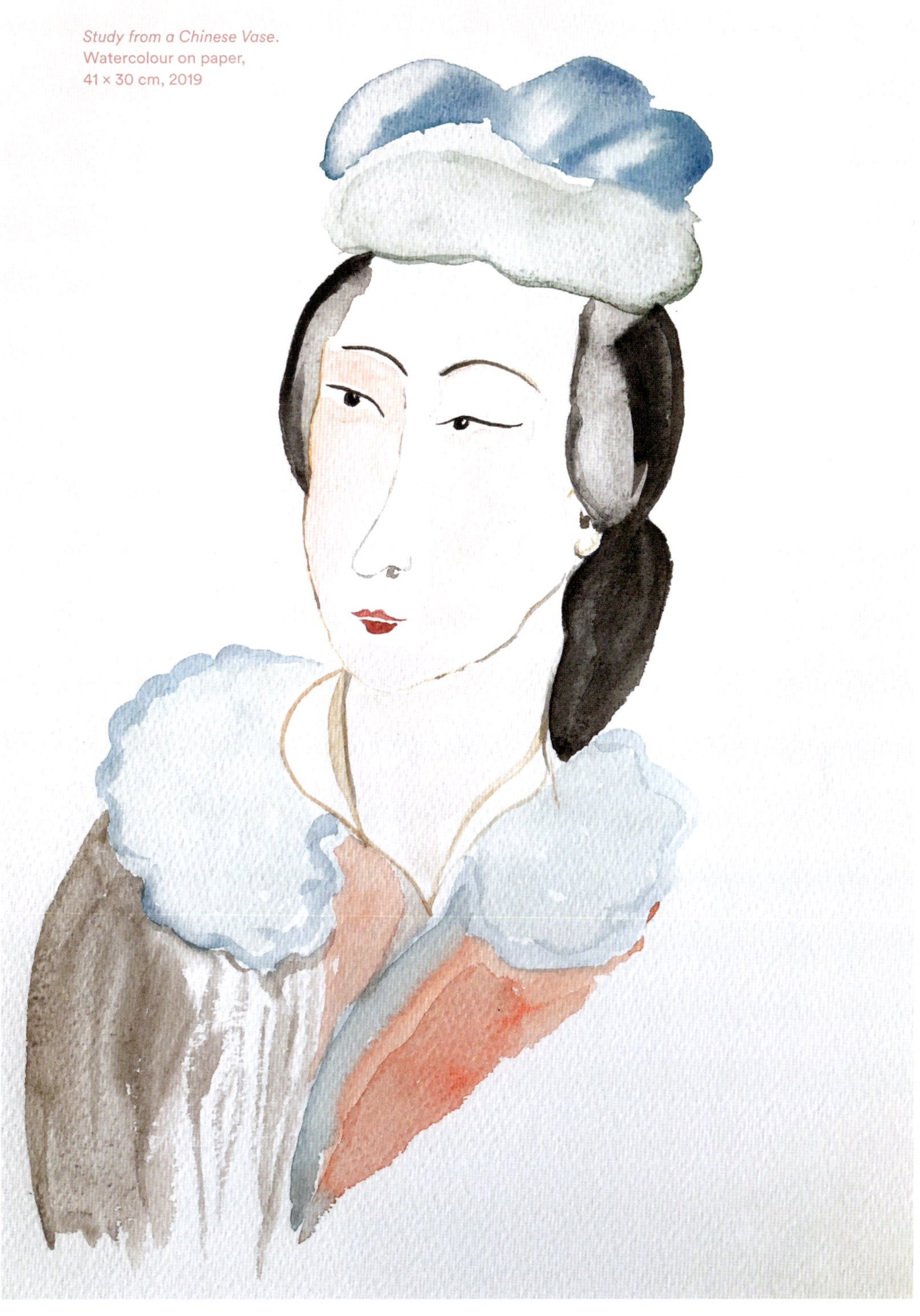

Once Upon a Time There was Tin-Glaze

Tanya Harrod

Maiolica or tin-glaze, the genre of ceramics described so eloquently by Rob Kesseler elsewhere in this book, belongs to the history of ceramics in Europe and the Middle East. In the case of Agalis Manessi, tin-glaze also relates to the story of British studio pottery and to the very special replicative nature of Renaissance maiolica.

In 1973 Manessi entered the Central School of Art and Design to study ceramics after a year's Foundation course at Hammersmith School of Art (*see page 11*). She was joining a department with a short, distinguished history, traceable back to the leadership of Dora Billington who had been appointed department head in 1938. At that date the relatively new art form of 'modern' or 'studio' pottery largely looked to early Chinese ceramics, to Korean ceramics and to medieval British pottery for inspiration. It was a canon of excellence set out concisely in Bernard Leach's *A Potter's Book* of 1940. Billington, however, wrote and spoke up for broader geographies.

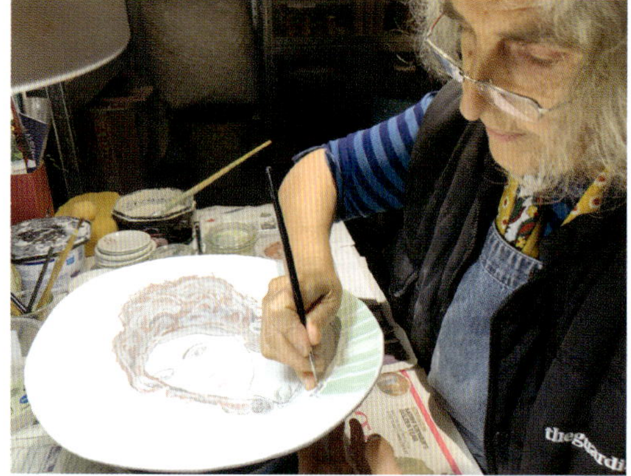

AM with Maurice Savin. Buste de Madame Rose Larock-Granoff. 1937. Musée d'art modern de Troyes.

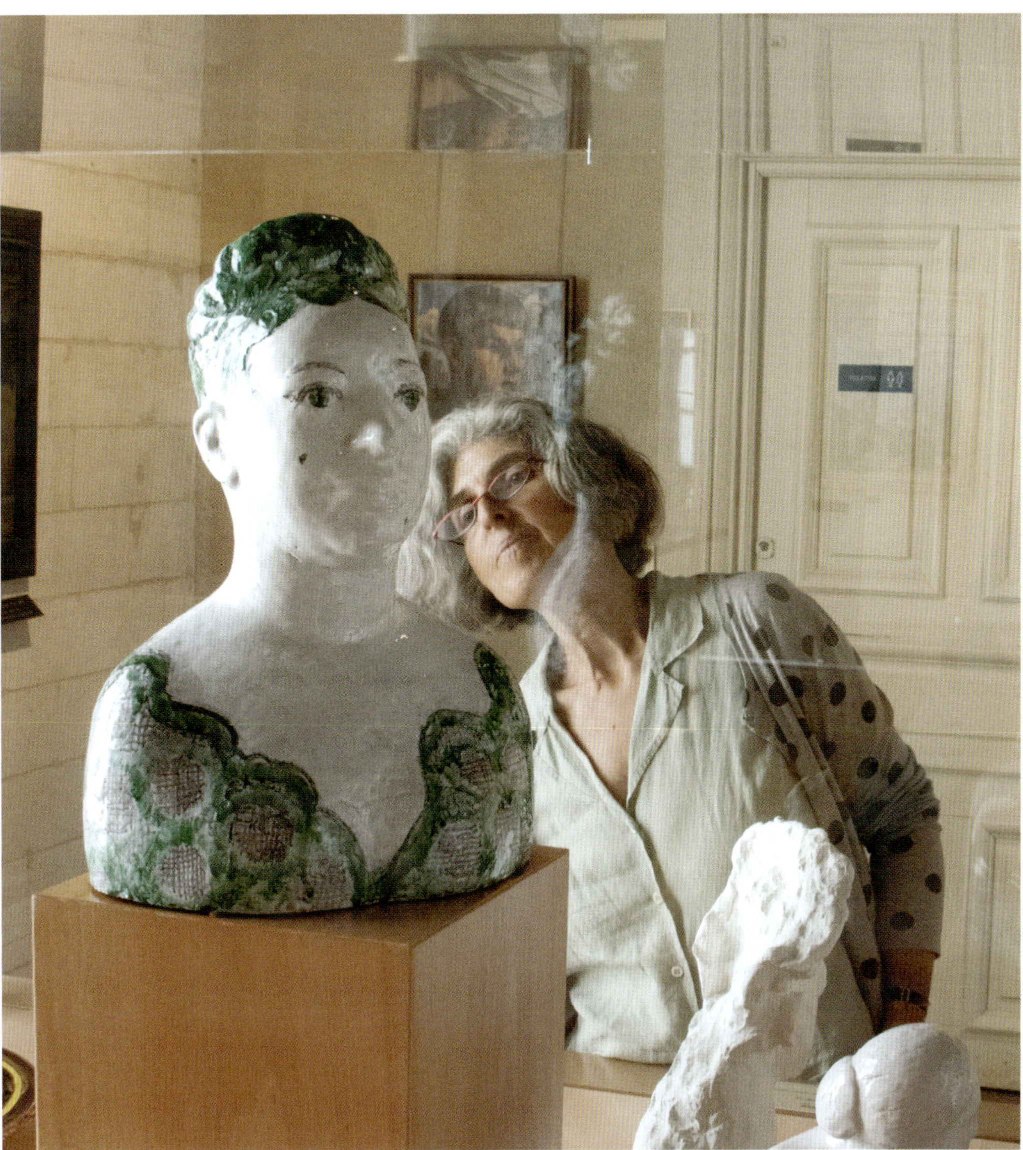

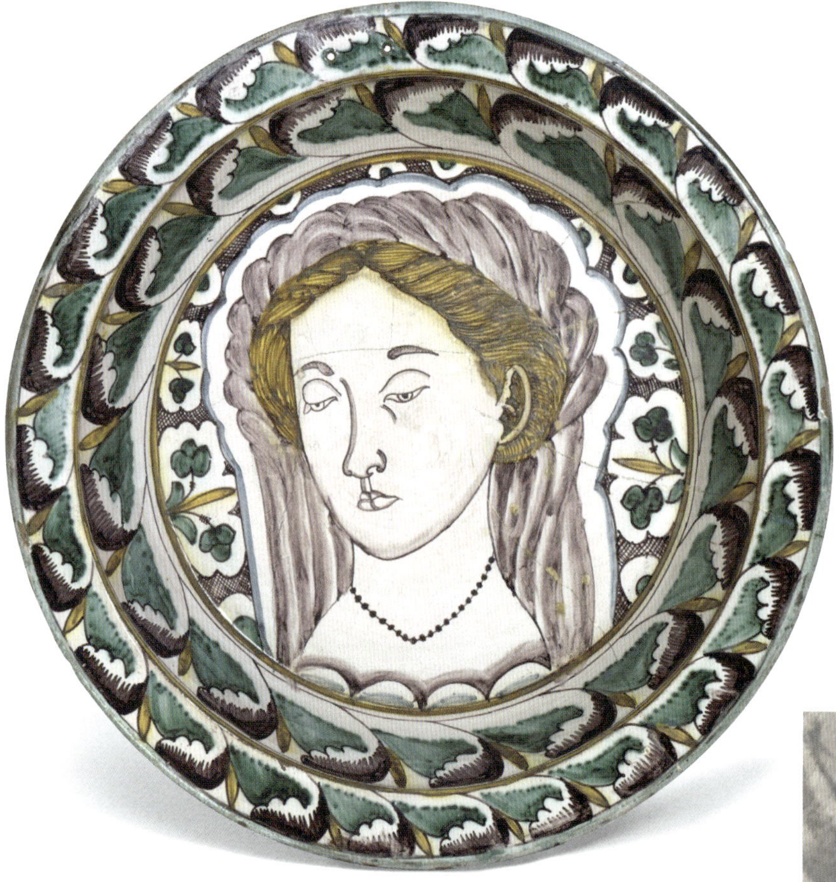

Large maiolica dish depicting the portrait of a lady in green, manganese and yellow and light blue glaze, made in Montelupo, Italy, between 1470 and 1490.

Glaze tests, tin-glazed earthenware with painted oxides.

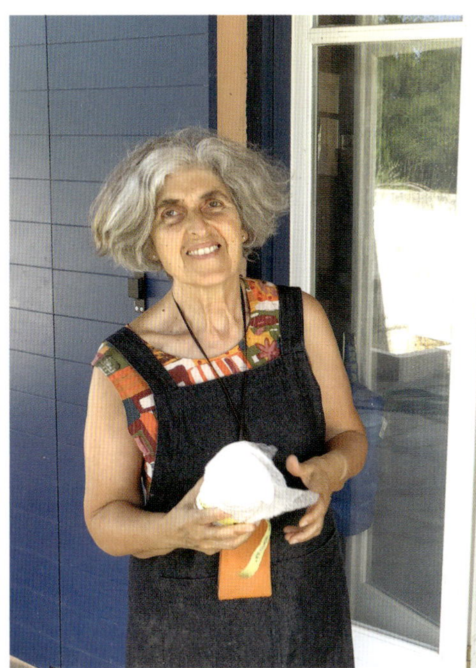

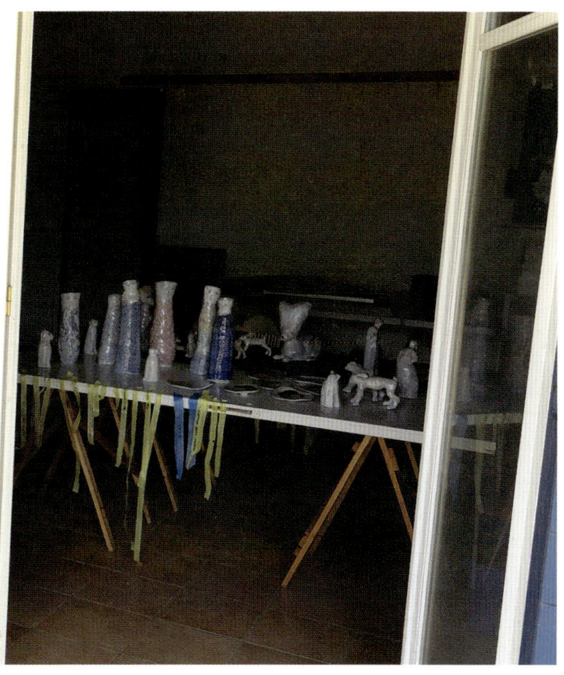

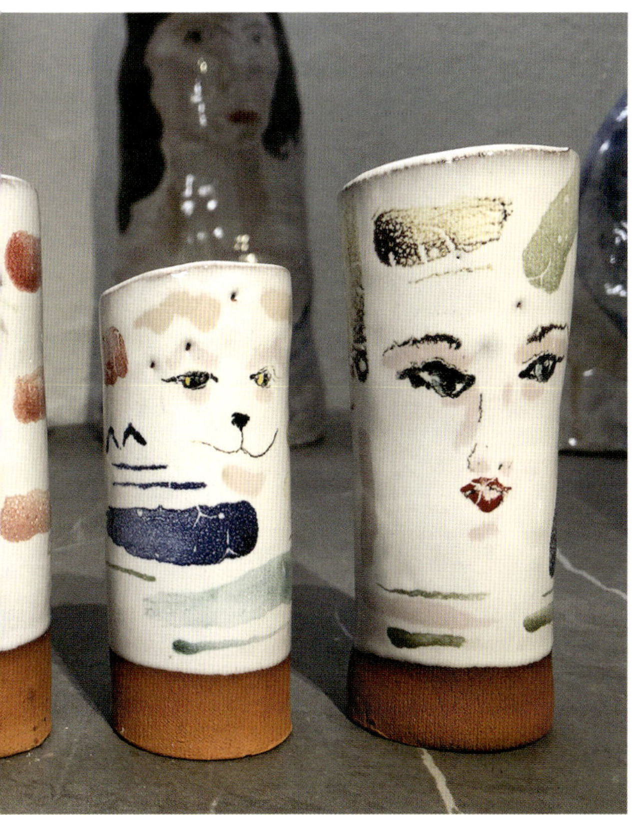

She urged her students not to overlook European traditions, in particular salt-glaze and tin-glaze. There were early modern precedents for her interests – in the form of the tin-glaze wares of William de Morgan and the work of the French Fauve artists who, with the encouragement of the dealer Ambroise Vollard, had painted on tin-glaze pots in a modernist spirit during 1906–1911. A group of these Fauve ceramics, including pots decorated by Henri Matisse and André Derain, had been included in Roger Fry's exhibition *Manet and the Post-Impressionists* of 1910. And when the Omega Workshops were set up by Fry in 1913, tin-glaze was seen as the ideal surface to be painted on by artists, including Fry himself, Vanessa Bell and Duncan Grant.

It was perhaps unsurprising that a group of students connected with the Central School began working in tin-glaze just after World War II. Aside from Billington's

Diamond Weave,
38 × 20 × 13, 2020.

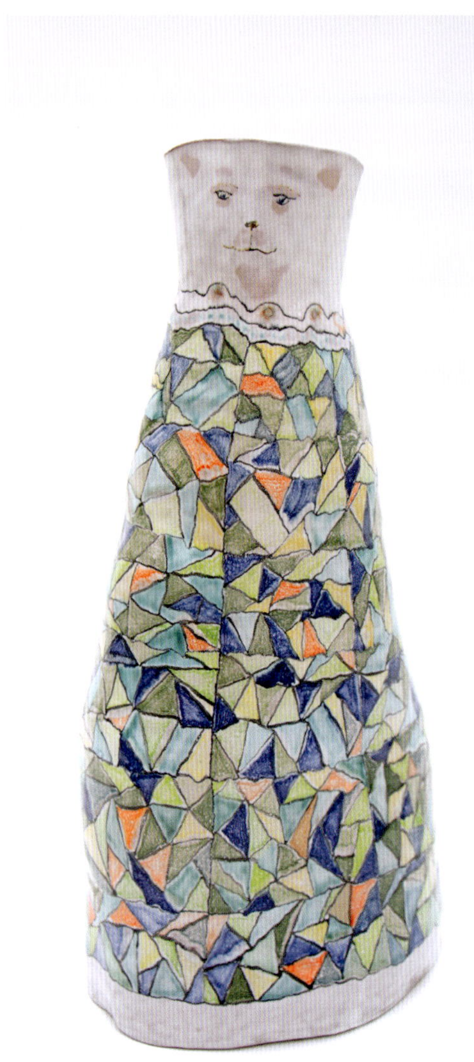

encouragement, another vital inspiration was the vigour and playfulness of the pots made by Pablo Picasso from 1947 onwards at the Madoura Pottery at Vallauris. Some were tin-glaze, many were manipulated forms thrown for Picasso, and he also painted with vigour on oval press-moulded dishes. Inspired by Picasso, William Newland, a New Zealand ex-serviceman who had taken evening classes with Billington, went on to teach Margaret Hine, James Tower and Nicholas Vergette at the Institute of Education. The group set in train a tin-glaze renaissance of decorated platters and figurative pieces – prancing bulls, owls and cats – all emblematic of post-war gaiety and endorsed by Billington as 'The New Look in British Pottery'.

By the time that Manessi arrived at the Central School the tin-glaze revival had receded, living on most convincingly in the ceramics of Alan Caiger-Smith, another Central School graduate. But a special kind of freedom still informed the teaching there, with a focus on sculptural hand-building. The staff included Gordon Baldwin, Gillian Lowndes, Eileen Nisbet, Kenneth Clark, Dan Arbeid and the painter Geoffrey Rogers. Every kind of technique was taught and, by the time she left the Central, Manessi was working in hand-built porcelain, making

Rosie's Sister,
25 × 9 × 6 cm, 2017.

objects of great tenderness, echoing the work of another recent student, Andrew Lord. But ultimately Manessi abandoned porcelain in search of colour, turning to tin-glaze on sculpted hand-built earthenware as a vehicle for painterly exploration.

The shift to tin-glaze opened up new worlds. Manessi makes tin-glaze figurines that reflect on the human condition and our generalised vulnerability. Perhaps it is not surprising that she makes angels also. 'Angels fly because they take things so lightly,' said G.K. Chesterton; but Manessi's angels are more grounded, accidental angels surprised at their otherworldliness, rather like the Staffordshire figures so admired by Herbert Read because they 'stumbled into beauty'. Manessi is also a sympathetic *animalière* whose dogs are generic, familiar and classical all in one, walking out of Renaissance hunting scenes and out of a painting by Franz Marc, *Dog Lying in the Snow*. Her cats are suitably poised. Some, however, have two faces, a drift into Surrealism that suggests mood and mystery. Her strangest creations are felines hand-built as tall vessels. These are objects that appear to reflect upon themselves, each with a cat face looking down at the complex patterns that adorn the body of the vase.

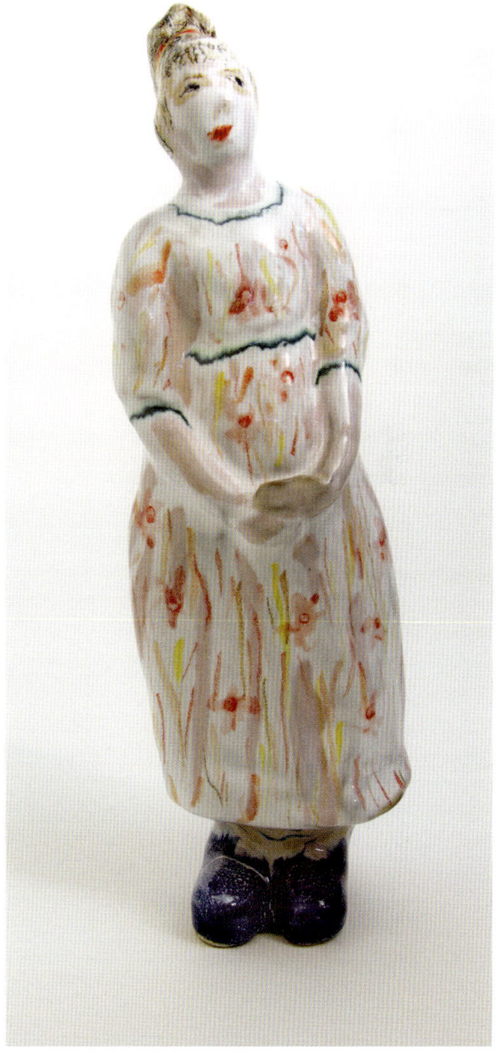

Renaissance maiolica is an important exemplar for Manessi, studied initially in the

Victoria and Albert Museum, the rich palette capturing her imagination. She is particularly inspired by one branch of maiolica, the *istoriata* wares made in Italy from around 1500 onwards. These are narrative paintings on pots, *istoriata* maiolica depending heavily on engravings and woodcuts after paintings and sculptures, antique and modern. In an age of infinite visual reproduction, appropriation and quotation, *istoriata* maiolica, in effect copies of copies, speak to us especially powerfully. Then again, British commemorative and portrait ceramics are also based on a catholic range of graphic visual information from the Toby Jug onwards. Manessi's work hovers between these two worlds – that of the Renaissance maiolica workshop and the homelier industries of English Delft, Staffordshire flatbacks and memorial wares.

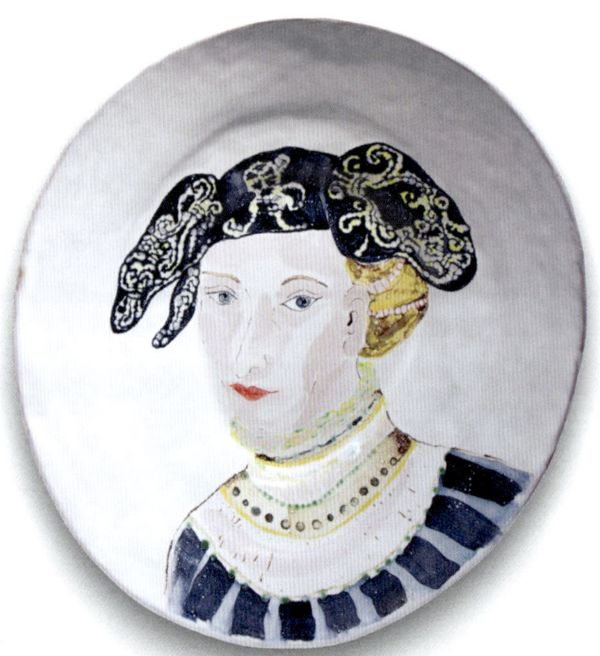

Lucas after Cranach the Elder, 30 × 27 cm, 2018.

Her portrait plates come close to *istoriata* platters and to British memorial wares, borrowing playfully from a great range of imagery. A portrait on a platter speaks to us in a very special way, being both grand and homely, while the fact that Manessi's platters are coiled rather than thrown gives them a special softness and presence. They look remarkable hung together on a wall, being tributes to artists as various as Cranach, Masaccio and Masolino, Gainsborough, Schiele and Sickert. The power of these plates lies in Manessi's choices as much as in her graphic skill.

As a group, the portrait plates have much in common with the *Famous Women* dinner service commissioned for the art historian Sir Kenneth Clark, some 50 plates painted by Vanessa Bell and Duncan Grant depicting women of letters, queens, great beauties,

Thoughtful Angel in Blue, 17 × 6 × 5 cm, 2015.

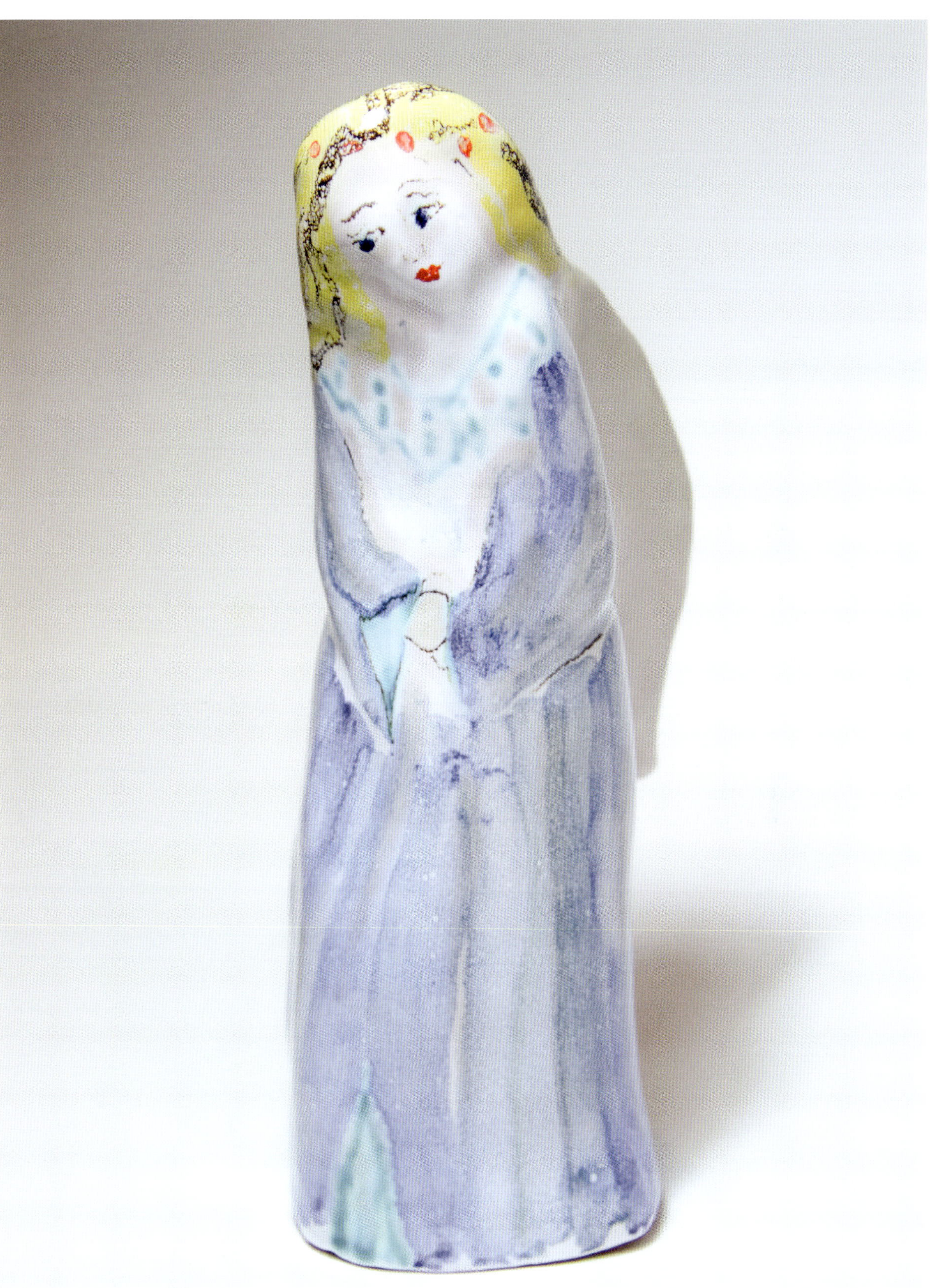

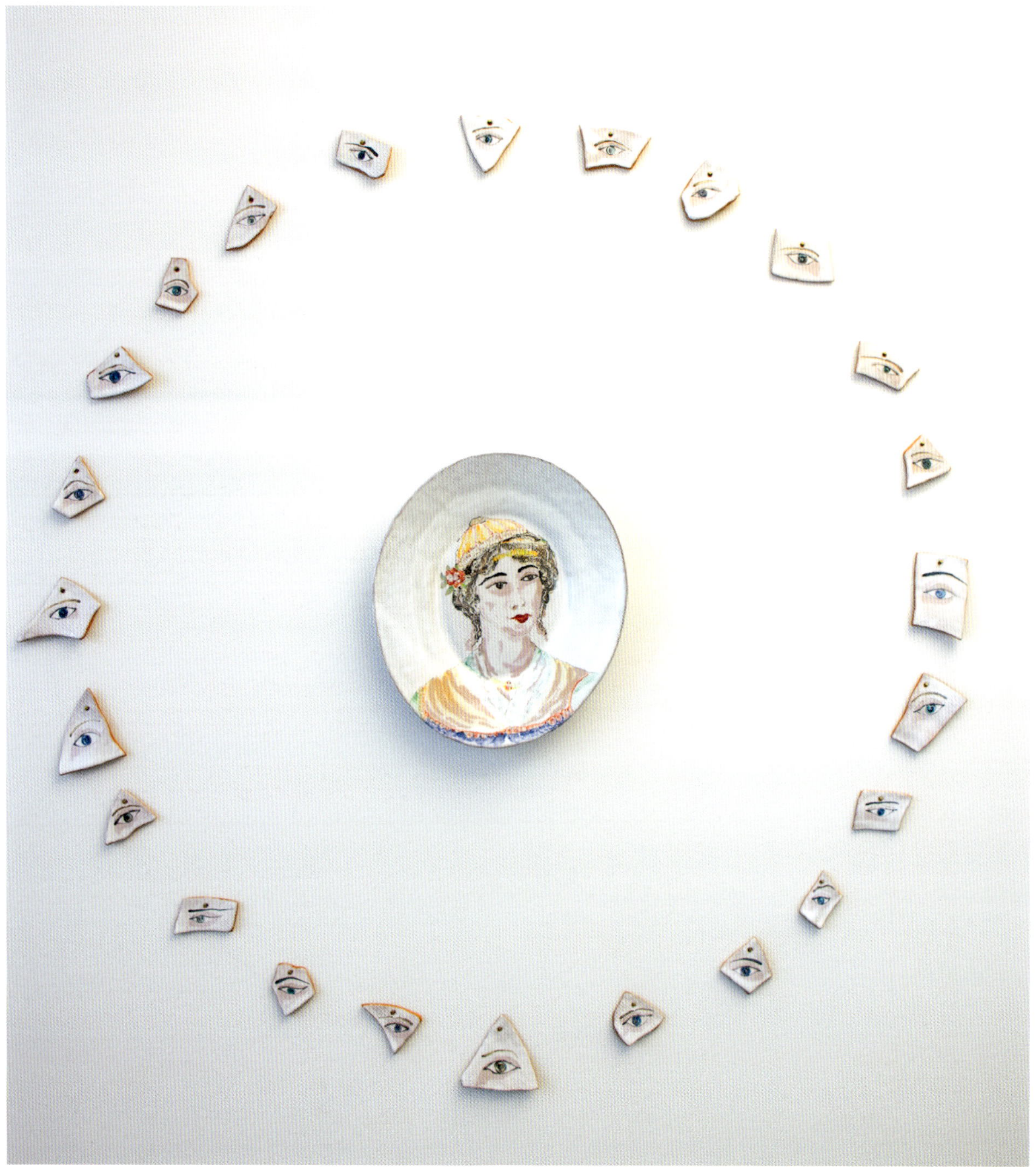

Manto Gazing at Liberty

Painted maiolica dish with 24 eye fragments. 100 × 100cm, 2021. Commissioned for the exhibition Ex-Stasis, Tinos, Greece celebrating 200 years of the Greek revolution. A Portrait of Manto Mavrogenous (1796–1848), an emancipated woman who with her actions gave everything for the struggle to deliver Greece from the Ottoman Empire. In her quest, Manto commissioned a collection of portrait plates of Hellenic Heroes that were sold to raise funds for the cause.

Young Woman, after Cranach, 33 × 33 cm, 2019.

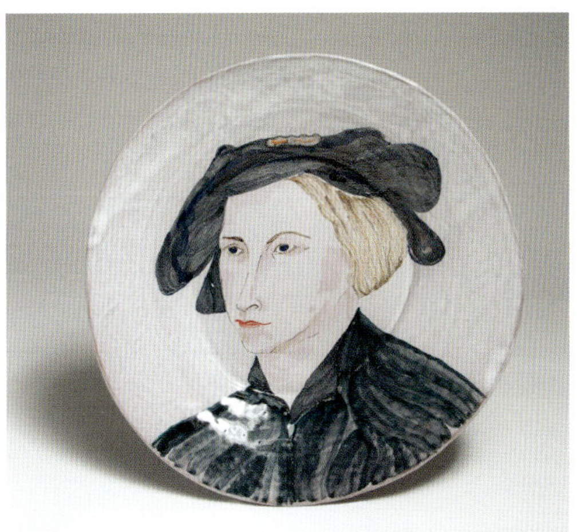

dancers and actors. But Manessi is working for her own pleasure, not for an art world panjandrum. Her appropriations move from Italian fresco to Austrian Expressionism, while her decisions as to whom to portray are more mysterious, being part of a series of journeys. These are literal journeys as she travels across Europe from London to her home in Corfu. But they are also spiritual voyages, as she seeks out the essence of existing works of art and transforms them, giving them a vivid permanence.

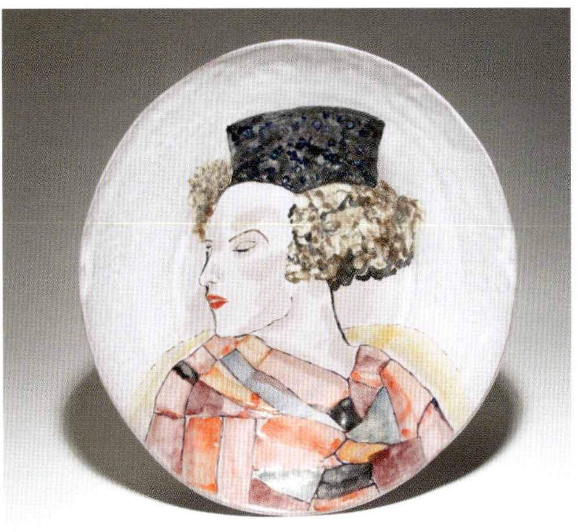

Looking at Egon Schiele, 33 × 33 cm, 2019.

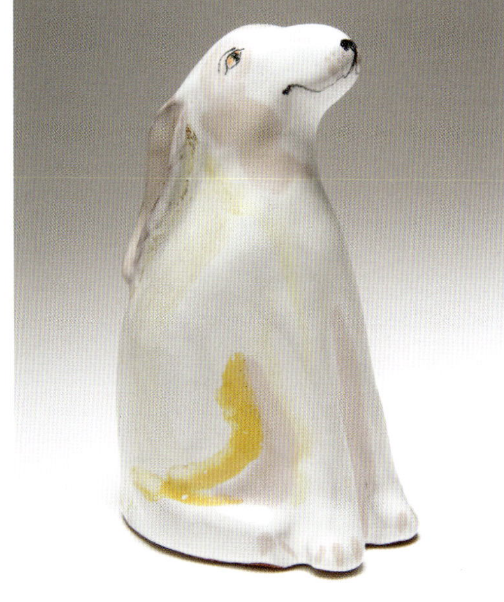

Sitting Hare with Yellow Patch, 22 × 14 × 8 cm, 2016.

A Studio Visit

Mina Holland[3]

Agalis Manessi's studio is reminiscent of a Dutch genre painting, a busy scene with limited but potent light that catches angles – cheekbones, knuckles, glazes, pages. We are in the cavernous basement of a Georgian house in Kennington, south-east London, at the end of which sits a desk illuminated by a rectangular beam of daylight streaming down from what was once a coal chute.

Several of Agalis' works – painted vases and ceramic animals – are also lit up, as are manifold jars and pots brimming with assorted paint brushes. Above the desk, she has tacked a few postcards of paintings, inspiration for one piece or another, among them some that evoke the very lighting in this room. It feels brilliantly meta.

Manessi makes and paints ceramics here in a technique called *maiolica*. Using red terracotta clay, she forms pieces – ranging from dishes to figures – and dips them in an earthenware glaze loaded with tin oxide, for a cloudy, opaque surface. She then paints onto this with metal oxides like copper, cobalt and iron. 'I love the way things look light and fresh and not labour intensive with it,' she says, 'but that belies the difficulty of the process. It's quite a gamble – lots can go wrong.' As she talks, I notice the economy with which Agalis moves – no gesture is wasted, each one graceful and considered.

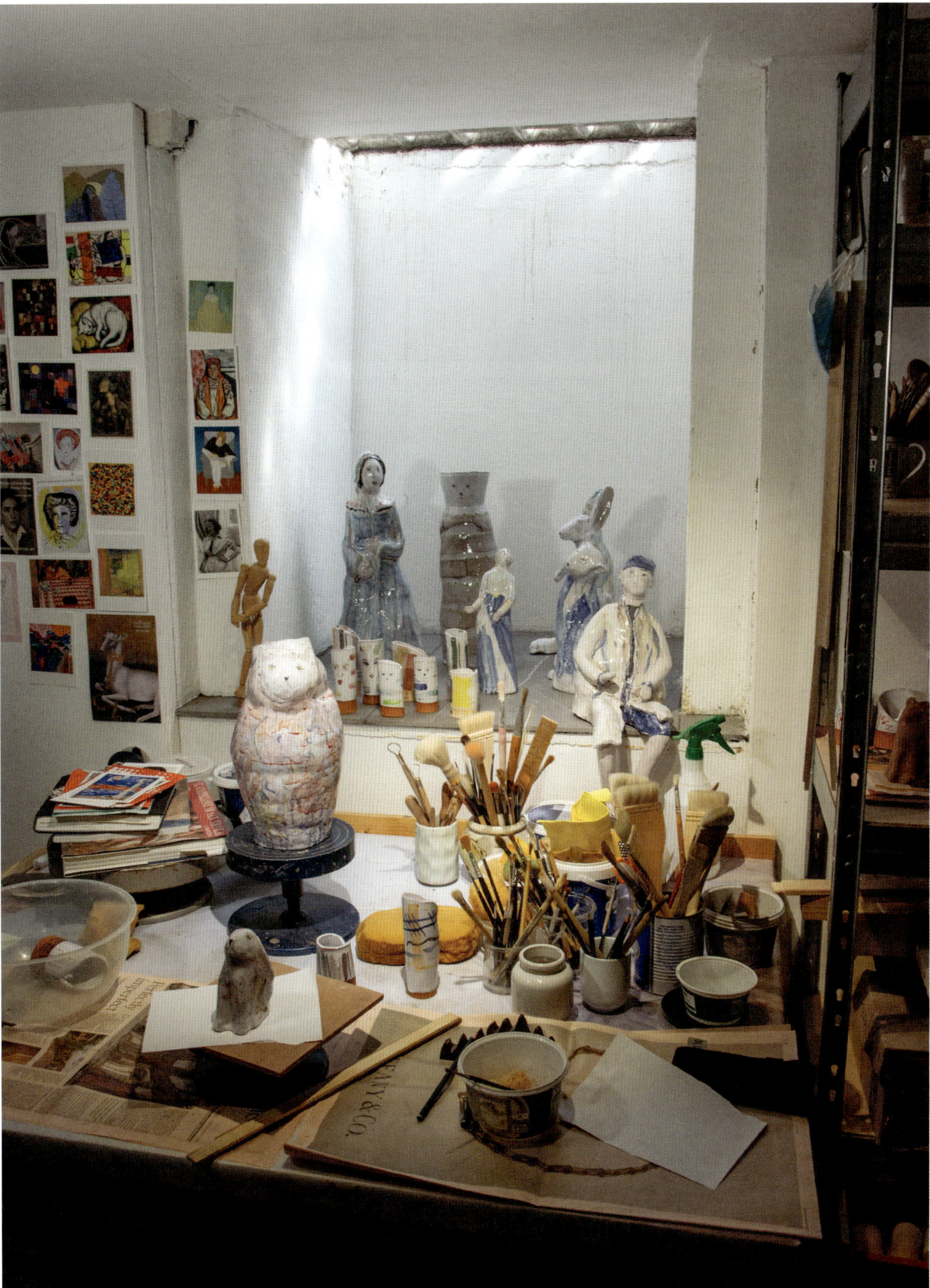
Perfectly
imperfect

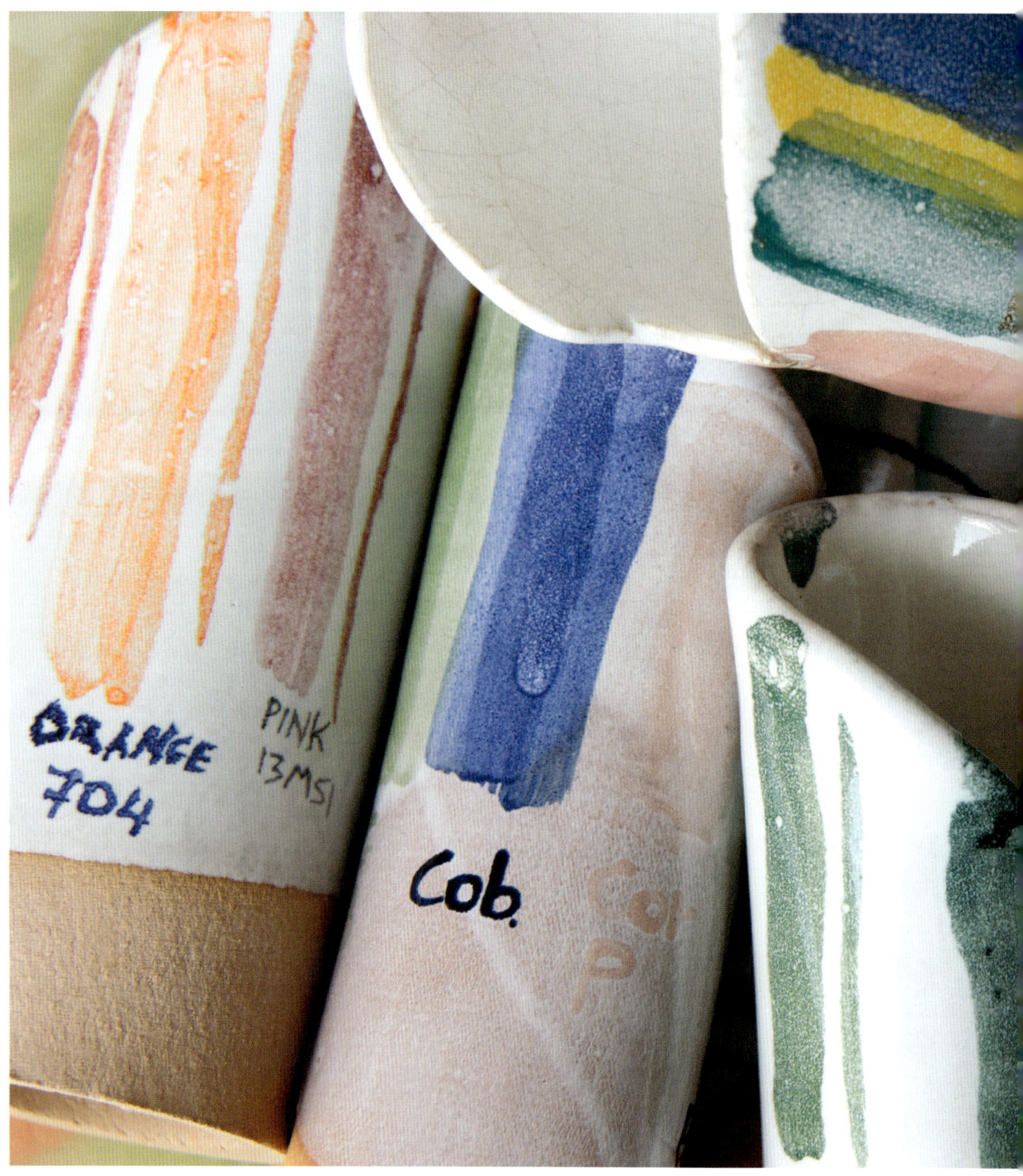

Glaze Tests. Tin-glazed earthenware with painted oxides.

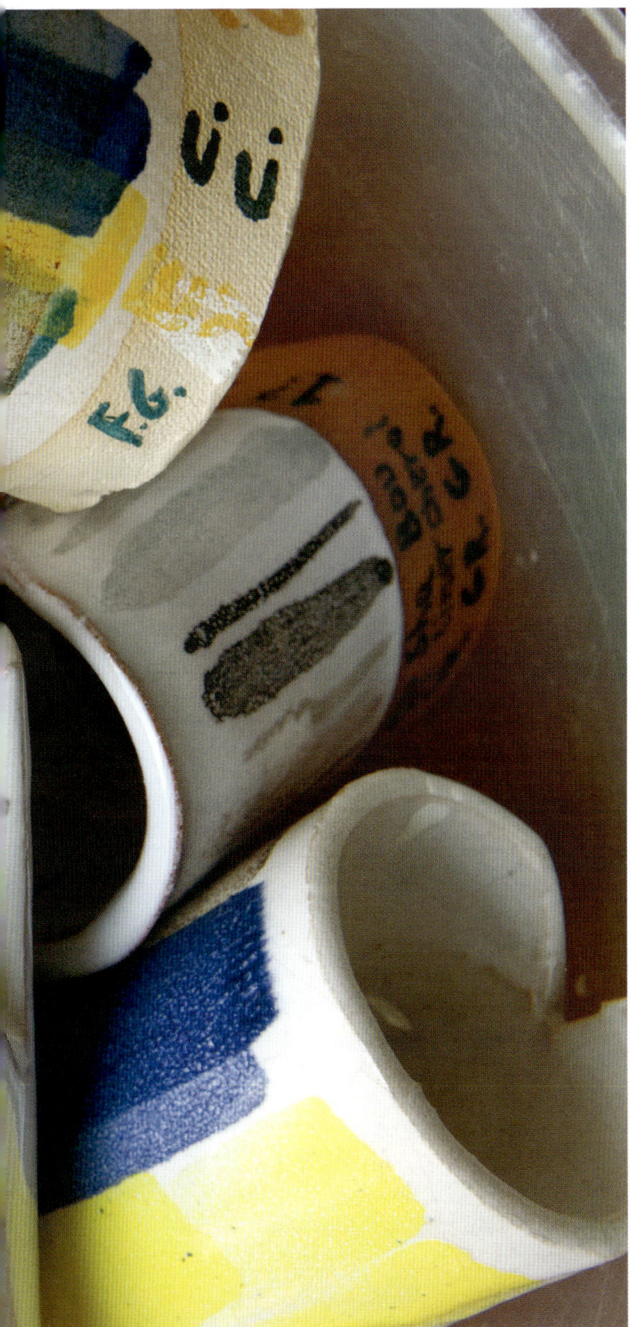

This soon makes sense. Growing up in Corfu, Manessi had her heart set on classical dance as a career, but after an accident, she took some time out to reconsider. She'd had no formal art education – it didn't exist in Greece at the time – but was drawn to it, particularly to ceramics, 'because it seemed a bit like dancing, a material that could move about.' In Greece, only Athens offered an opening into the world of pottery, and only as an apprentice. Manessi wanted to study and, having heard about British art foundation courses, applied, among others, to Hammersmith and Chelsea College of Art. 'I stuck with the idea of ceramics, partly because it was something I could get my mind round. The concepts and the language of art were like Chinese to me, but ceramics felt more practical.' Her career started and continued with an intuitive flow: she has worked with clay ever since.

The two-part process of making ceramics and then painting onto them always interested Manessi. For the first few years, she worked with porcelain, using a method called *sgraffito*, scratching lines into raw clay before filling them with oxide. Drawn to the range and intensity of colours, she then experimented with maiolica – a process which, by definition, is far less forgiving than

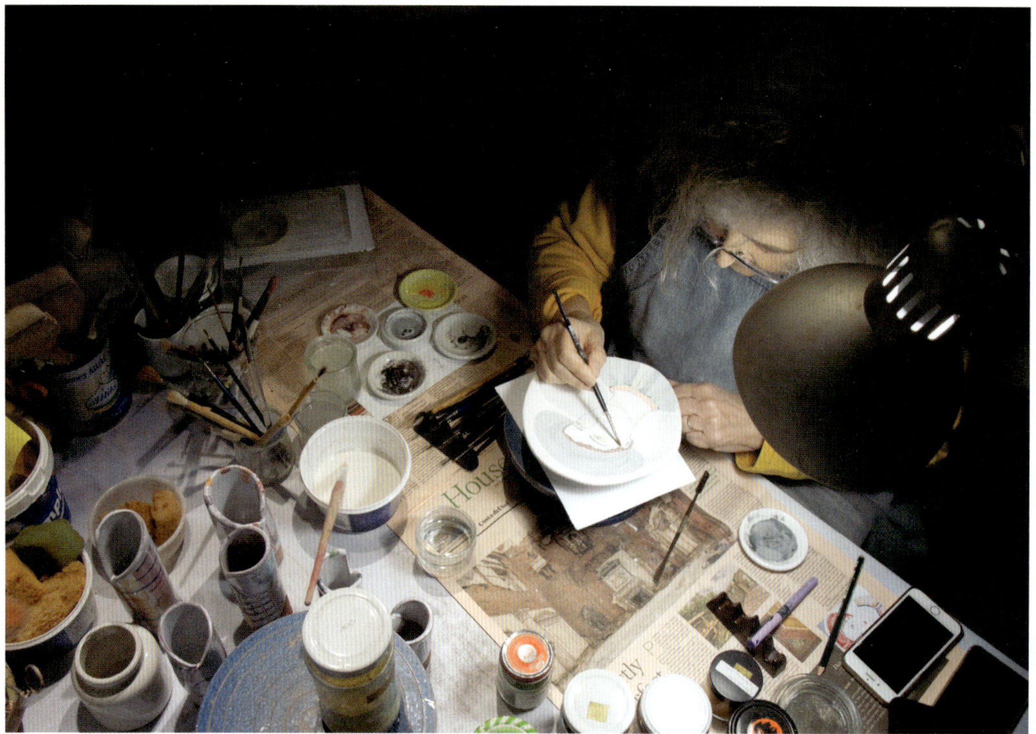

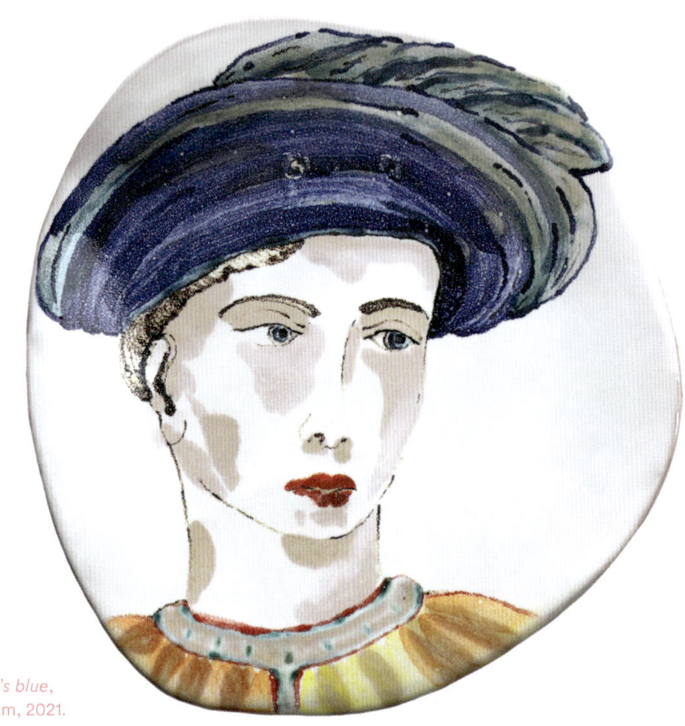

Masolino's blue,
20 × 20 cm, 2021.

sgraffito because things can't be undone. From a single, initial piece of clay, she moulds platters and vessels, models and figures; as forms, they are chunky, rustic, peculiarly at odds, I think, with the delicacy of Manessi's painting. It is as though, with these two phases to her process, she is exercising two parts of herself.

Her shelves are peppered with sprawling whippets and hovering bunnies, also ducks, chicks and sparrows with openings in their beaks – designed, she says, to be placeholders for a wedding – their bodies and faces looking out from tins of paint powder arranged by colour families – blues/greens, reds/pinks. And then there are the cats – 'I've always liked cats' – which range from figurines to vases she describes as 'catamorphic', inspired by the British Museum's collection of mummified cats. 'They are like the cats' apparitions,' she says, each with its own character. Some sleep, others smile, others still have a knowing look. I feel I might have been plunged into a book by Lewis Carroll, a poem by T.S. Eliot. Beneath dream-like faces, the cats have whimsically patterned bodies, untidily geometric, their stars or flowers, or hexagons suggestive, I think, of a reptile's skin. There is a kind of wonder to them and to this room, it fizzes with ideas.

The piece that turns my head, however, is a small plate picturing a glamorous, dark-haired woman. 'She's called Fritza,' Manessi tells me, 'and she was one of Gustav Klimt's muses.' The starting points for her portraits are diverse, inspired by what the artist might have read lately – the poetry of Sylvia Plath, Isabella Blow's biography – or special commissions, 'someone once sent me a picture by Cranach the Elder to paint – and I thought what a fantastic hat he had.'

Agalis clearly planted roots deeply in Hackney, however, and during her years as a resident, no matter how far her work took her, always took part in local exhibitions, such as Ceramics in the City at the Geffrye Museum. 'I could entice people I knew from the community, who would never have travelled into central London for a show,' she says, alluding to her teaching work at Homerton hospital. For almost three decades, she combined teaching with making her own art. She worked alongside the hospital's occupational therapy team to provide classes for local people with mental health issues, 'in which I have no training, but which the hospital saw as a strength.' Patients could shed their medical labels and become simply ceramics students.

For Agalis, too, the experience offered the chance to reframe, shedding light on her own work, just like the coal chute in her studio. 'I learnt a lot about what was possible with my material. In the ceramics world, there's lots of emphasis on how things *should* be done – but I watched as people who had never touched clay produced beautiful things simply through play.'

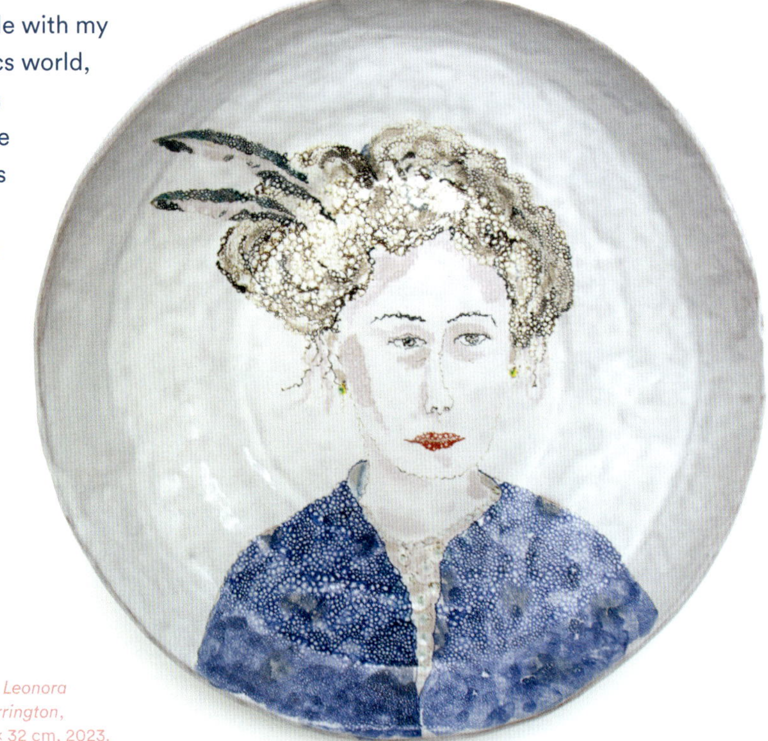

For Leonora Carrington, 31 × 32 cm, 2023.

Fritza, 18 × 15 cm, 2021.
After *Portrait of Fritza Riedler*, Gustav Klimt, 1906.

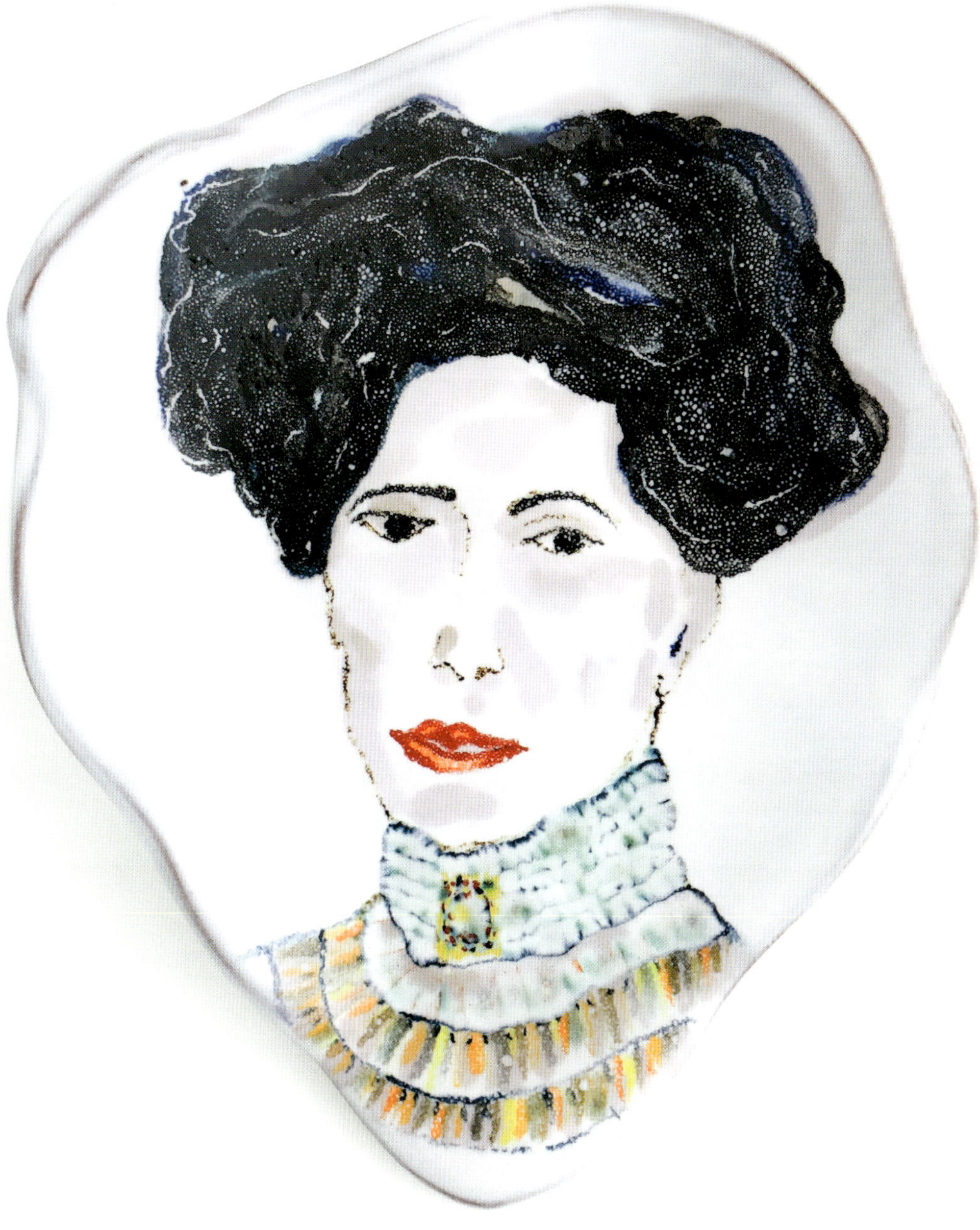

The Before and After

Rob Kesseler

Tin-glaze painting, or maiolica, as it is also known, is a technique of painting with colouring oxides and stains on to an unfired glazed surface loaded with tin oxide to give an intense and subtle spectrum of colour against a bright white surface. Its roots can be traced back to ninth-century Iraq, where the potential to add colour and pattern to functional form ensured its rapid reception throughout an expanding Islamic world. In contrast to the duller, earthen tones of medieval pottery, the colourful potential of this new technique ensured its spread in popularity across North Africa, the Mediterranean and up into northern Europe. With the flowering of the Italian Renaissance in the 16th century, the skills of the artisan potters exploited the potential of such a vibrant palette to create complex narrative compositions borrowed from classical paintings, and bold stylised portraits. With the complexities of wrapping an image around a form or across the curved space of a dish, such works were elevated to a higher art form, with painters seeking equal status with other artists of the day.

For Agalis Manessi, the art of maiolica lies somewhere between the haptic and happenstance, where the painting belies the difficulty of the process. Striving for poetic mastery through pictorial representation and a freshness of palette, she has built up her practice from a repeated engagement and understanding of how colours will behave in the firing. There is no reliable recipe, no formula that will guarantee a certain result, just experience and intuition. The powdery unfired glazed surface is an unforgiving, absorbent canvas where the weight of the brushstroke, the dilution of the oxide, the effect of one colour on top of another are not apparent until after the firing. Potassium dichromate in varying strengths looks yellow on the unfired ware and may give anything from a pale flesh tone to a murky yellow in the firing. Cobalt carbonate, a dull pink powder, turns a vibrant blue; copper oxide turns from black to green as it fuses with the glaze when it melts in the kiln.

At times, even the years of experience count for little, as control is relinquished in the kiln. The constituents of clay bodies and glaze recipes that have stood the test of time may subtly alter

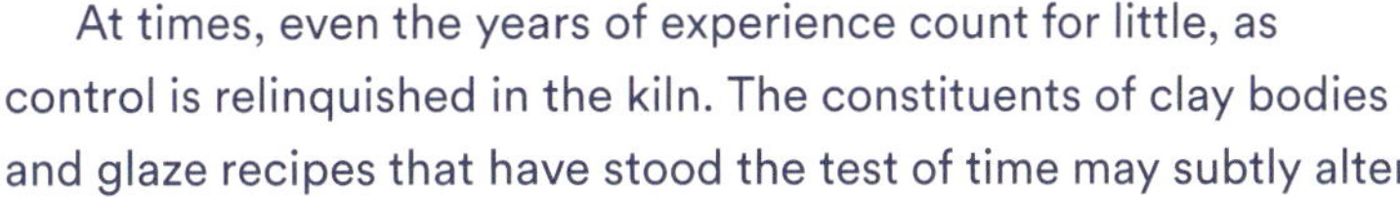

Klimt Girl, 2020. Left: Detail of unfired glaze painted with oxides. Right: After firing to 1085°C.

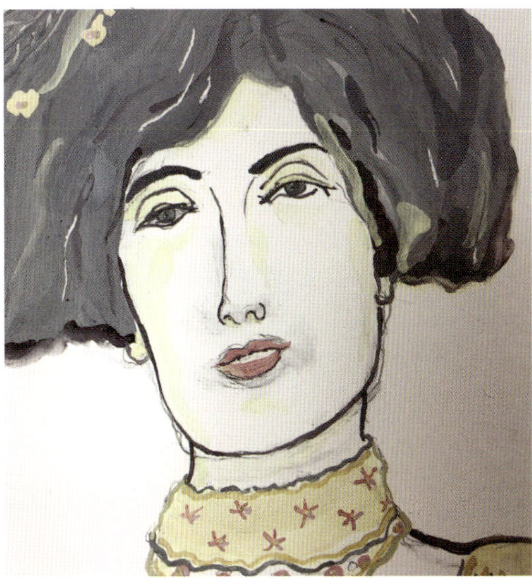

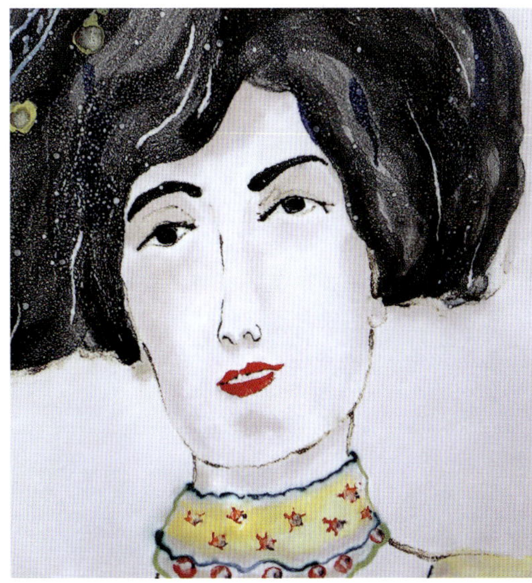

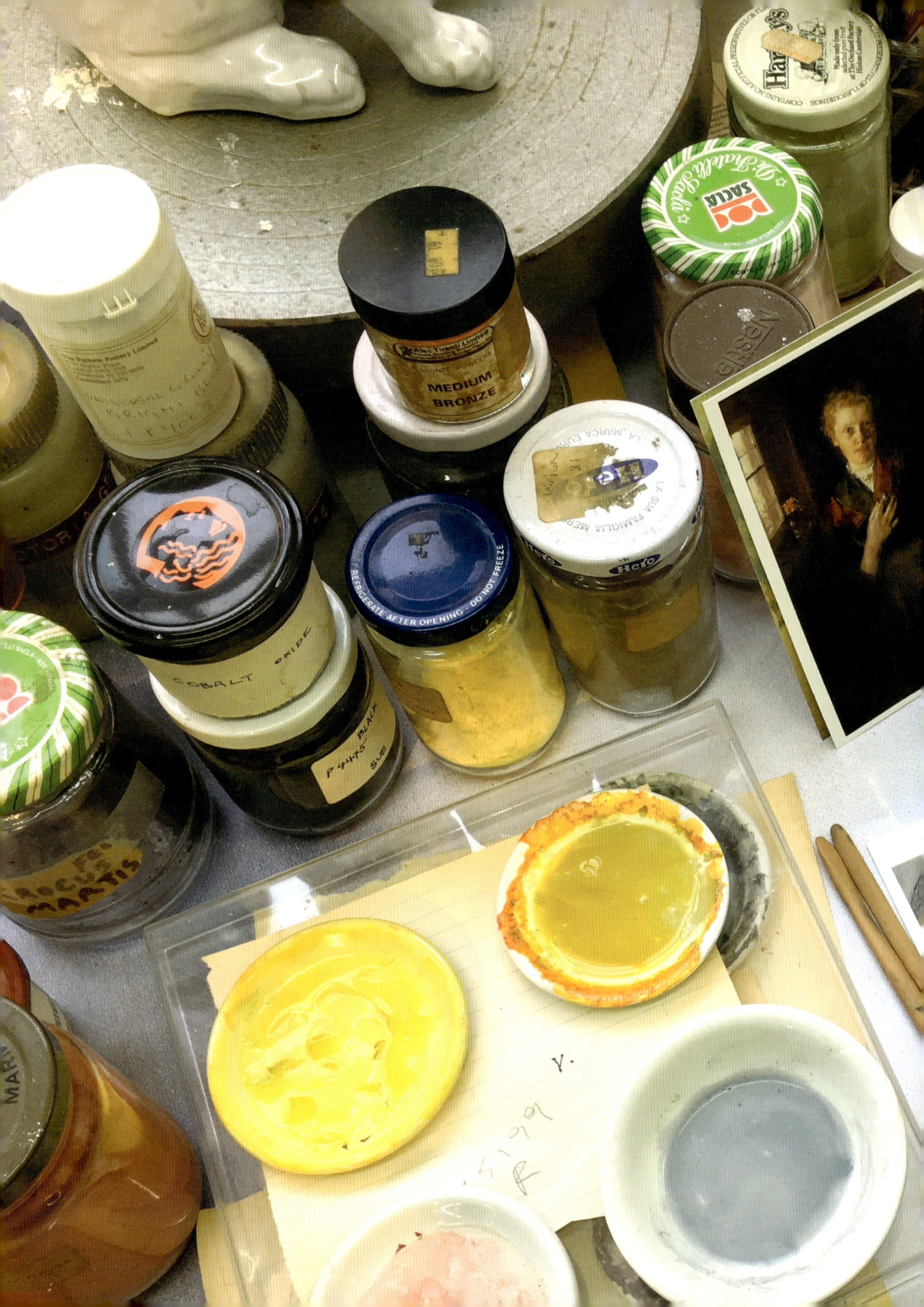

MEDIUM
BRONZE
COBALT OXIDE
REFRIGERATE AFTER OPENING · DO NOT FREEZE
Hero
LA SUA FAMIGLIA MERENDA
SACLA
BLACK
P4475
SUE

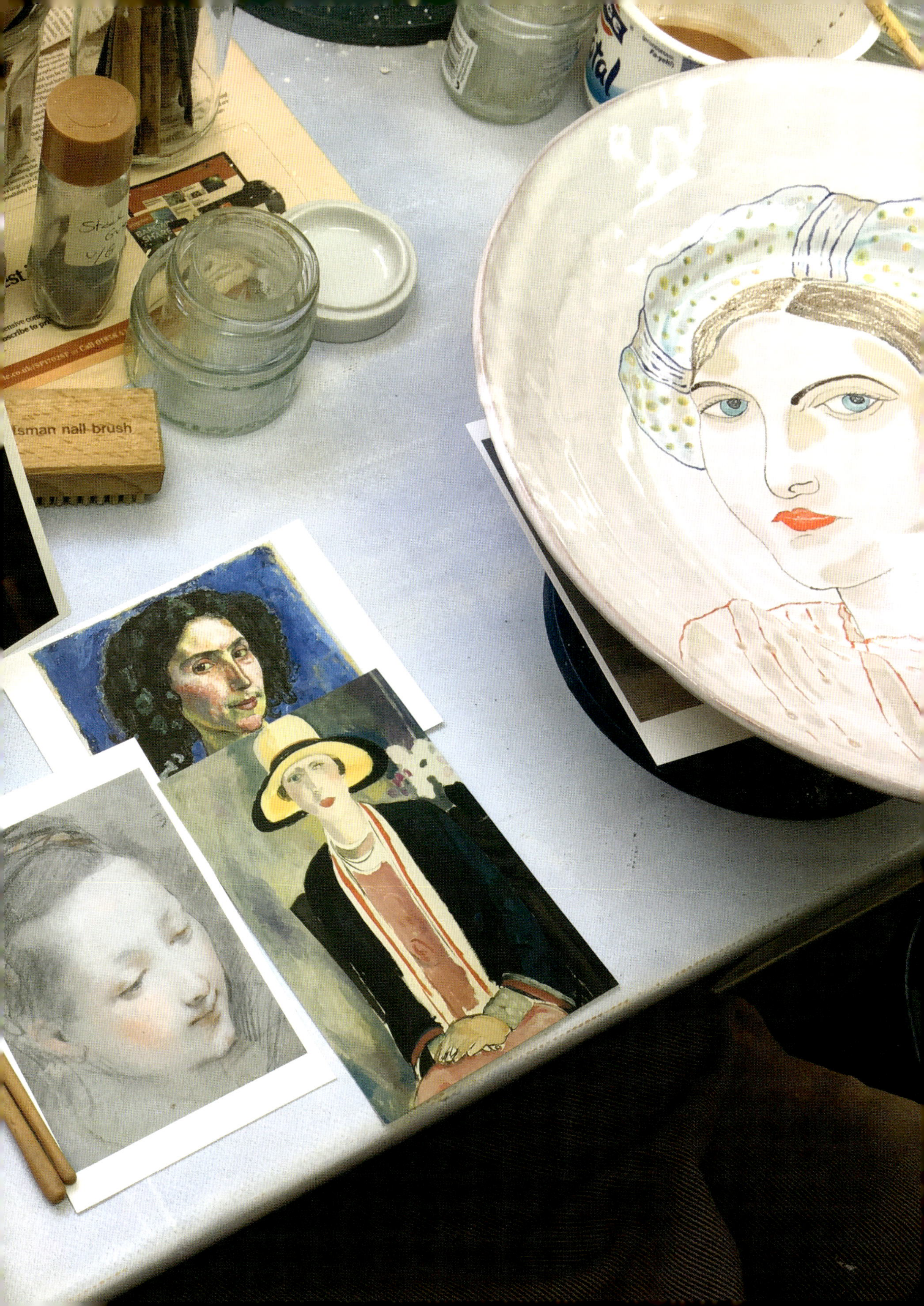
nail brush

Woman from Ukraine,
34 × 34 cm, 2022

with unexpected and seemingly irredeemable consequences. When the kiln reaches temperature, the dry glaze gradually turns to a molten glass on the surface of the work, the painted oxides sink and fuse within the glaze, linear drawings shift, brushstrokes soften. At the time of the conflict in Ukraine the artist painted a dish with the portrait of a Ukrainian woman in national costume with an elaborate headdress. Previous firings had suggested the glaze was starting to behave differently, but nothing quite prepared her for what she found on opening the kiln. The carefully painted contours of the face and fine details in the costume had all shifted and blurred and appeared as though being viewed through dappled glass. These unintended and unwanted consequences take time to remedy, and many pieces have been lost in the process of trying to correct the behaviour of the materials. In the case of the Ukrainian portrait, however, the distressed surface seemed wholly appropriate, a sympathetic resonance with the plight of the people of Ukraine.

Journeys are undertaken by artists and the works they create. Objects travel to new homes and new lands to reside with other objects, within other collections. In 2018 when the artist relocated her studio in Kennington, in the borough of Lambeth, she was moving into an area rich in ceramic history. Ten minutes' walk away, the Royal Doulton Factory was one of many potteries to have emerged in previous centuries on the banks of the Thames, the importance of the river providing a conduit for the transportation

Geo cat in Blue (detail), 2019. Top: Unfired glaze painted with cobalt oxide. Below: After firing to 1085°C.

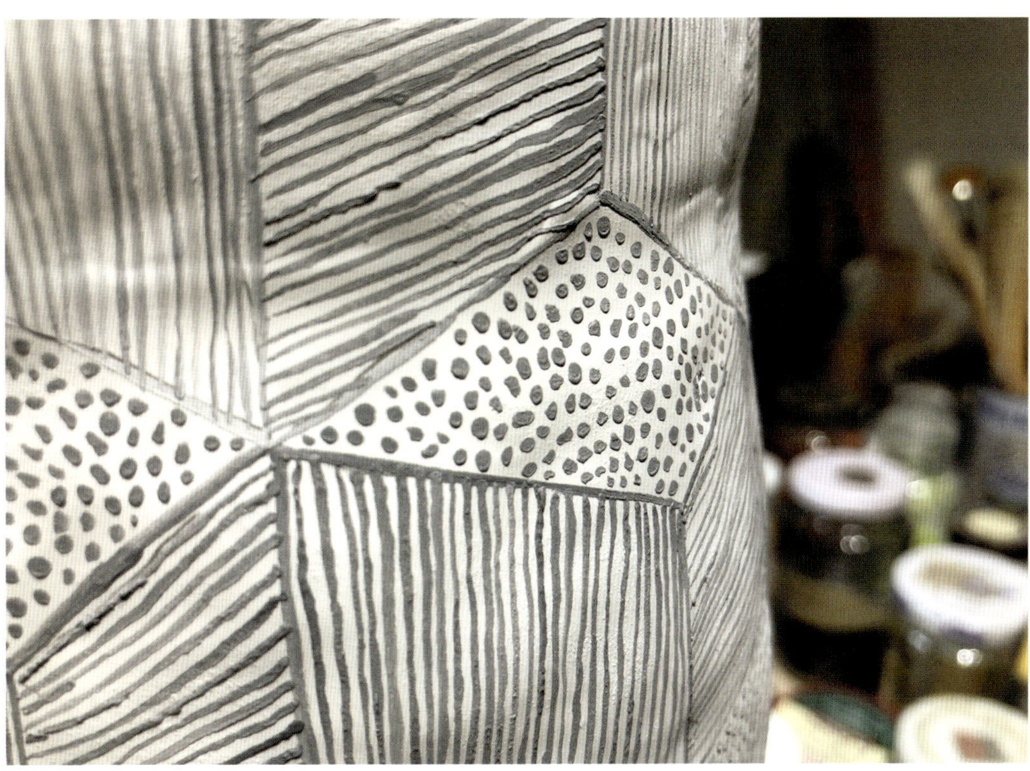

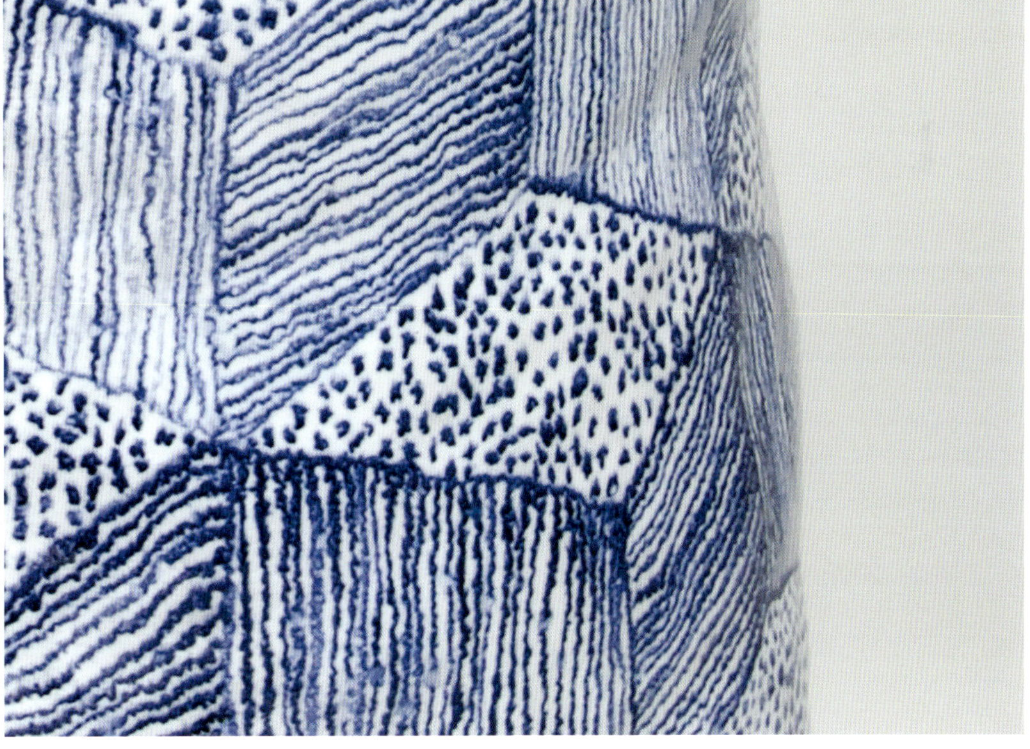

of raw materials and shipping of goods. It is not surprising that two of the primary characteristics of ceramic, its durability and fragility, have left a tell-tale trail along the foreshore of the river. Now at low tide shadowy figures can be seen meandering along the water's edge, mud-larking in search of sherds sifted and brought to the surface of the sandy riverbed. Broken fragments of English Delftware from the Lambeth pottery, clay pipes, Roman slipware, handles from Victorian chamber-pots and roof tiles from the Great Fire of London, all become archaeological mementoes, a before- and after-life for the ceramically curious.

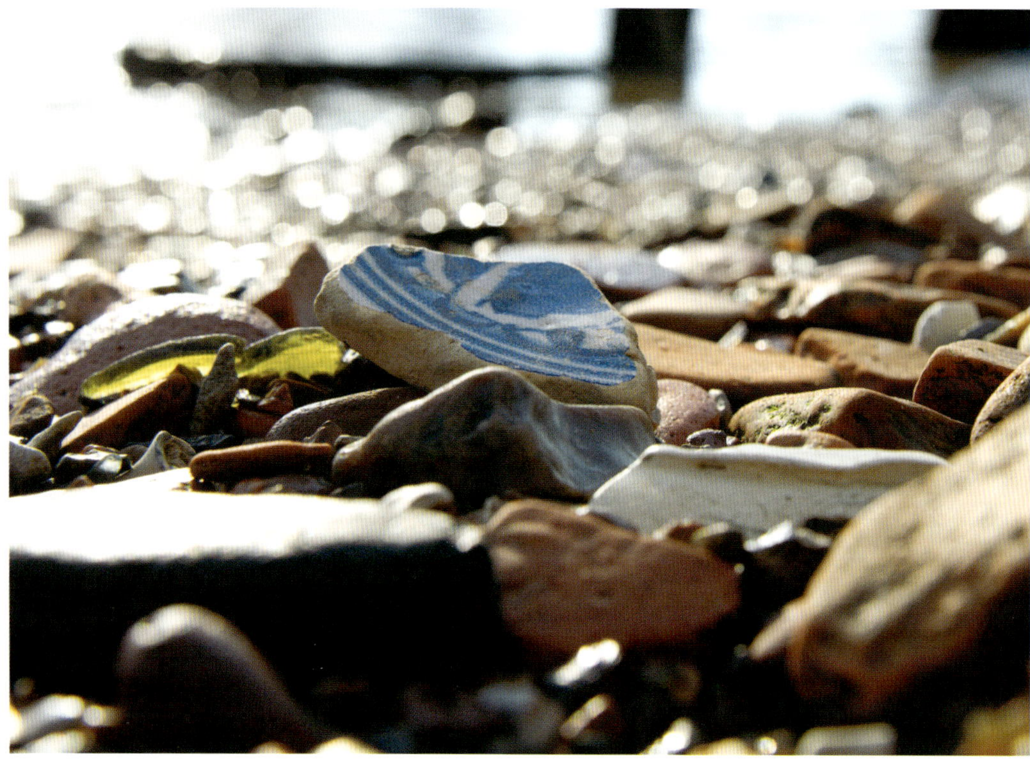

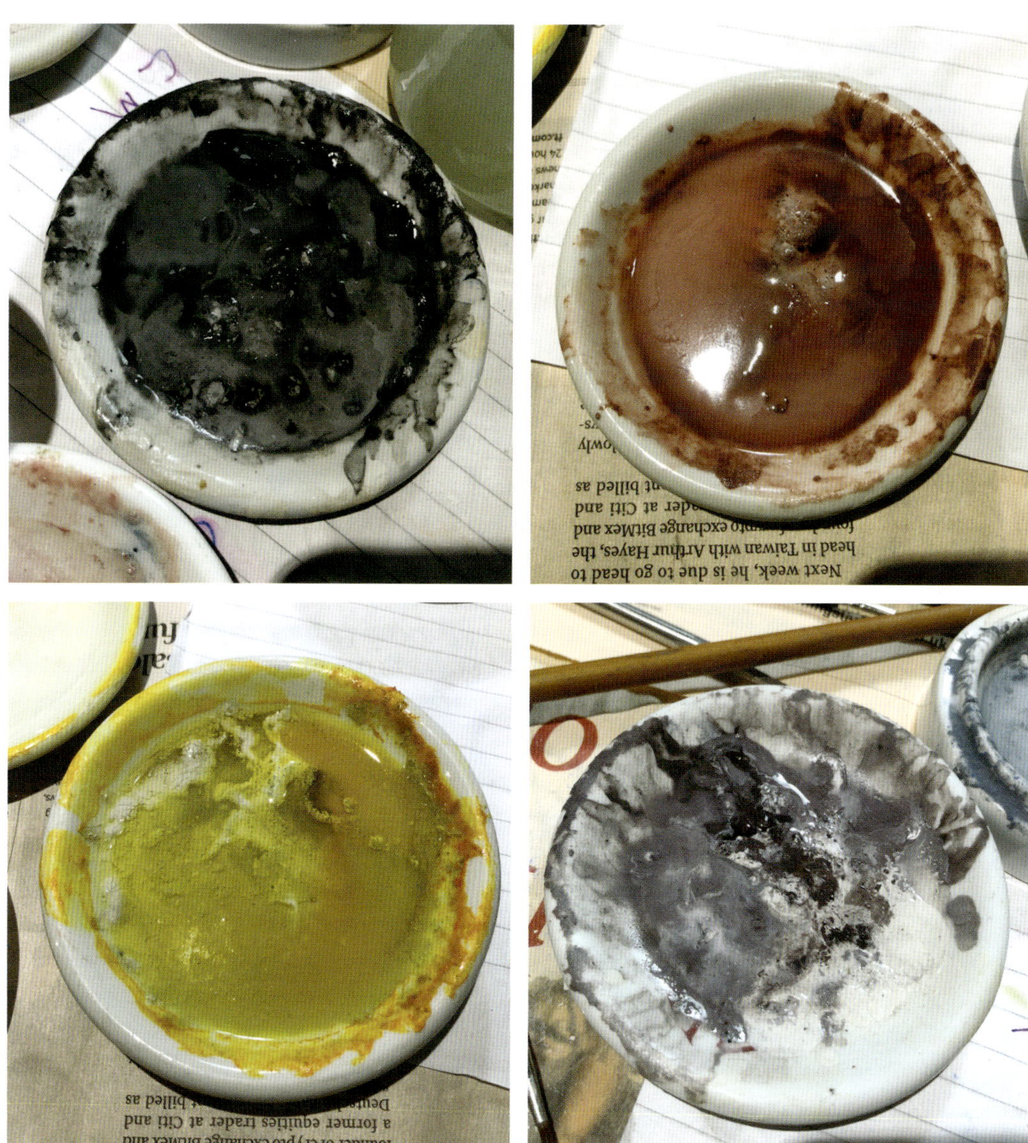

Oxides, clockwise from top left:
Copper; Iron; Crocus martis; Vanadium.

Platter Portraits: Found in Translation

Liz Rideal

In England the eighteenth-century Toby jug is the epitome of the portrait vessel, and indeed these were originally manufactured in quantity for use, but the portrait plates that Manessi makes are of a different order, hers tend towards the bespoke unique, like the handmade Renaissance platters that inspire her. Originally these tin-glazed platters were made to impress those who had the privilege of commissioning and looking at them; they were part of dowries or were expensive gifts and like the humble Toby jug they often represented real people or a famous royal or religious person with specific recognisable characteristics.

Manessi's objects are designed as individual original items and relate more to Susie Cooper's (1902–1995) self-portrait ceramic mask[5]. Her first venture into the genre was in response to a commission and for this she used photographic portraits and the information about the sitter related by the commissioner. This first plate had such an impact on the family who had invited Manessi to take this experimental step that it provoked tears when unveiled. This work was mainly appreciated by that family, in the same way that Renaissance works would have been understood by the educated. This privileged group would also know and understand the narratives

For Isabella Blow, 29 × 29 cm, 2019.

Every portrait that is painted with feeling is a portrait of the artist, not of the sitter.

The sitter is merely an accident, the occasion. It is not he who is revealed by the painter;

it is rather the painter who, on the coloured canvas, reveals himself.[4]

Oscar Wilde

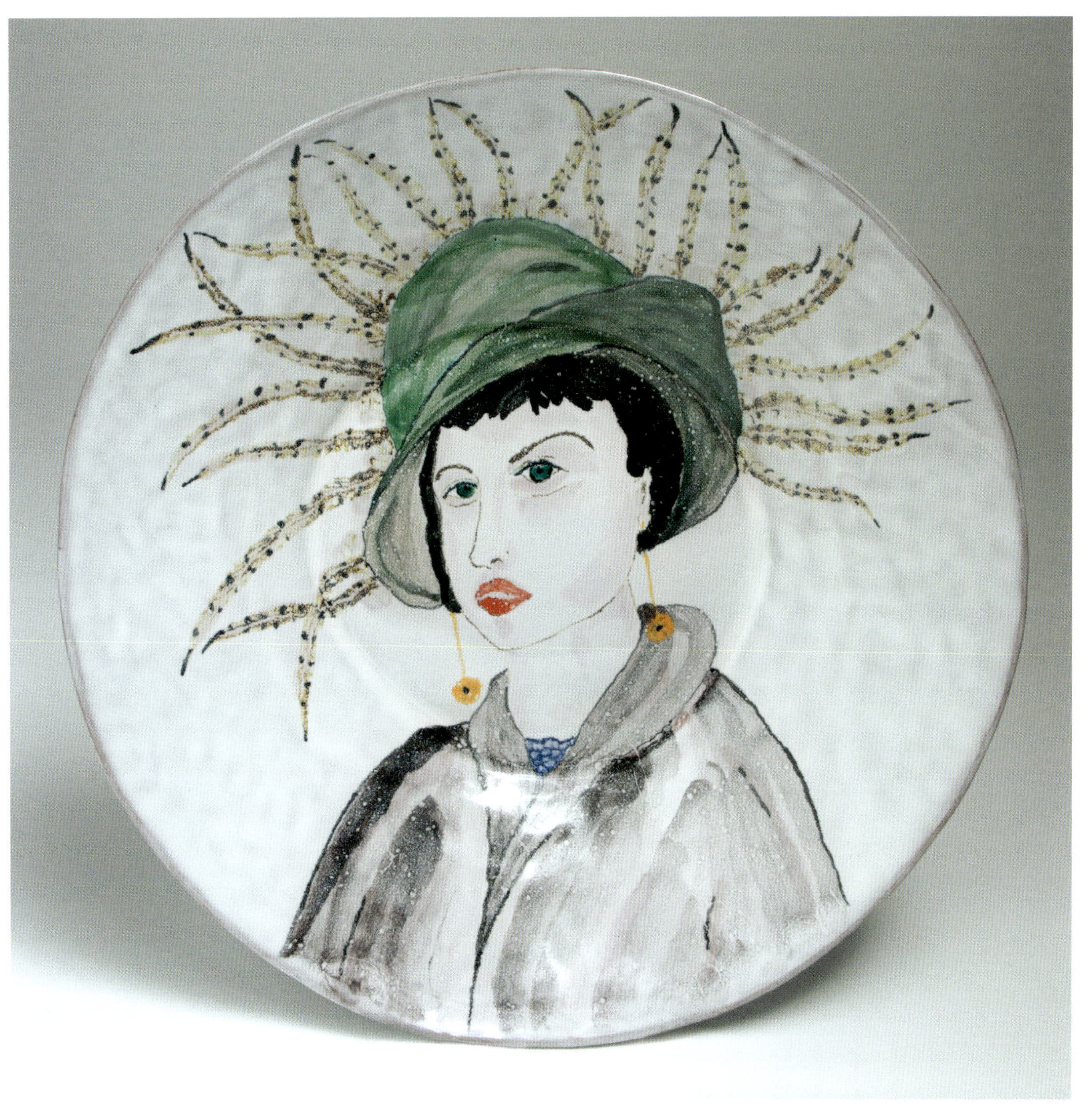

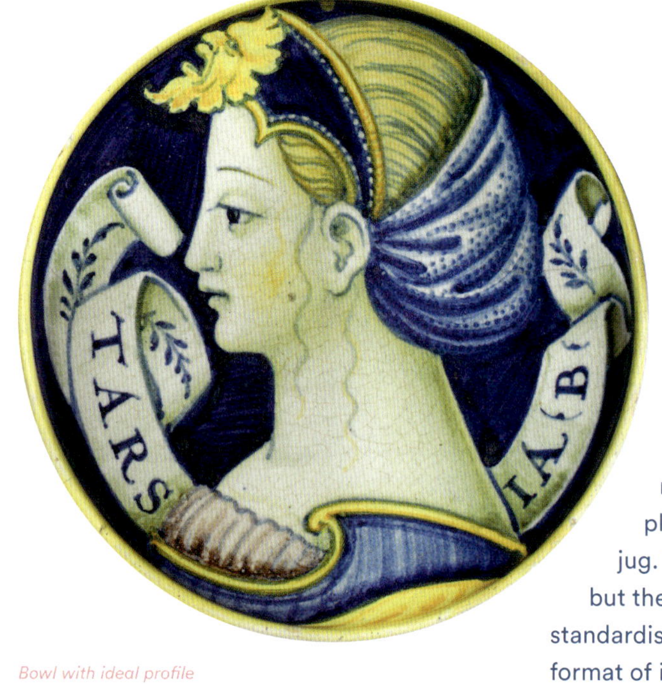

Bowl with ideal profile of a woman, Castel Durante, Italy, c.1520–25. Tin-glazed earthenware.

of hand-woven tapestries or paintings. In this fashion Manessi's work relates to the maiolica genre, although those plates are more akin to the Toby jug. They relate stories and portraits, but their parameters of expression are standardised, with specific ranges of colour, format of illustration on the plate, and often they display repetitive decorative borders. One can compare the Courtauld[6] profile plate depicting 'Tarsia' (a possible portrait of a real life beautiful, 'Bella' Italiana) with Manessi's ceramics and register the difference. Manessi operates more like a painter than a paintress[7], there is little pressure in her studio to fulfil a recognisable brief. Once her support (be it large, up to 33cm diameter or her smaller sketch size) is ready and she has dipped it into the tin glaze, she can pick up her brushes and jump in, sometimes following a light pencil trace to guide her eye or else using a digital photograph or a post card. Her guides are the famous artists that she is drawn to, whether Kahlo or Cranach, Klimt or Sickert.

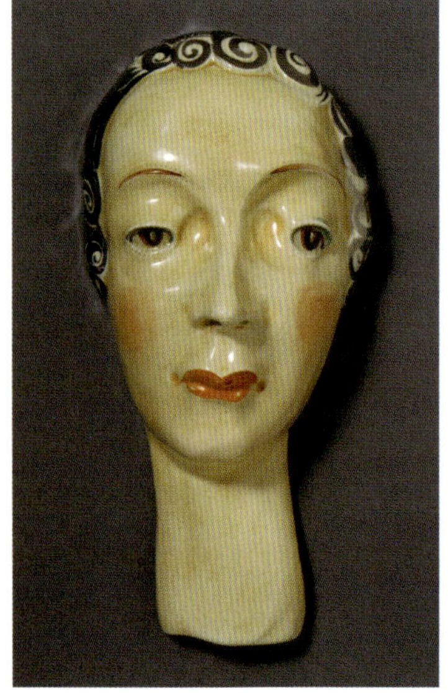

Susie Cooper, by Susie Cooper, ceramic mask, c.1933. The mask was in the artist's collection and hung at first in her London showroom, and later in her studio.

Artemis with hound, for Meg,
39 × 39 cm, 2019.

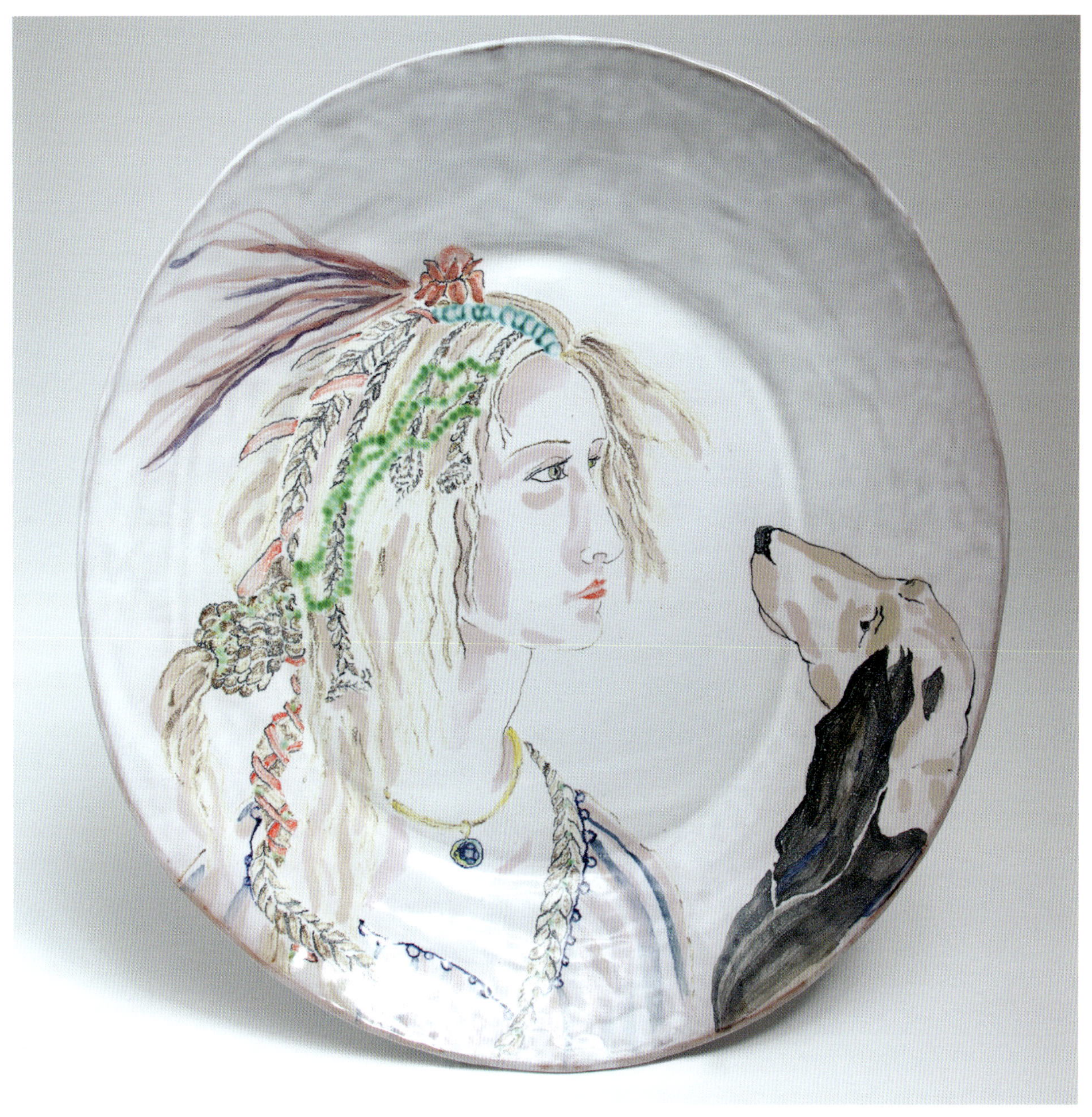

The roots of Manessi's portraits lie in fine art and the tradition of drawing from the master. At the British Museum, the Van Dyck (1599–1641) sketchbooks give us an insight into this method of working and gathering information. Through Van Dyck's drawings we can follow his Italian journey in the 1620s, as he pursued Titian's paintings in an artistic learning adventure. However, Manessi warms to a plethora of well-known portraitists offering us her interpretations of readymade iconic faces. Some are famous and with others she riffs on their form and enhances certain aspects, introducing her new perspectives on familiar paintings.

The surface of these platter paintings is basic; the red clay is coiled and once fired, covered in a cool white glaze, no canvas or wooden support underpins these portraits. Once prepared, the inflexible and powdery surface is ready to receive the magic of mixed glazes of pure elements in the form of metal oxides suspended in water and deftly applied onto the absorbent surface and then fired 'blind' onto the biscuit base. As with the print process, the surprise lies in the reveal. Similarly, as the artist develops their skill and technique, the results grow more confident and predictable. The specific process of creating ceramics dominates and determines results with the opening of the kiln as the final reckoning.

Perfect control of colour with this method is impossible, but, as in oil painting, subtle unexpected blends and mixtures are possible but unpredictable. *Minnie Cunningham at the Old Bedford*,

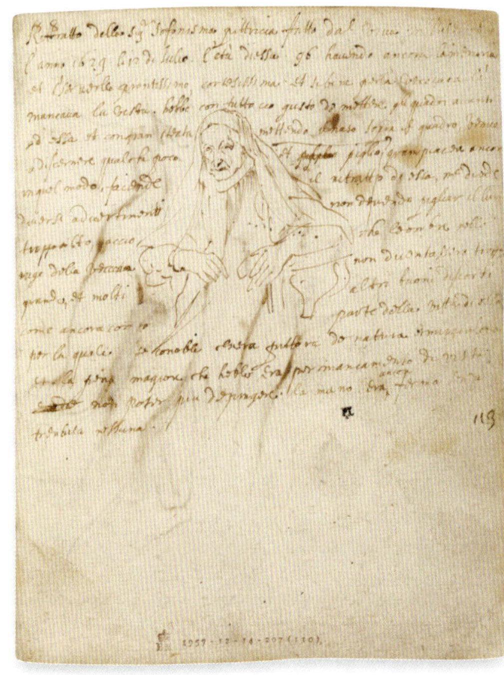

Van Dyke, after Titian, 1624. Pen and brown ink. The painter Sofonisba Anguissola, seated in a chair, frontal view and half-length; leaf from van Dyck's Italian Sketchbook (containing 121 leaves); half-length seated in a chair.

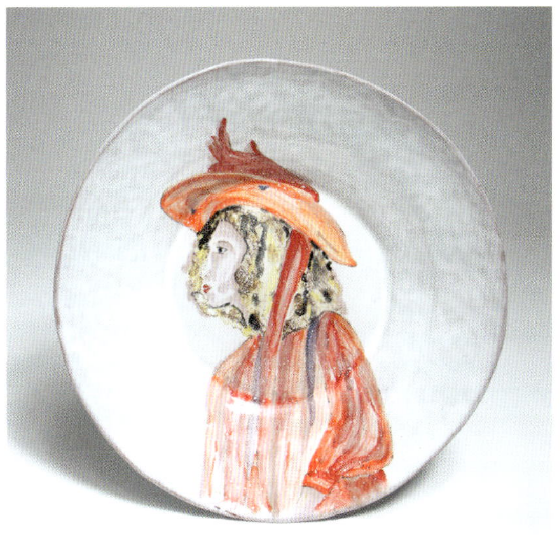

Looking at Minnie Cunningham,
30 × 30 × 8 cm, 2019.

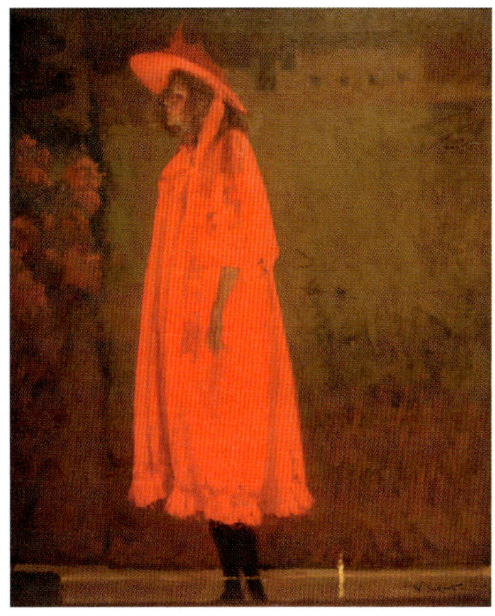

Minnie Cunningham at the Old Bedford,
Walter Sickert, 1892.

1892, after Walter Sickert (1860–1942), repeats his image of a tiny waif conjured from drawings he made in situ. Small in scale, the red of her dress sings out together with the sitter. When first exhibited it bore the subtitle from one of her songs; 'I'm an old hand at love, though I'm young in years'. Manessi revels in the 'intense red on Minnie Cunningham's dress (that) made me look at her again and again'. That intense colour was the hook for this piece which enabled her to broaden the scope of these ceramic portraits by tackling the abstract balance within the formal portrait. The hat and dress have equal weight to the profile portrait. Loosely painted brushstrokes are obvious within the strident orange and red glaze. 'I am drawn to Sickert's use of colours, there is always a sense of mystery in his brushstrokes and colour choices… I wanted to have a go at depicting her on one of my portrait plates[8].'

One might think that the Bell/Grant *Famous Women Dinner Service*[9] would be a relevant comparison here, however, these all bear decorative borders and the names of the sitters, they are painted onto mass produced Wedgwood plates and pay tribute to famous women, from Pocahontas to Georges Sand, Greta Garbo to Queen Victoria. The likenesses when taken from known portraits,

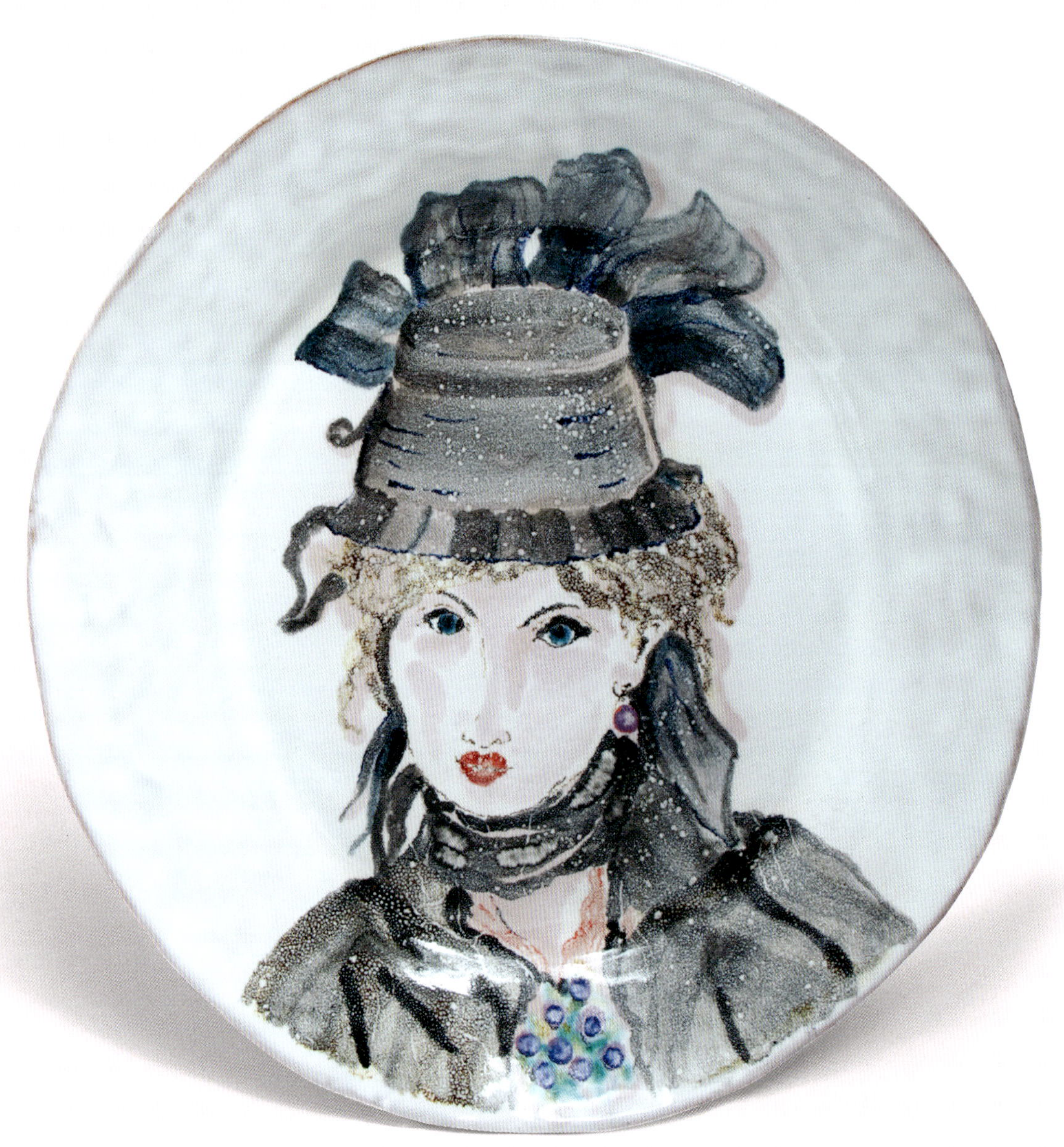

Berthe,
28 × 25 cm, 2019.

are reliable, but the whole project feels like a pantheon of postage stamps, the uniformity of design suffocating the individual. By contrast G.F.Watt's (1817–1904) *Hall of Fame*, testifies a repetition of illustrious Victorians, but because he is a painter of rare talent, his equivalent to these plates is far more successful. Manessi is to Watts what Charleston is to Toby.

It is the painterly quality of Manessi's work that strikes us when we look carefully at the surface of the plates. We retain the notion that these are paintings in glaze and that they remain experimental and edgy precisely because of the insecurity of their process. What reads as line, form, accident and colour is both a chemical and visual amalgam. If we take for example, the direct and confident stare of Berthe Morisot (1841–1895) painted by Édouard Manet (1832–1833) in 1872, when transmuted by Manessi another picture entirely is revealed. The gaze of the sitter is present, the reference to her distinctive hat, hair and ribbons enables us to recognise the person, but the presence of that reiteration is other. Manessi makes the portrait her own, allowing the freedom of expressive glaze to bubble and meld, to pool and spot. Morisot and Manet provide the reason for an exploration into portraiture. Because the sooty blacks employed by the oil painter cannot be immediately recreated, we delight in the alternative shifting Prussian blues and greys. In terms of glaze, these are created with a cocktail of iron and copper oxides into the mix of alumina, silica, and

Berthe Morisot with a Bouquet of Violets, Edouard Manet, 1872. Oil on canvas, 21.9 × 15.9 cm.

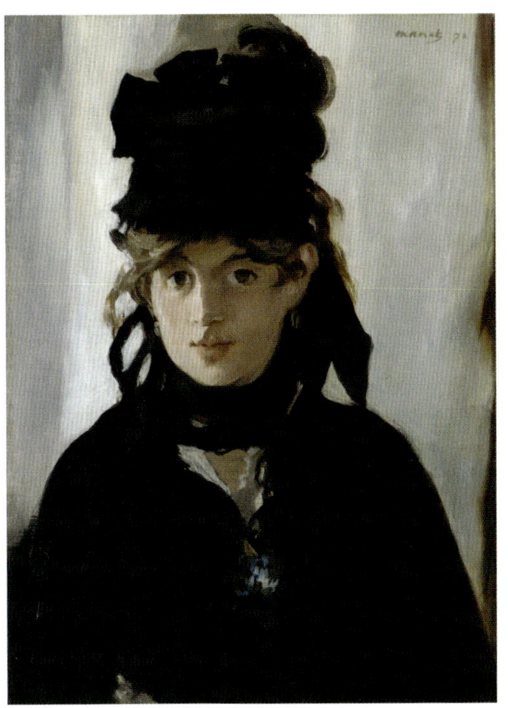

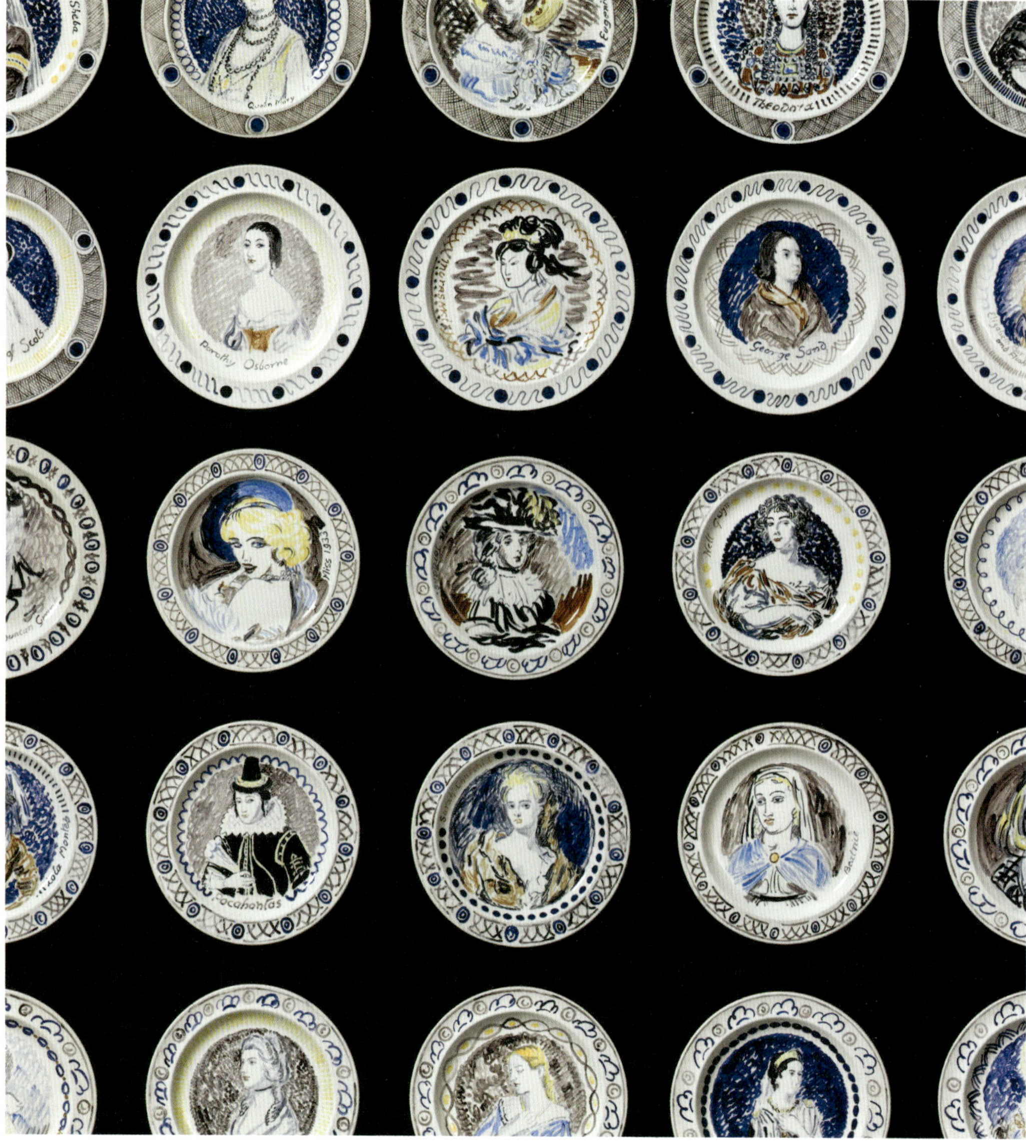

Part of a dinner service of fifty hand-painted Wedgwood plates by Vanessa Bell and Duncan Grant at Charleston House, Sussex between 1932 and 1934.

flux. What becomes increasingly apparent when comparing the two, is that it is the medium and technique of each artist that shines out through their common subject matter. Manessi uses a light pink for areas in the face allowing parts to remain white. In this way she suggests three-dimensional form, much as one would leave a mid-tone on an oil canvas to give a neutral point from whence to make gradations of light and shade. She continues the pink into the overall composition allowing it to colour the throat and neck travelling up through the unruly hair, and further, using this as an

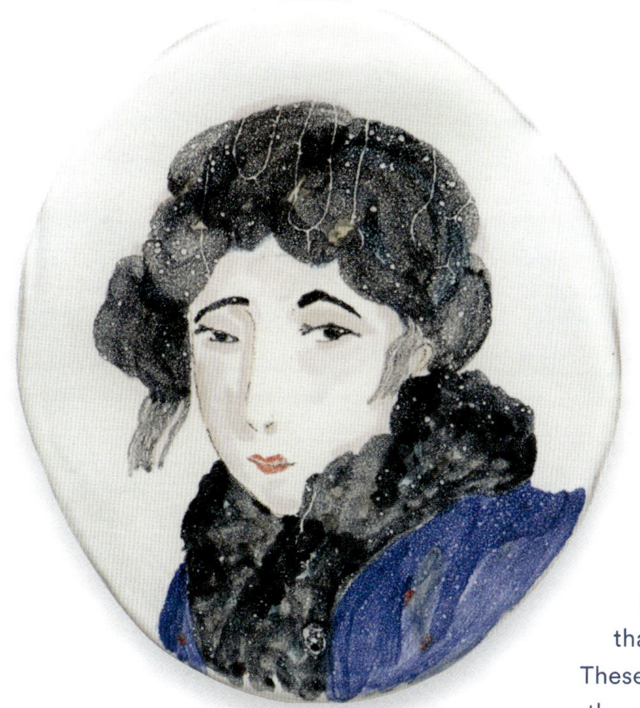

Mrs Nobuko with Fur Collar, 20 × 19, 2019. The development of colour lithographic printing in Japan in the early years of the twentieth century led to the emergence of 'Bijin Kuchi-e': beauty for the masses. Women's magazines were filled with illustrations of kimono-clad beauties. My discovery of these sparked a collection of platter portraits.

under colour in the hat and a light 'shadow' around the splayed ribbons. An earring: the mauve sphere, becomes a more prominent addition and relates to the similarly coloured blobs of mauve and viridian green that masquerade as the violets. These coloured dabs take this portrait in another direction entirely as they are jaunty and decorative, whereas Manet's abstract indigo brush marks are mere suggestions of light within his sombre composition. In *Mrs. Nobuko in a fur collar,* the difference between blue and black is more apparent, the black more distinct with a light peppering of Cerulean blues twinkling through. These sparkle and seem to gravitate upwards into the sitter's hair. Once we start to become attuned to the surface quality (reminiscent of shagreen) the work becomes more intriguing and seductive. There is a meandering white line that curves and wanders along *Mrs.Nobuko*'s hairdo, suggesting form and also bringing to mind Hogarth's (1697–1764) famous *Line of beauty and grace.* He recommended the inclusion of a serpentine line within artworks in order to guarantee their beauty. *Mrs.Nobuko* also reminds us of Japanese cultural traditions of ceramics and societal reserve.

Adele Bloch-Bauer sports the same kind of volcanic black hair pin-holed with white showing the under-glaze activity that suggests movement through rhythmic bubbling creating patches of light. This headdress-hairstyle echoes the red and black spotted triangles that hang from her shoulders like bunting. This part of the plate is in dialogue with the triangular head of hair above, separated by the jewelled golden choker. The substrate is more obvious in this piece

Adele through Dappled Glass,
32 × 32 cm, 2021.

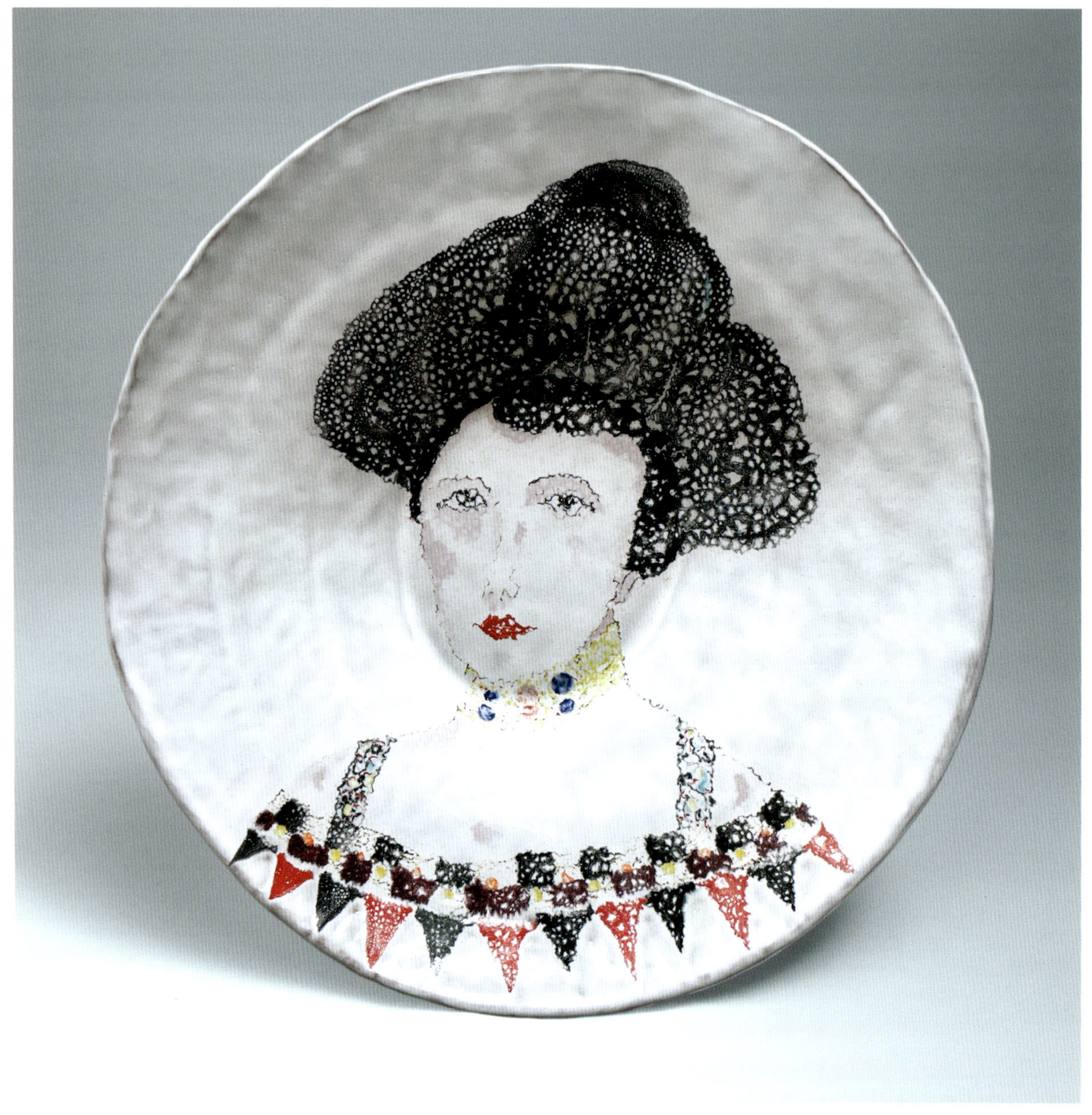

Woman with Headdress, after Andrea Piccinelli,
30 × 27 cm, 2018.

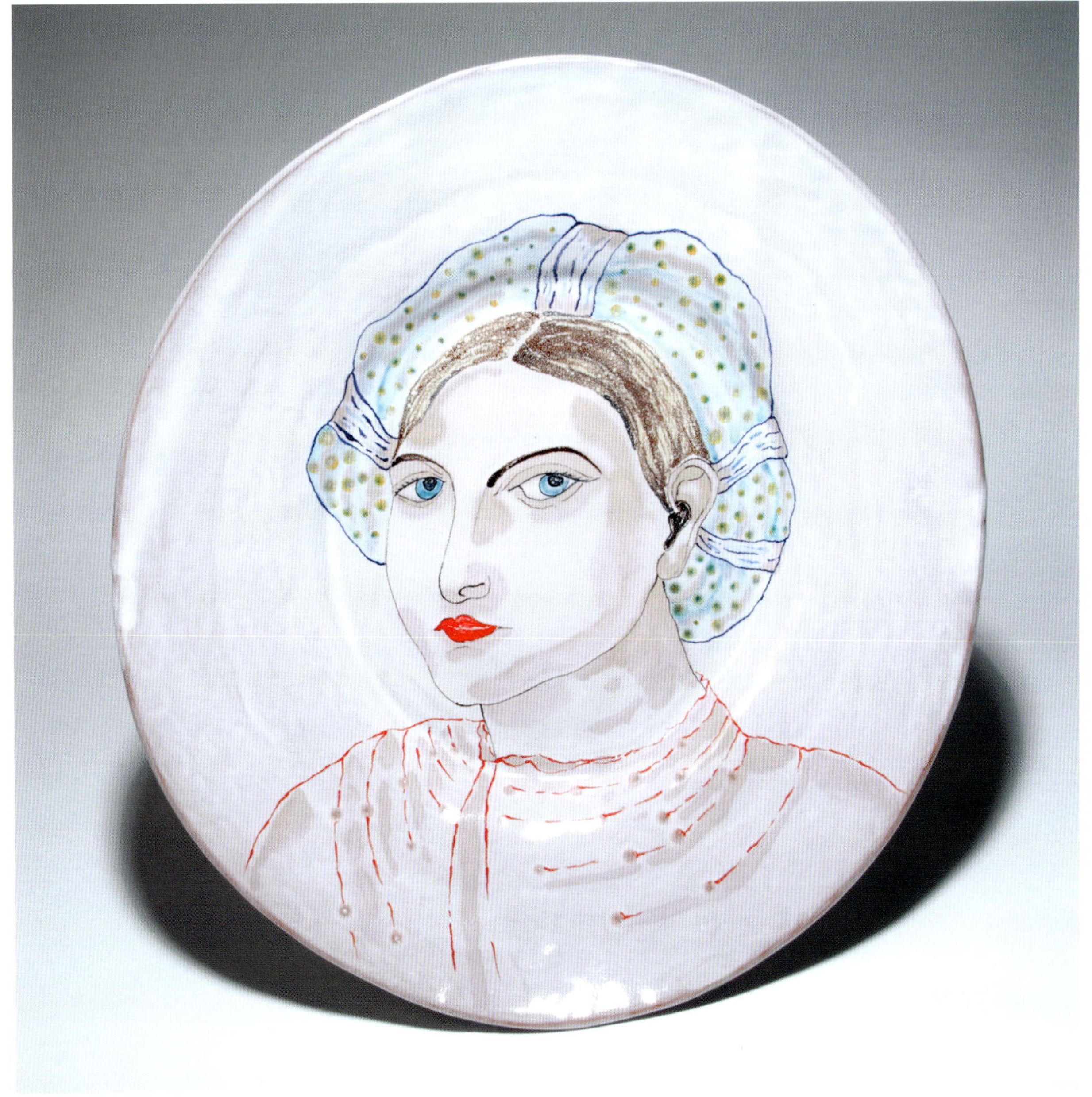

and we can almost sense the way that the plate has been made by the squashing and joining of the soft coils. This in turn influences the way that the tin glaze has taken to the undulating surface. This element adds a ripple effect which combined with the winking colour of the patchy glazes and the red-black dynamic, provides another twist of movement for the eye to catch.

Manessi's portrait plates are more complex than they appear. Even the seemingly simple works like *Madge with a straw hat* (after Edward Wolfe, 1897–1982) and *Woman with Headdress* (after Dei Piccinelli) are fiercely and independently different from their associated painted originals. Their purported inspirations seduce us into thinking that we know the portrait subject concerned, but somehow, we find that we have entered another type of unrelated visual world. The very nature of the substrate obliges us to look more questioningly. The sitters who look back at us refute our preconceptions and offer a different space for contemplation. Manessi's art is skilful and her profound manipulations of material do more than create clay portraits, they show us a way to suspend our disbelief.

Madge with Straw Hat, 30 × 27 cm, 2018. After *Portrait of Madge Garland*, a fashion editor at *Vogue*, by Edward Wolfe, 1926.

1.

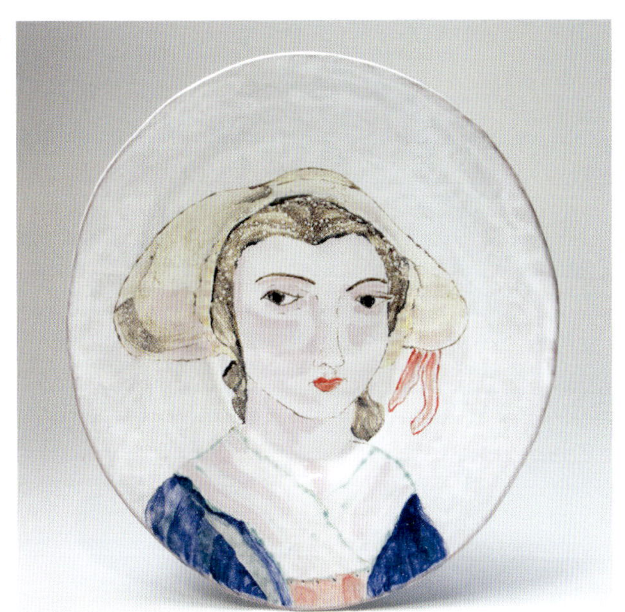

2.

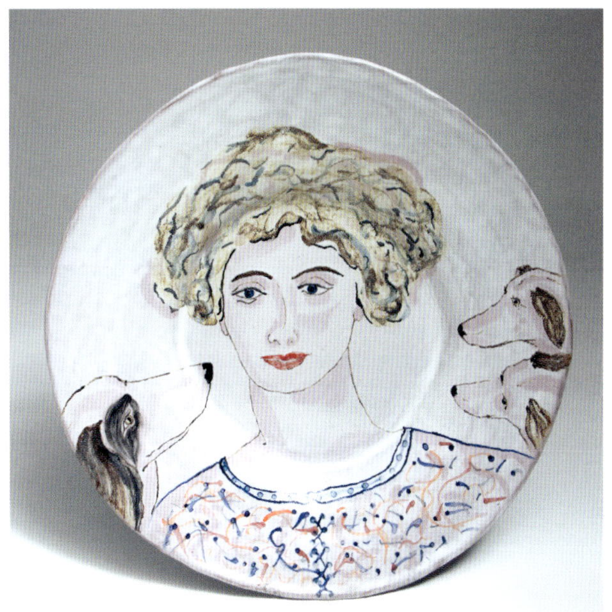

3.

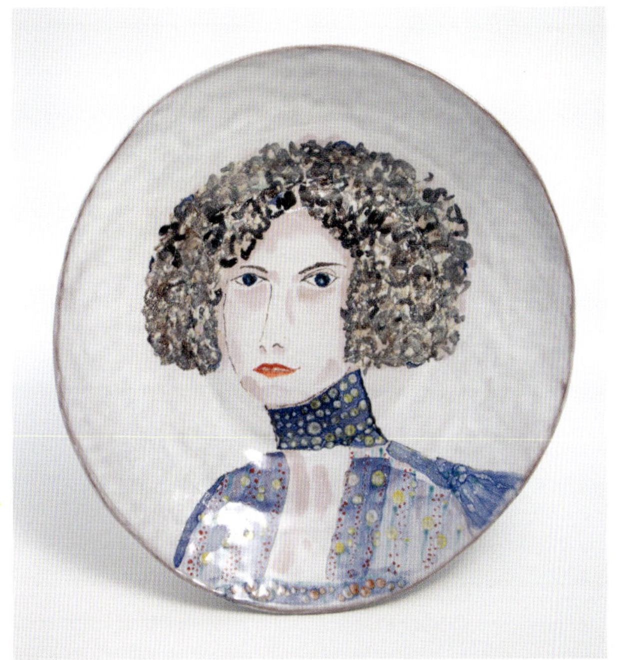

4.

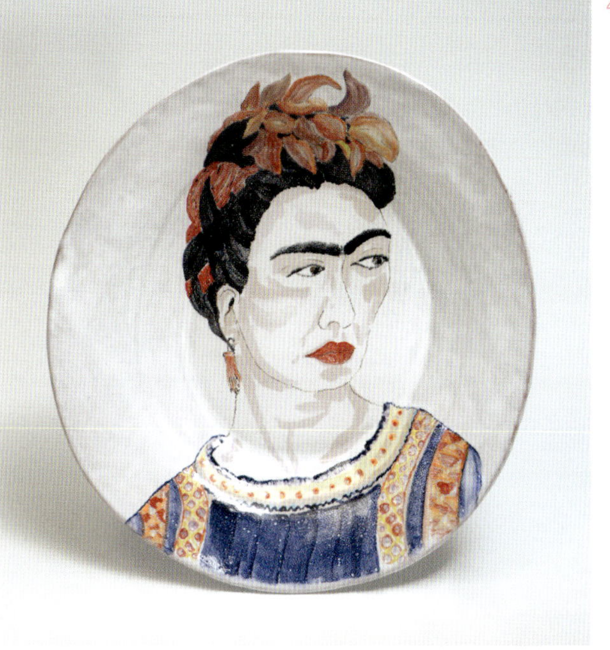

1. *Looking at Mrs Andrews*, 32 × 28 cm, 2018.
2. *Contemporary Artemis with Hounds*, 30 × 30 cm, 2019.
3. *Emilie Flöge*, 29 × 29 cm, 2019.
4. *Frida*, 30 × 30 cm, 2018.

Dogs Never Bite Me …

Michael Petry

In Lucian Freud's painting *Eli and David* (2006), we see a large, well-built, naked man sitting in an armchair while on his lap is a wonderfully sleek dog, definitely with a bit of greyhound or whippet in him. The dog is quietly sleeping as the man sits still for the famous painter of human flesh. The handsome man has a slightly worried look about him, and I am not surprised. I have had dogs for the whole of my life, for the past 25years black and tan Manchester terriers. Many people do not know this breed, but if they have ever seen a Lowry painting they will have seen the stick dogs as well as the stick men, women and children. Perhaps the most famous owner of the breed was Sir John Soane, who built a tomb for his pet inside his London complex of town houses, now open to the public. Should you visit, you will see the marble tomb with the inscription 'Alas poor Fanny'. They are wonderful pets and even better guard dogs; they leap and attack the door, barking at the slightest rustle of noise. They were bred to be ratters. I have never sat naked with my dogs on my lap.

I would be terrified of any noise.

I keep their nails clipped but even so, dog nails on exposed, sensitive flesh are a nightmare in the making and I am sure Eli, or is it

Dogs never bite me. Just humans.

Marilyn Monroe

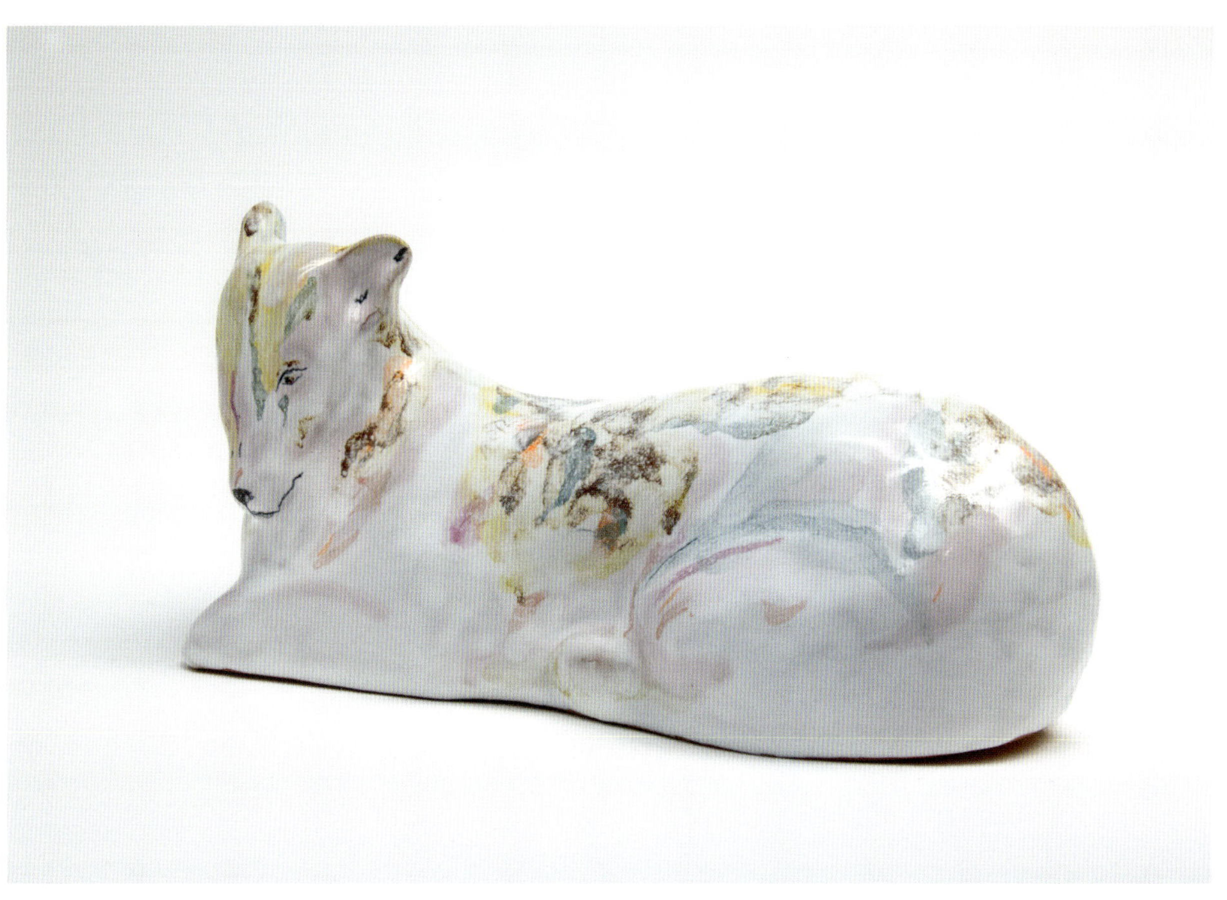

A Dog for Lucian (Freud),
22 × 10 × 9 cm, 2015.
After Lucian Freud,
Eli and David, 2005.

Dogs are our link to paradise.

Milan Kundera

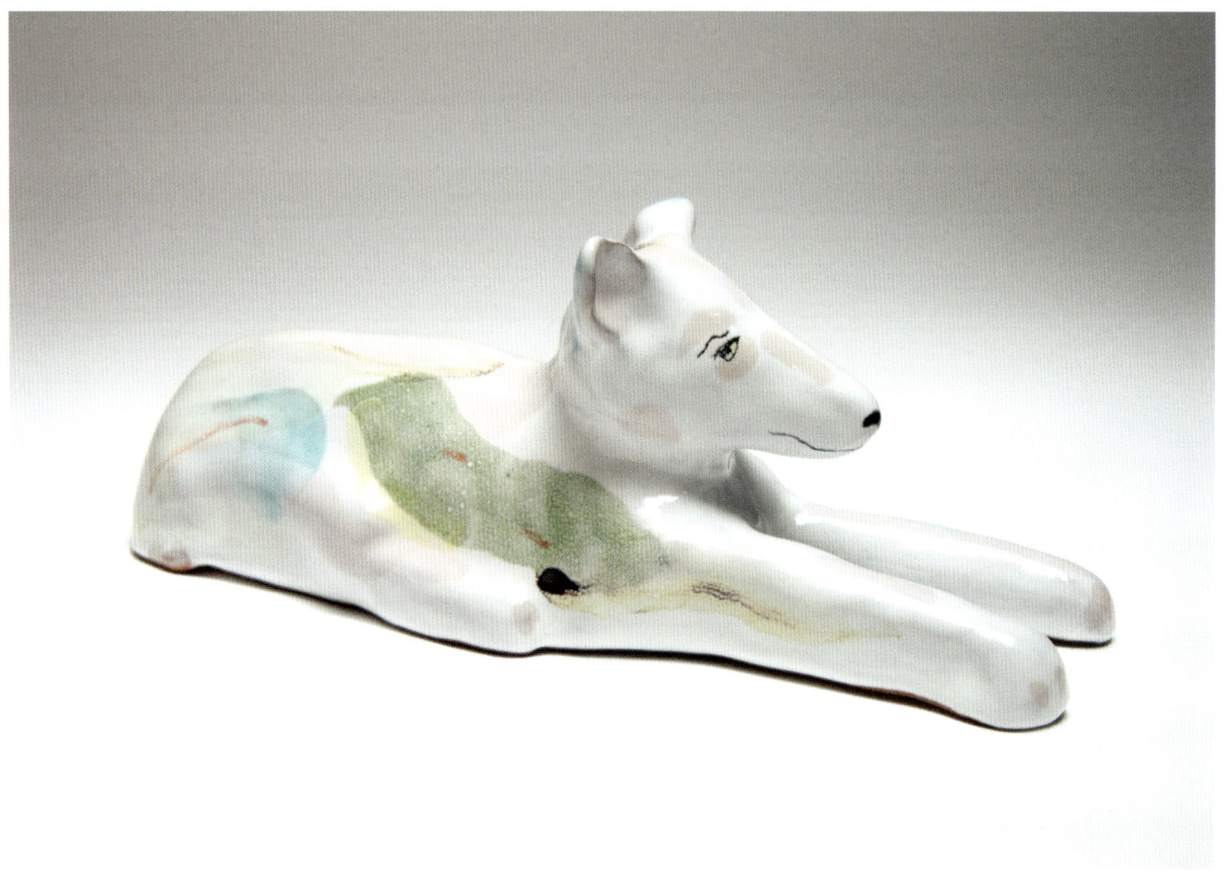

Stretching Dog in Green,
21 × 10 × 8 cm, 2016.

*Dogs are better than human beings
because they know but do not tell.*

Emily Dickinson

David, is thinking the same thing. Agalis Manessi has translated this two-dimensional image into a three-dimensional ceramic sculpture. But she has made only the dog. It sits quietly, awake, but curled up, waiting, in this case for Freud as its title is *A Dog for Lucian* (2015). Its glaze is mainly white with a few pink and blue pastel markings recalling, but not mimicking, the painted version of the real dog: a translation of a translation. I think that is at the core of her work: she interprets the animal world through her own particular gaze, and always seems to get under the skin of the animal. They are rather anthropomorphic, but then domestic animals usually are.

Manessi not only makes divine dogs: she makes rabbits, and cats, and hares, and all of them seem to have their own personality, just as real ones do, if you have spent any time with our four-legged cousins. I always worry about people who don't like animals, whether cats or dogs or the more exotic kind. It seems to show a lack of empathy for the wider world beyond the man-made. I consider babies to be part of the man- (or rather woman-) made world, so concern for them is rather more self-interest than concern for the environment as a whole. We know that there are whole countries of selfish self-centred people who deny the effects of man-made (yes, man-made, usually) pollution and worse on the global environment. These people refuse to look at scientific data or worse, dismiss it and say they have done their own research (usually on a smartphone while sitting on the toilet) and don't care what happens to the rabbits that run wild in the forest or the prairie. People who care about their offspring, but not the world they live in, astound me. The unexpected look of a dog in my direction can astound me, and Manessi seems amazingly capable of capturing such a look.

It is a combination of sculptural form allied with a painter's touch that brings Manessi's ceramic creatures to life. Her *Shy Hare* (2016), based on the famous Albrecht Dürer watercolour (1502), is a

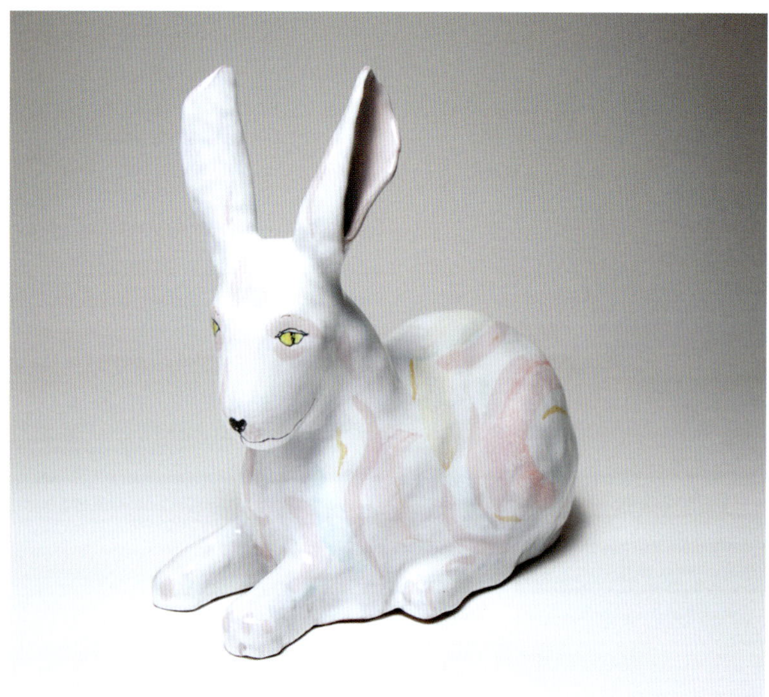

Shy Hare,
26 × 23 × 12 cm, 2016.

perfect example. The ears stick straight up, facing odd directions, listening out for the possibility of danger and the need to bolt from its comfortable resting place at a moment's notice – they look as if we might even see them twitch. But it is the face painted on in black and yellow glaze that perhaps makes it more human or makes humans feel attracted to such an object. No artist in their right mind would try to copy or simulate Dürer's insanely precise and beautiful drawing – it is a master work of observation – and one that can only be interpreted, translated into another medium. Manessi uses it as the basis for her sculpture but then makes it into something very different. Its markings and colour change it not into a cartoon rabbit (a shout-out to Bugs) but certainly a creature of the imagination. Dürer's is 100% real, we see it hair for hair and the brown colour of it, and its twitching whiskers leave us in no doubt that he sat observing it live. Manessi has sat thinking about it, then she has made one for herself, one that speaks of her, and for her, to the viewer.

Most of these works are small and can easily be hand-held: they are not anywhere near the size of a real dog or a cat. But like such animals Manessi's ceramics want to be picked up, held in the hand, stroked, and it is no wonder they seem to catch their spirit. Some of her animals have a genesis in the paintings of Franz Marc. He has said:

I am drawn to Franz Marc, the German Expressionist artist who painted many animals using vibrant colours and energetic brushstrokes. His own dog, Rossi, is depicted lying in the snow with a calm, well-observed facial expression. From this I have made multiple versions and repeatedly return to.

Agalis Manessi

'Is there a more mysterious idea for an artist to imagine how nature is reflected in the eye of an animal? How does a horse see the world, how does an eagle, a doe or a dog? It is a poverty-stricken convention to place animals into a landscape as seen by me; instead, we should contemplate the soul of the animal to divine its way of sight.'

Manessi has made many three-dimensional animals based on Marc's painting, such as *Three Animals (Dog, Fox and Cat)* (1912), where she has sculpted a similar white dog, red fox and grey cat. Her animals again are not copies but are inspired by Marc's brushstrokes, his ideas about seeing the natural world through the eyes not of others, but other beings that we share the world with. Her fox is mute, like a wild one, and as for cats, they never respond to human inquisition or orders, they are independent and only deign to interact with us.

Dogs on the other hand do seem to love us, humans, that is. Anyone who has had a dog will know that to be true and Manessi's

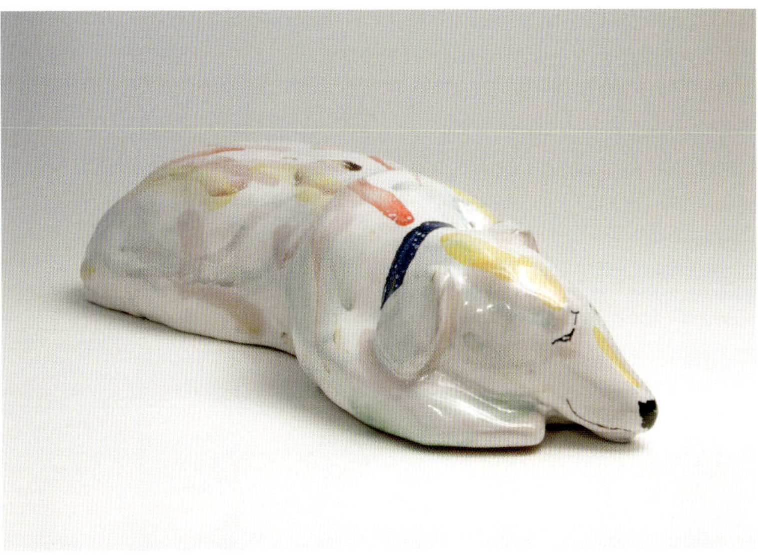

Sleeping Dog in Red and Yellow, 27 × 11 cm, 2016.

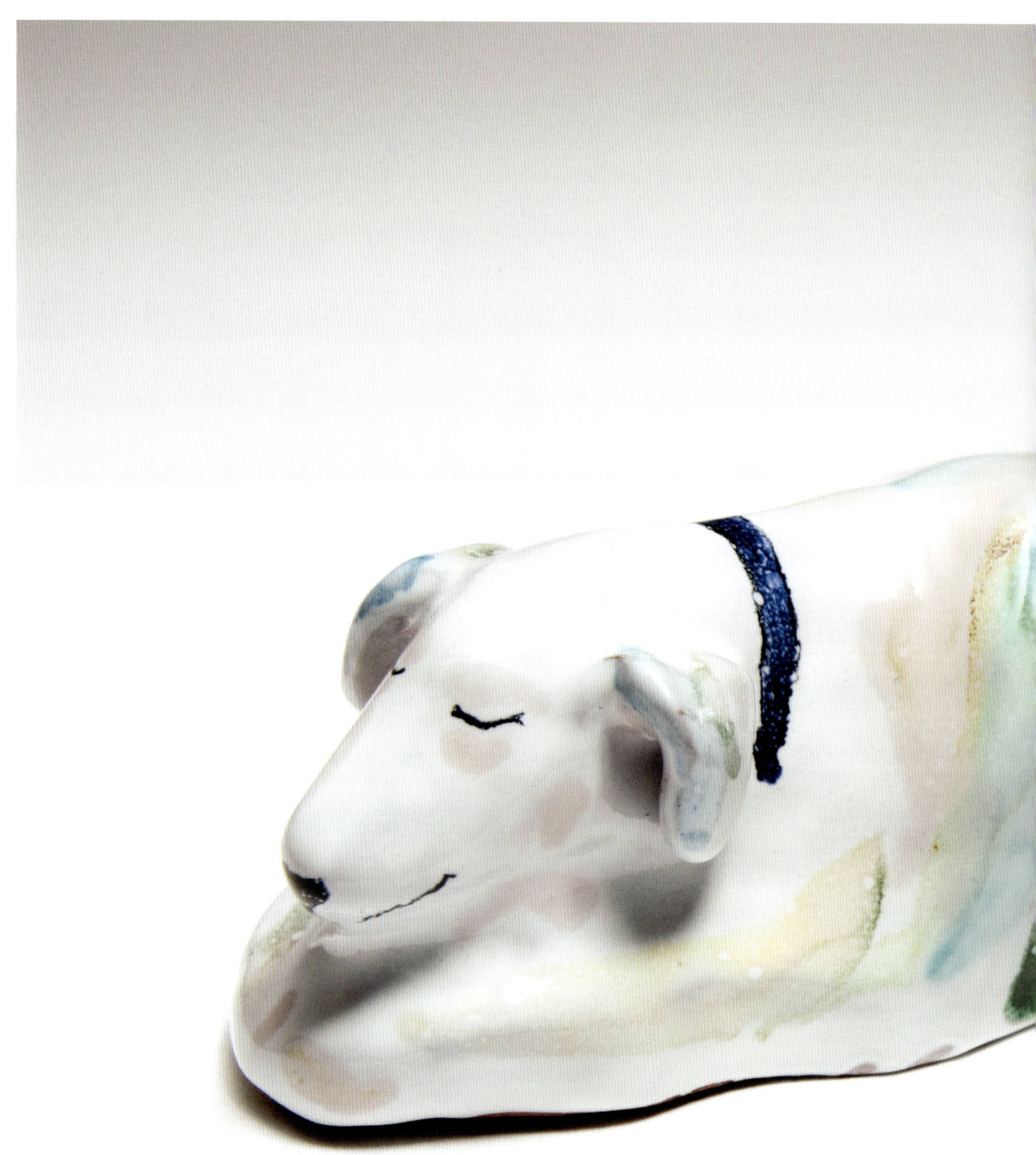

Sleeping Dog in Blue and Green,
25 × 8 cm, 2016.

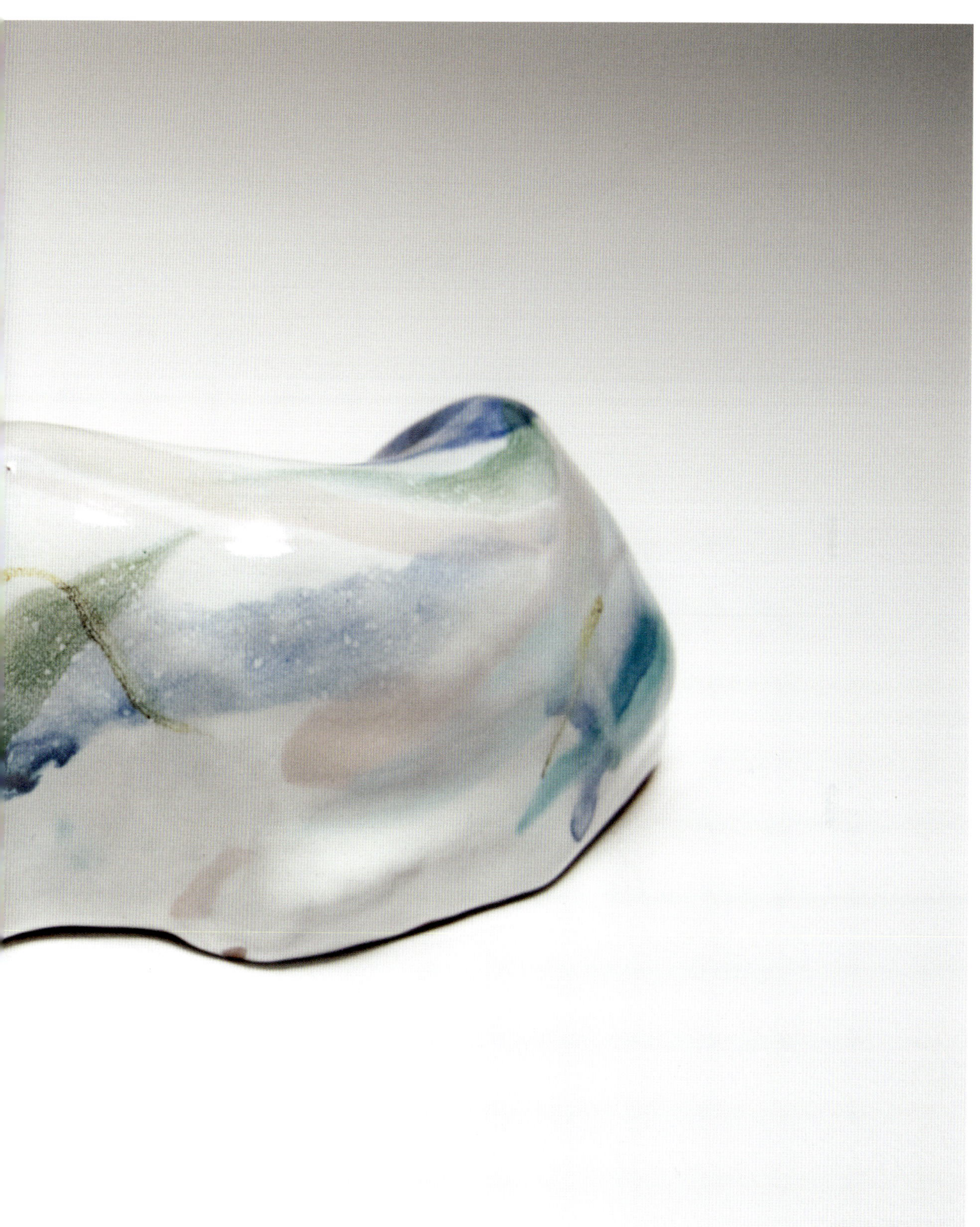

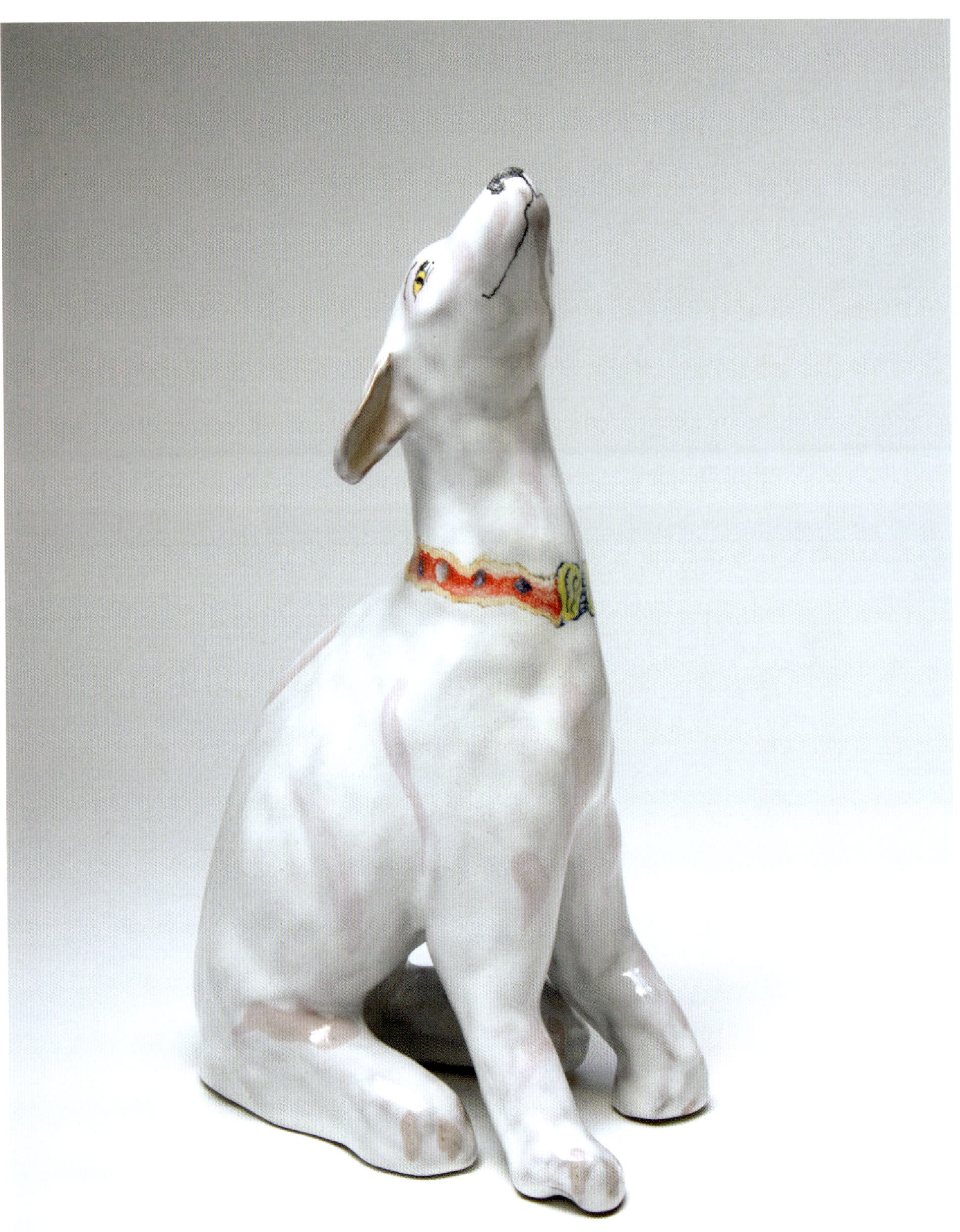

One cat just leads to another.

Ernest Hemingway

dogs all look as though they long for, and deserve, a good home, one where their love will be returned. One of my favourites of her dogs is *A Dog for Van Dyck* (2017). In the original painting of James Stewart, his faithful greyhound looks up to him lovingly, longing for a stroke or a pat of reassurance: 'What is going on, James, who is that odd man with the smelly potions?', he seems to ask. The dog is of good breeding and is strong; he wears a stylish and expensive lead (or necklace), and Manessi places a bright red one around the neck of her dog. His head also looks skyward up at his missing master and while he is a bright white (Van Dyck's is a sandy brown with a white neck patch), he so recalls the painting, the feeling of what the dog is looking for and longing to find. We might see the world through either of these artists' dogs' eyes.

Fox Cub, 10 × 4 × 3 cm, 2022.

Making dogs in art is really a sucker's game, because no matter how real to life or true to the spirit of the animal, nothing can ever come close to a paw in your hands, a tail wagging unconditional love at you and a happy lick to the ear in a big cuddle. Cats, well, cats – they certainly are much more aloof and if you capture an image of them in a drawing or even a photograph, they simply look at you as if to say, 'of course', or 'no paparazzi please', as they shade their eyes from view or flick a dismissive tail in your direction. That is not to say all cats are unloving, if not unloveable, but they are independent of humans, they live with us, because we act as concierge, they often go from house to house to find the best food available and are put out if you are not up to their standard. Dogs, well, dogs – dogs will do anything for a human. They often save them from the Outback, or from wells they have fallen into, or they sit upon the graves of

A Dog for van Dyck, 26 × 13 × 9 cm, 2017.

their fallen masters, and cats laugh at them. Christopher Hitchens has said: 'Owners of dogs will have noticed that, if you provide them with food and water and shelter and affection, they will think you are God. Whereas owners of cats are compelled to realize that, if you provide them with food and water and affection, they draw the conclusion that they are God.' Manessi gives both her cats and her dogs the dignity of ancient Egyptian deities (Bastet and Anubis) and, like their depictions of the gods, her dogs and cats hold similar poses to those observed in nature by artists over 5,000 years ago.

Like those cats and dogs, many of Manessi's works look as if they are merely asleep, or waiting for a human to feed or stroke them. They look as if they could get up at any moment. All of them have her signature light base glaze, which gives them a sculptural form on which she draws other features either in black or pastel washes. Her drawing on the forms often links them to the paintings or drawings that she uses as source material, but her marks are not mimetic, they are generative. Her works are small sculptures that also slide into the world of craft, as they are ceramic. This liminal world of objects that defy easy categorisation always disrupts the given

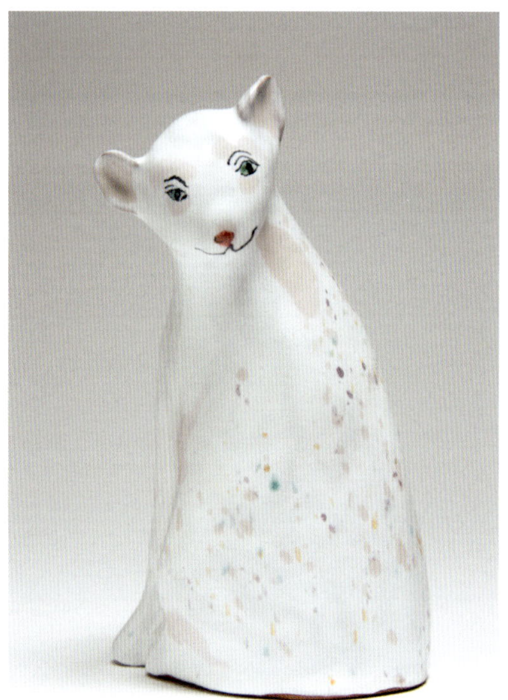

Splattered Cat,
16 × 10 × 7 cm, 2016.

Sly Cat with Sleepy Owl,
13 × 8 × 7 cm, 2016.

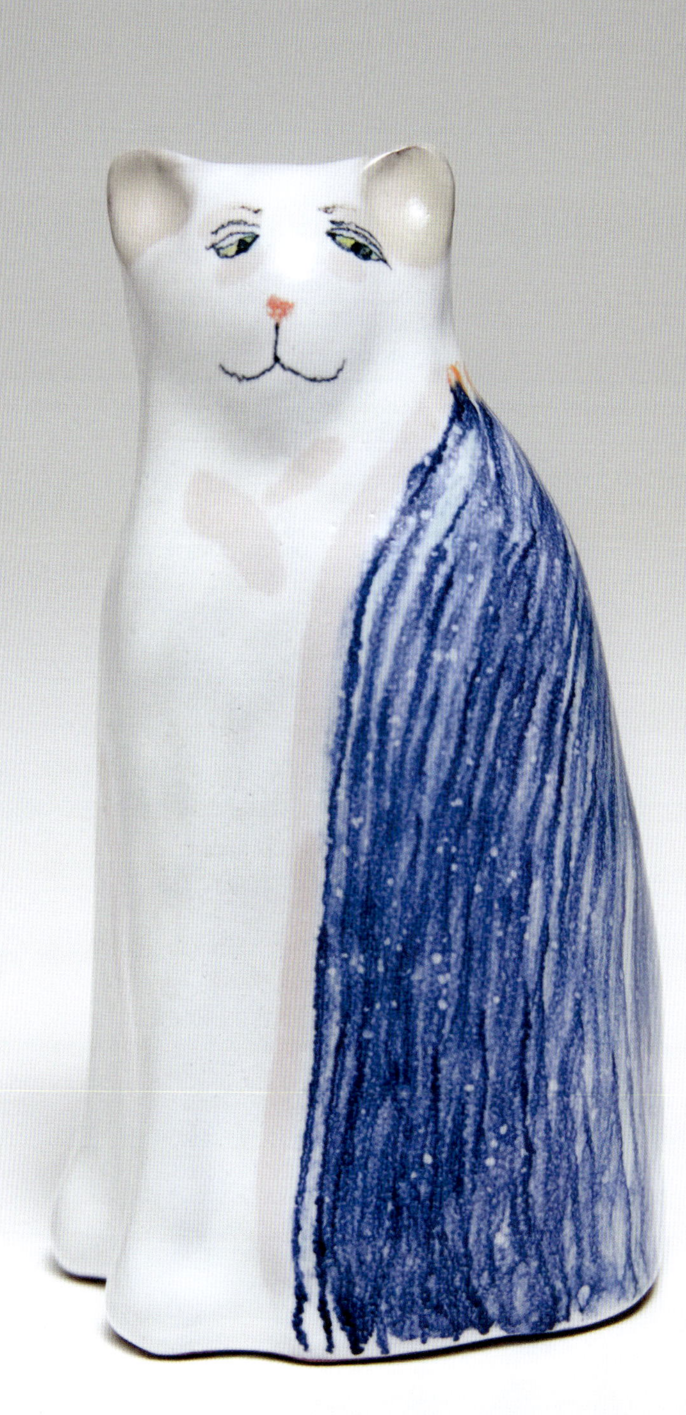

Some of my best leading men have been dogs ...

Elizabeth Taylor

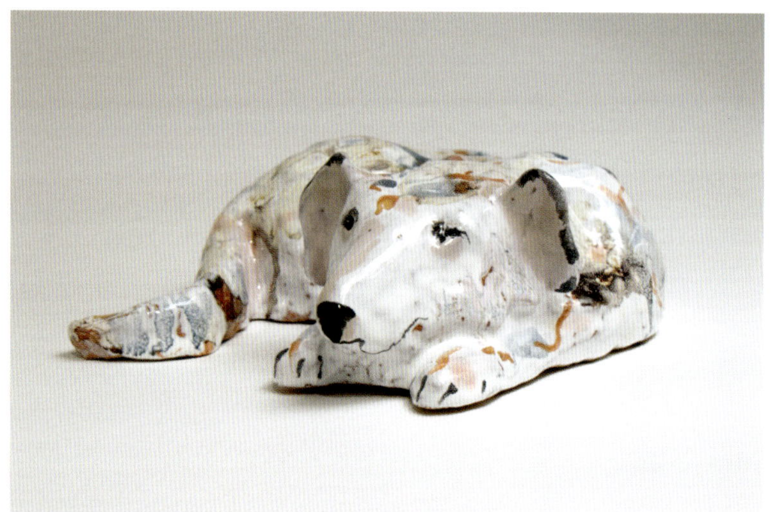

David's Dog, 36 × 20 × 14 cm, 2012.

order of handwork, and work made by women, and so often falls into what is seen as the lesser category of *craft*. While this is problematic primarily in the dominant Western cultures of representation, ceramics and fibre-work, long given over to women, are now truly coming into their own and those makers are rightly being courted and lionised by high art institutions such as the Tate (which recently presented a retrospective of the Polish artist Magdalena Abakanowicz, six years after her death).

Warnings about playing second fiddle to a dog (or a cat or a fox or a bunny) have long been the norm in the theatrical world, and *craft* has long played second to *fine art*, but happily this dichotomy is changing, and the world of objects is opening out to embrace a much wider variety of hand- and even computer-generated work. As all aspects of our lives slide in and out of social media's view, what is art, who is an artist, what is allowed to be seen as art or where it can be seen is ever changing. While it might not be for the best in

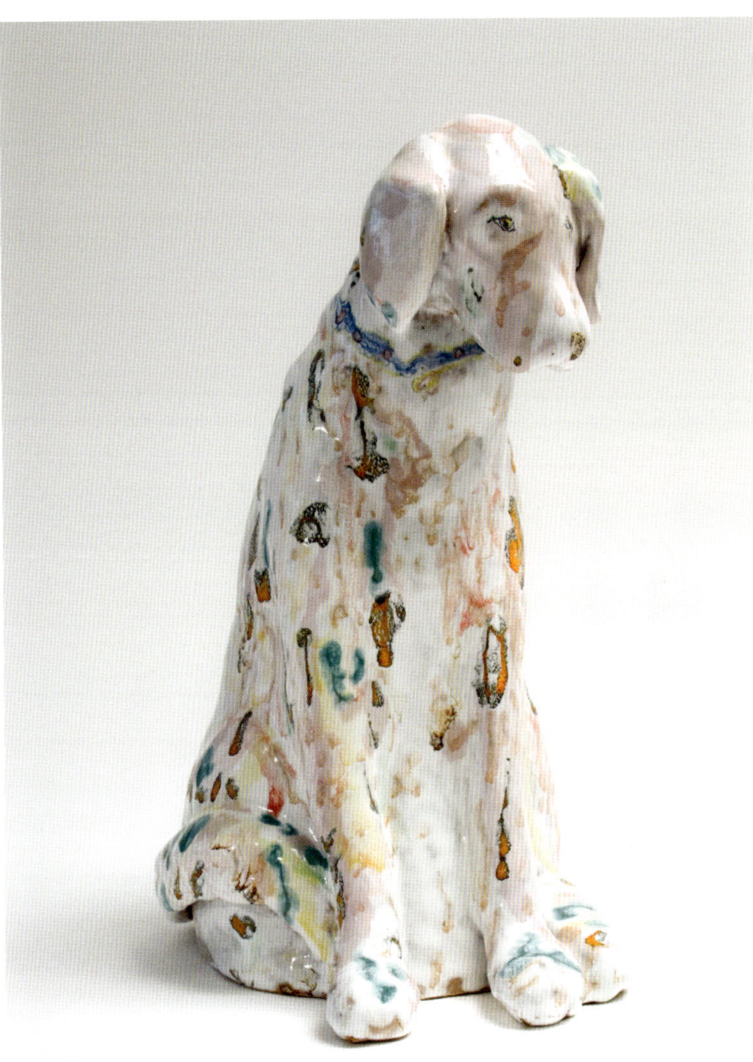

Pensive Painter's Dog,
39 × 20 × 18 cm, 2013.

the long run, it is a runaway train, and those foolish enough to stand in front of it will be mown down. Instagram is the new leveller in the art world and a beautiful ceramic at around two square inches is rather the same as a wonderful painting at the same resolution. How we, and if we ever, view these works in the non-digital world is at the root of the next step in the development of the art world, if not the world of art and artists. Happy are those who have a real dog to sleep in their lap or by the side of their chair – the next best thing is one of Manessi's on a shelf or a side table.

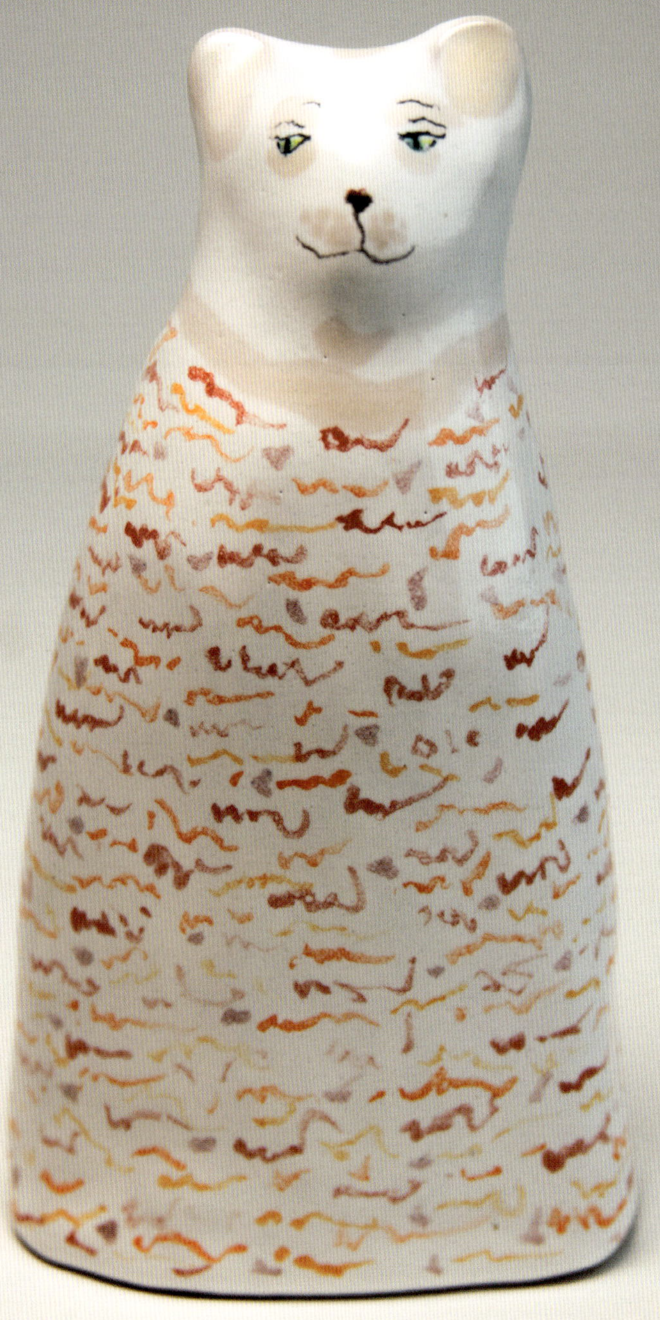

Owl Cat with Script,
16 × 9 × 7 cm, 2016.

...Tom is an old theatre cat....he puts his front paw
on his breast and says they don't have it any more...
once i played the owl
in modjeskas production
of macbeth
i sat above the castle gate
in the murder scene
and made my yellow
eyes shine through the dusk
like an owls eyes
modjeska was a real
trouper she knew how to pick
her support i would like
to see any of these modern
theatre cats play the owls eyes
to modjeskas lady macbeth
but they haven't got it
here
mehitabel he says
both our professions
are being ruined by amateurs

Don Marquis, *Archy and Mehitabel*

Owl Cat with Script (rear view),
16 × 9 × 7 cm 2016.

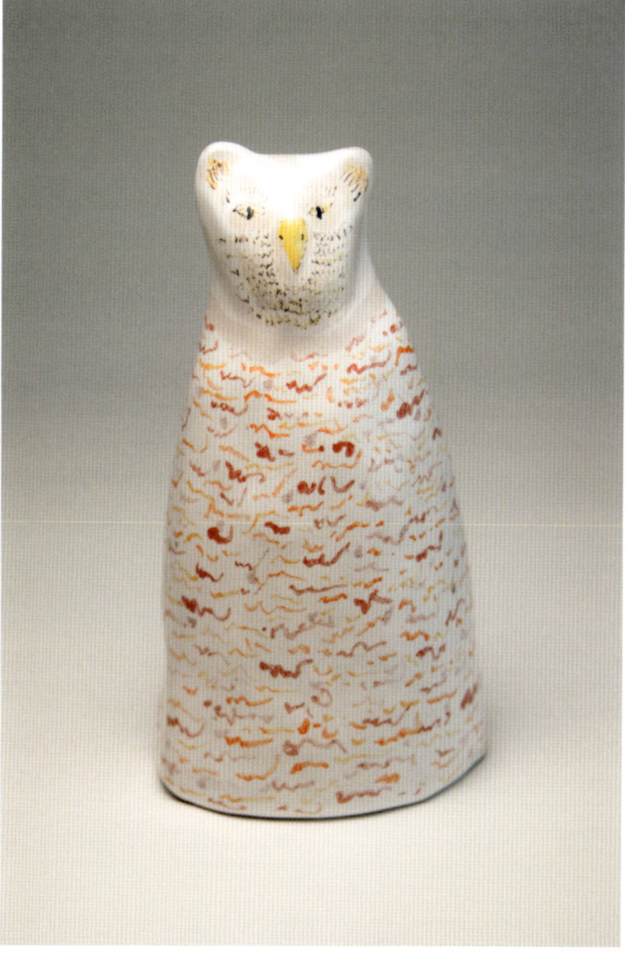

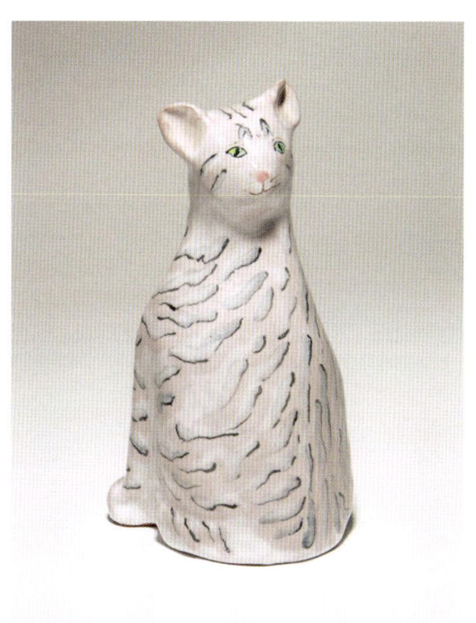

Perky,
13 × 7 × 6 cm, 2018.

Animal Encounters

Megan Brooks

Colourful Cat with Sleepy Owl,
15 × 9 × 8 cm, 2015.

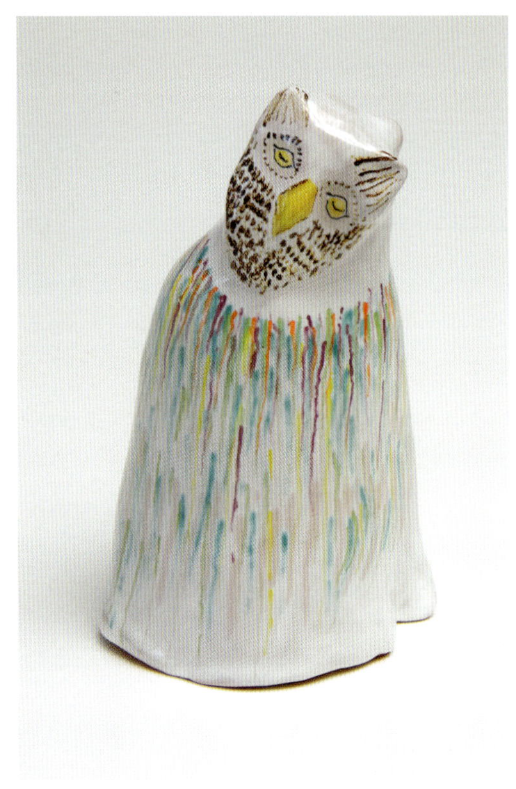

Swallows lift from the buildings with the last of the day's heat. Skimming the rising thermals like dolphins, with jubilant clicks and whistles. With the fever of midday broken, cats stretch and slip along city streets. Myriad colours from a genealogy that spans centuries, some pied, others striped and marbled.

It is possible that the first forms of life emerged from clay. A vessel for molecules that may have catalysed the first micro-organisms and the origin of all animals. This theory finds its parallel in ancient myth, in which life was shaped from clay by the hands of the gods and placed upon the earth. There is a living quality to the material that belies its inert matter, it moves and is changeable. It can stretch, compress, and coil around itself to become innumerable forms. Long-limbed hares and hounds, little

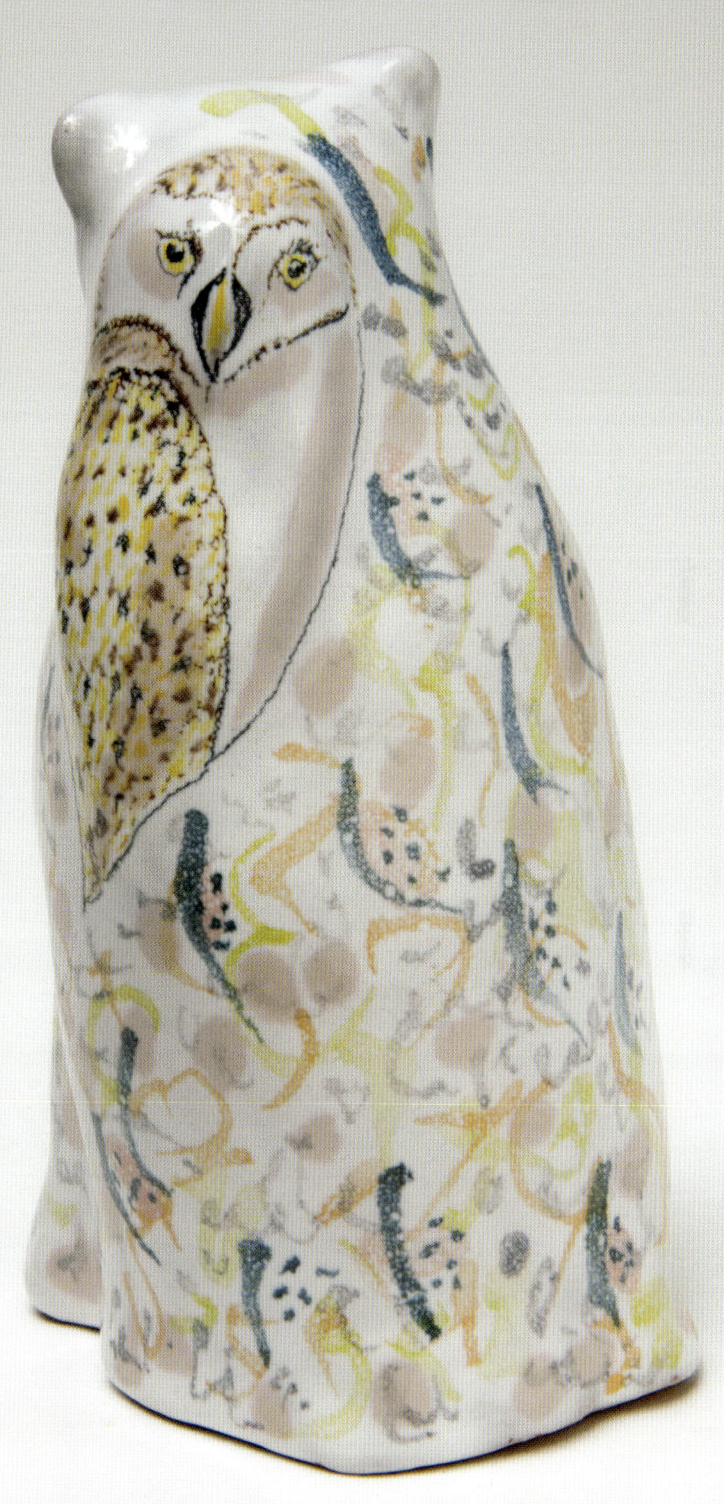

Passenger, (rear view),
14 × 9 × 8 cm, 2014.

1.

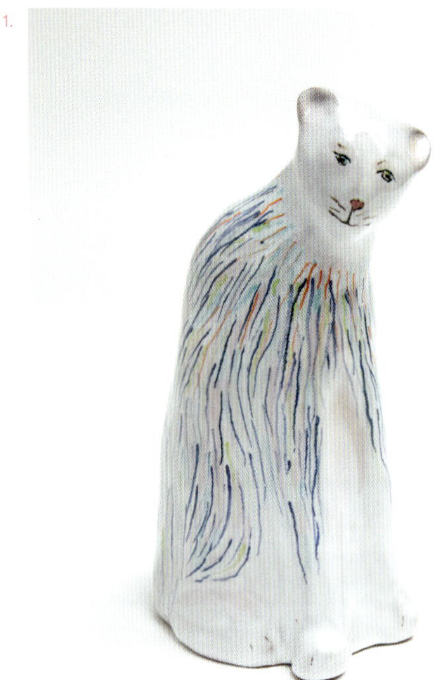

2.

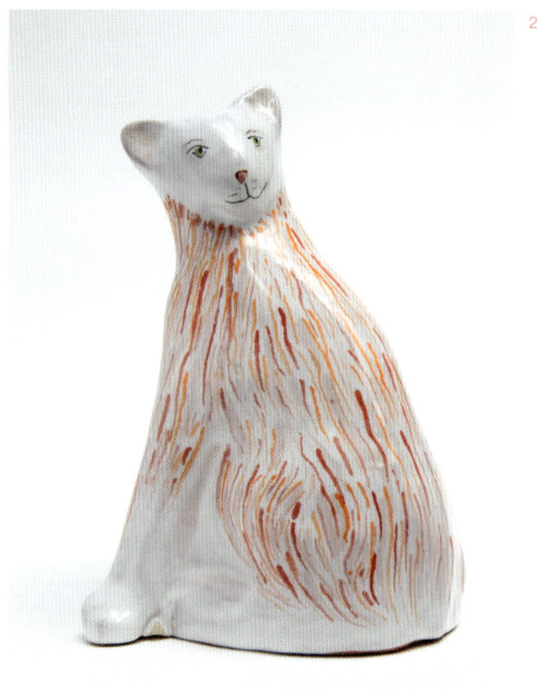

3.

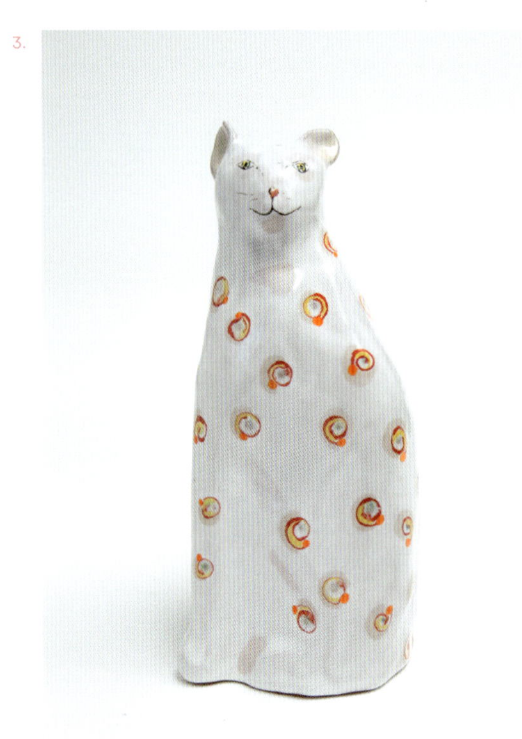

4.

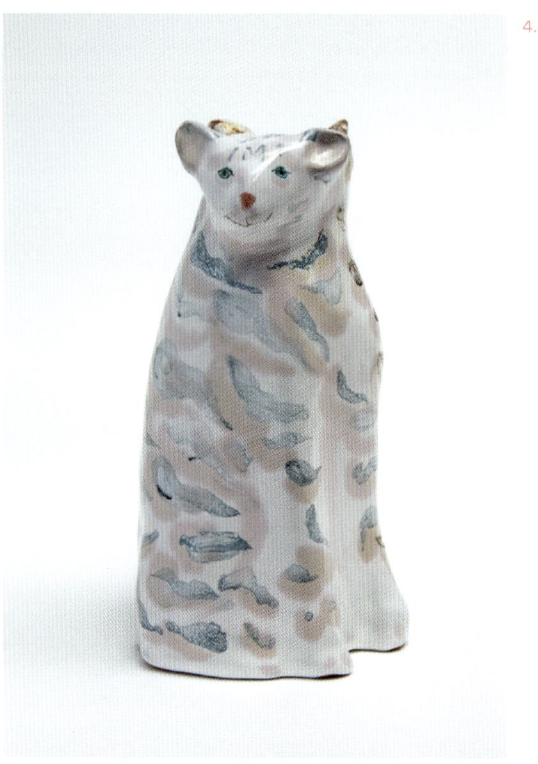

1. *Colourful Owl Cat*, 14 × 9 × 6 cm, 2015.
2. *Owl Cat in Red*, 14 × 9 × 6 cm, 2015.
3. *Firecracker*, 15 × 8 × 7 cm, 2015.
4. *Back to Back*, 15 × 8 × 7 cm, 2015.

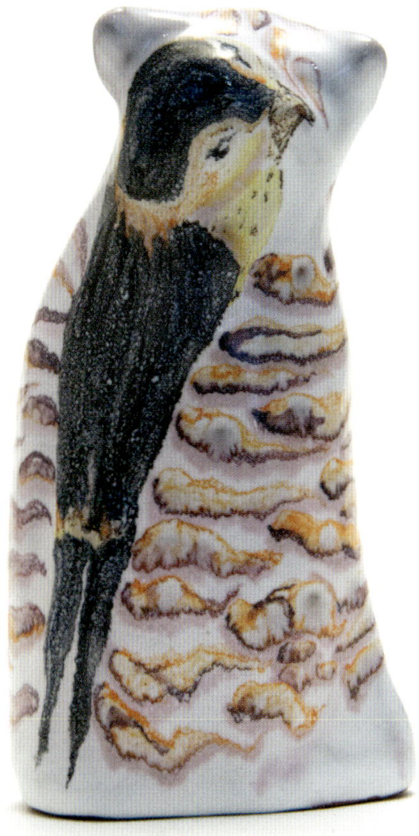

Red Rumpy,
16 × 8 × 6 cm, 2022.

birds, the composure of a cat. Each reveals itself in the clay, finding form against the palm and under finger and thumb. Holding a gentle suggestion of their anatomy in the curve of a spine pinched and smoothed or the tension of extruded haunches mid-leap. To uncover them is to know how they move, how they hold themselves in fleeting stillness, how they sprawl in the sun. An intimacy that is the result of a deep attentiveness to the non-human.

In the studio the tapering bodies of catamorphic vases lean dreamily. Like the mummified cats that first inspired them, there is the suggestion of a living presence, containing something of the enigmatic independence of cats looking out at the world. A ginger tom on the harbour wall or the face of a Bengal just visible in a thickly flowered meadow. Moments that are pressed into the clay impart a tenderness to their character that also dimples its surface. The expressive marks of maiolica accentuate their humour, and its unpredictable alchemy brightens the eye or softens the line of the mouth.

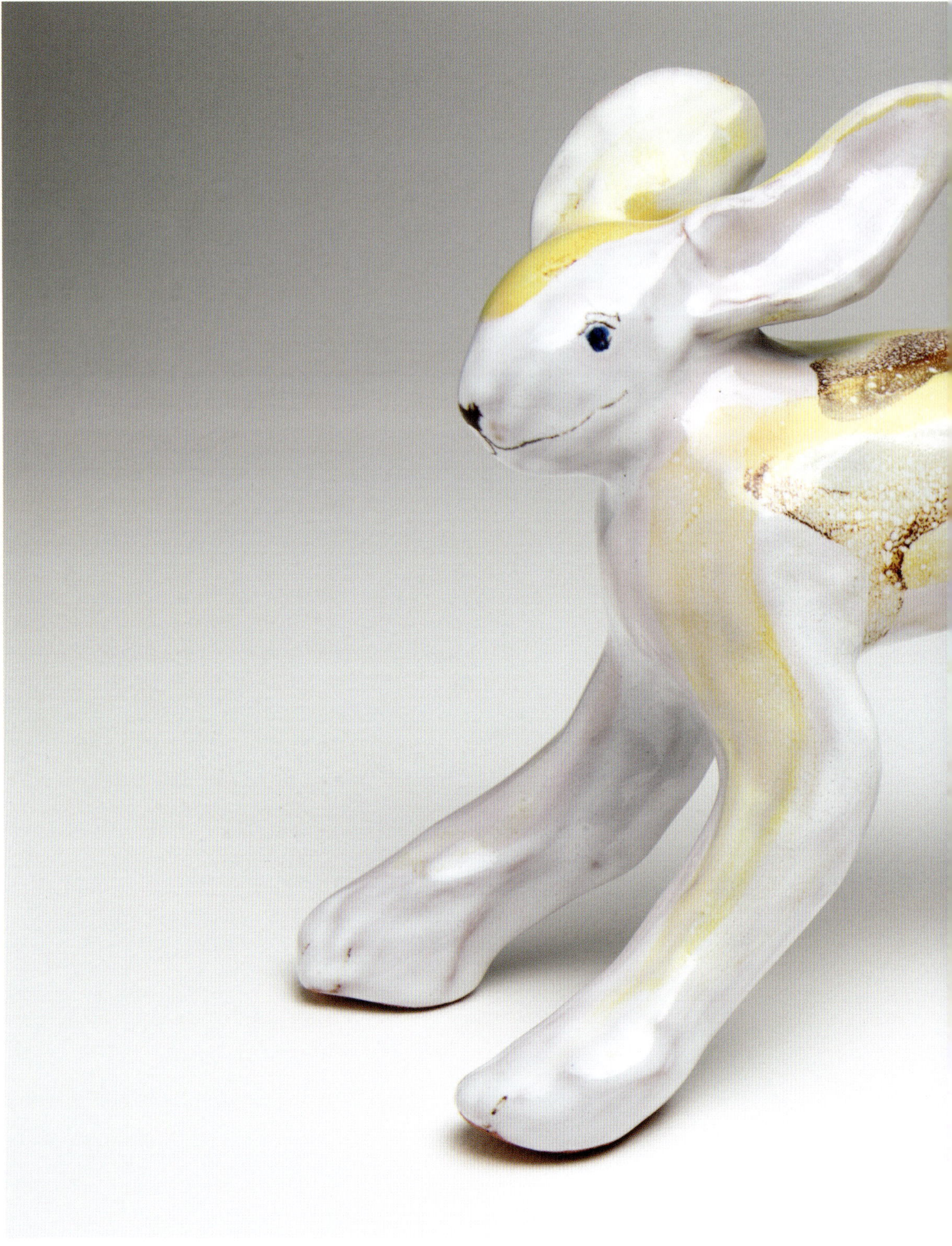

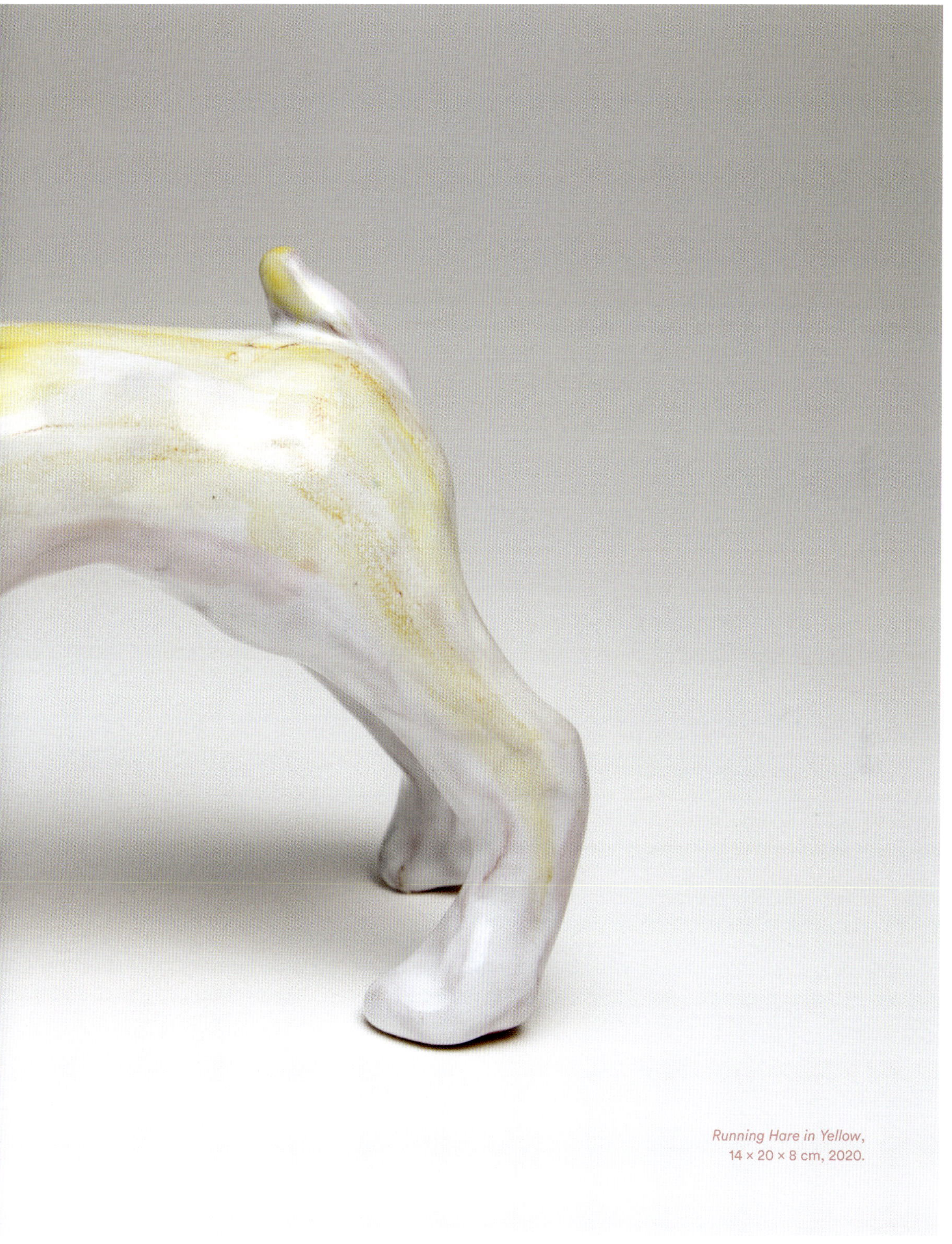

Running Hare in Yellow,
14 × 20 × 8 cm, 2020.

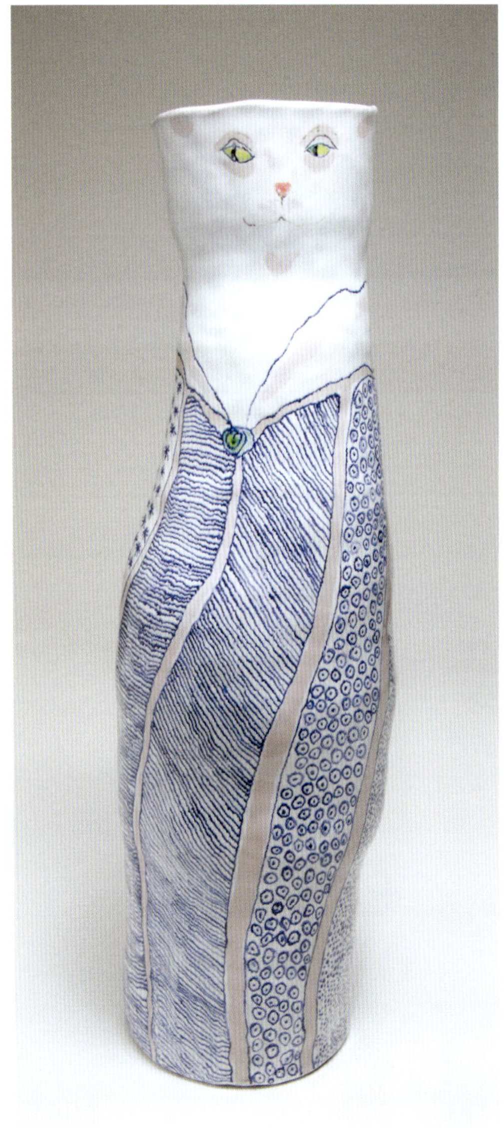

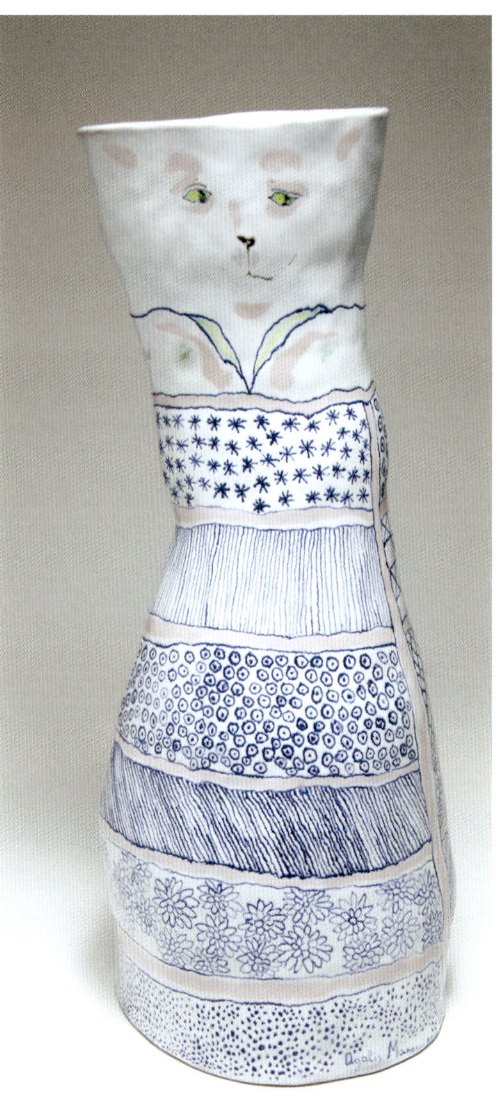

Twisted Willow,
39 × 12 × 12 cm, 2016.

Banded Willow,
35 × 14 × 13 cm, 2016.

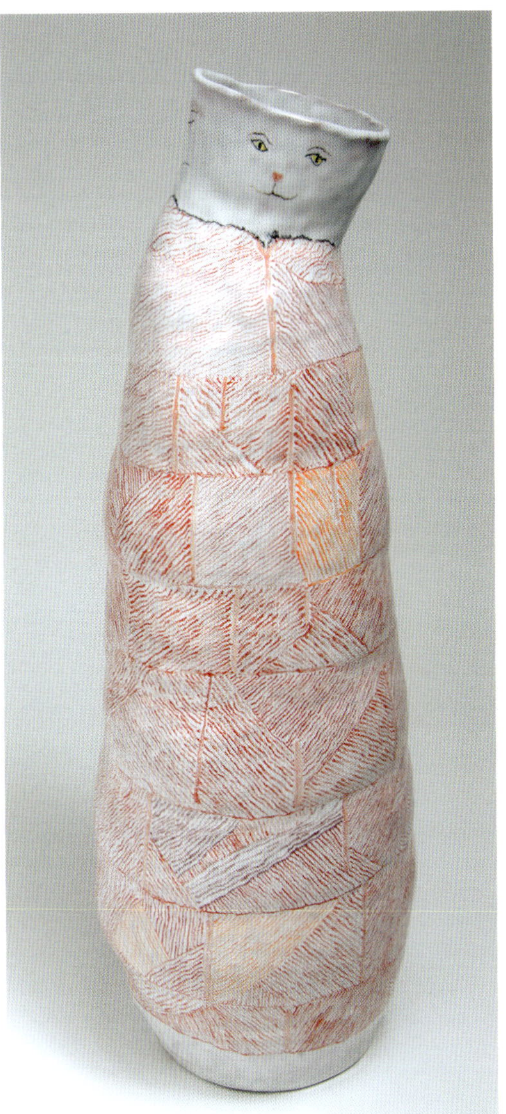

Geo Cat in Red,
45 × 16 × 13 cm, 2019.

There is a joyful but uncertain potential found in both this material and an animal encounter. The chance meeting with a fox as it disappears into the gloom between streetlights akin to the unknown possibility of the piece when it descends into the kiln. This liveliness remains even after it is fixed and fired, an animism that holds the apparition of breathing bodies.

Ripple Crowd,
40 × 14 × 14 cm, 2015.

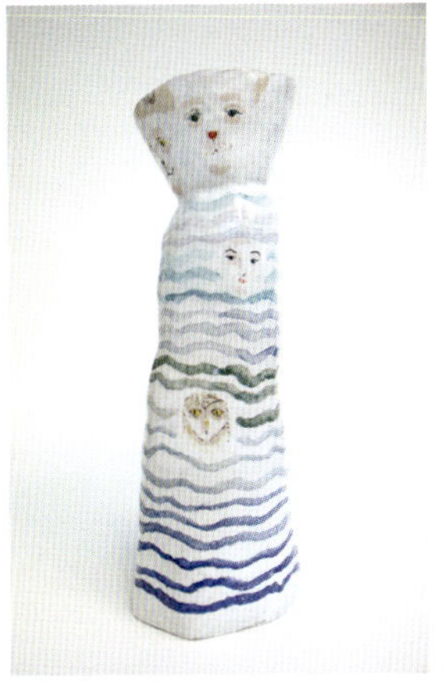

Tapestry Cat for Anni Albers,
40 × 18 × 18 cm, 2019.

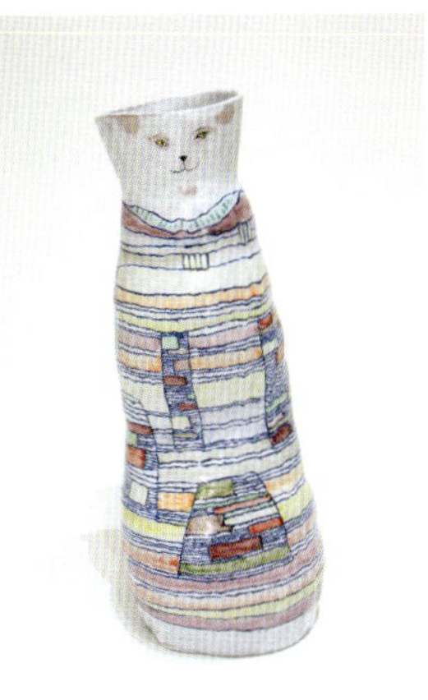

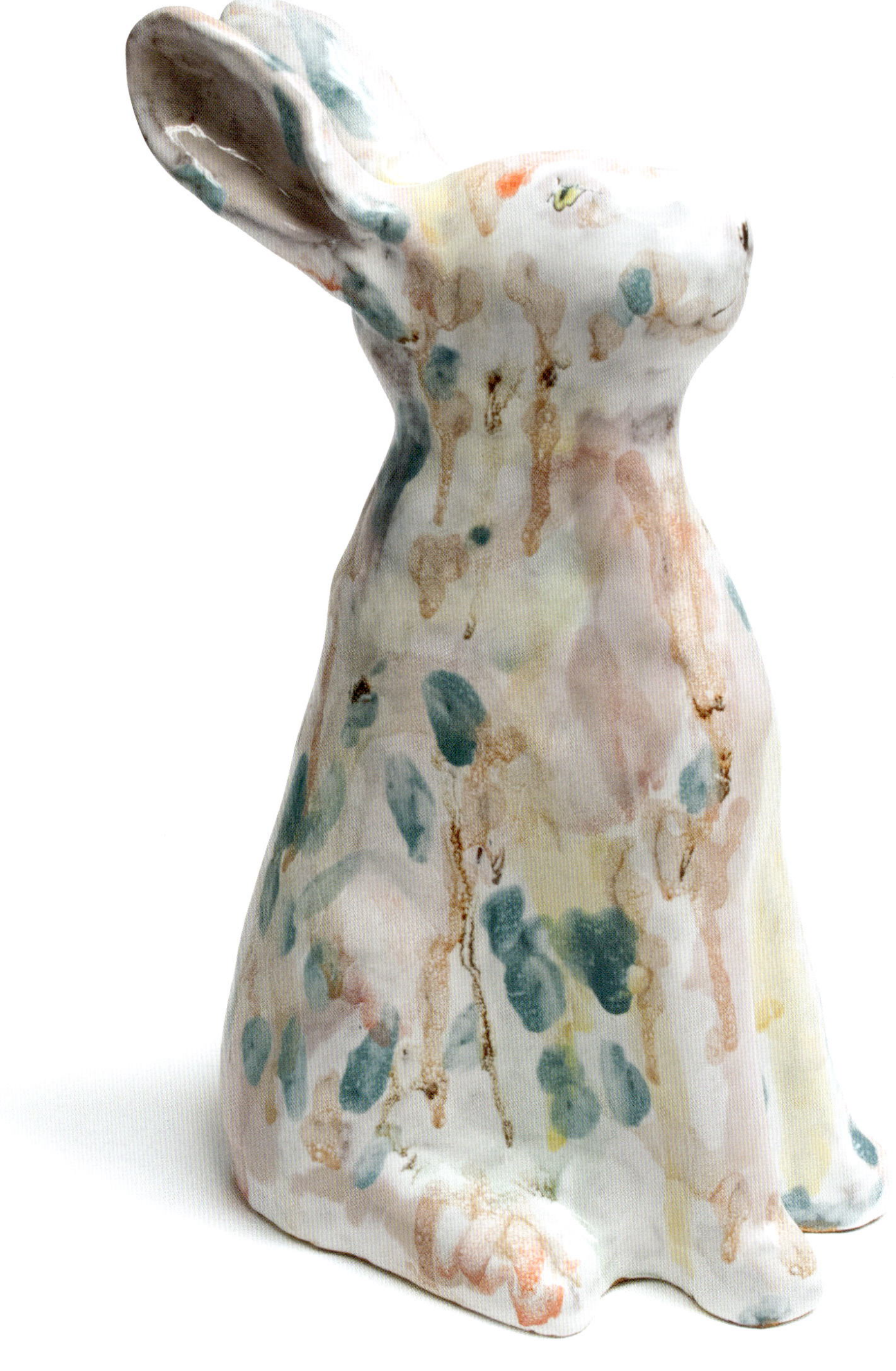

Polychrome Rabbit,
28 × 14 × 11 cm, 2013.

Painter's Cats,
33 × 20 × 16 cm,
2017–2022.

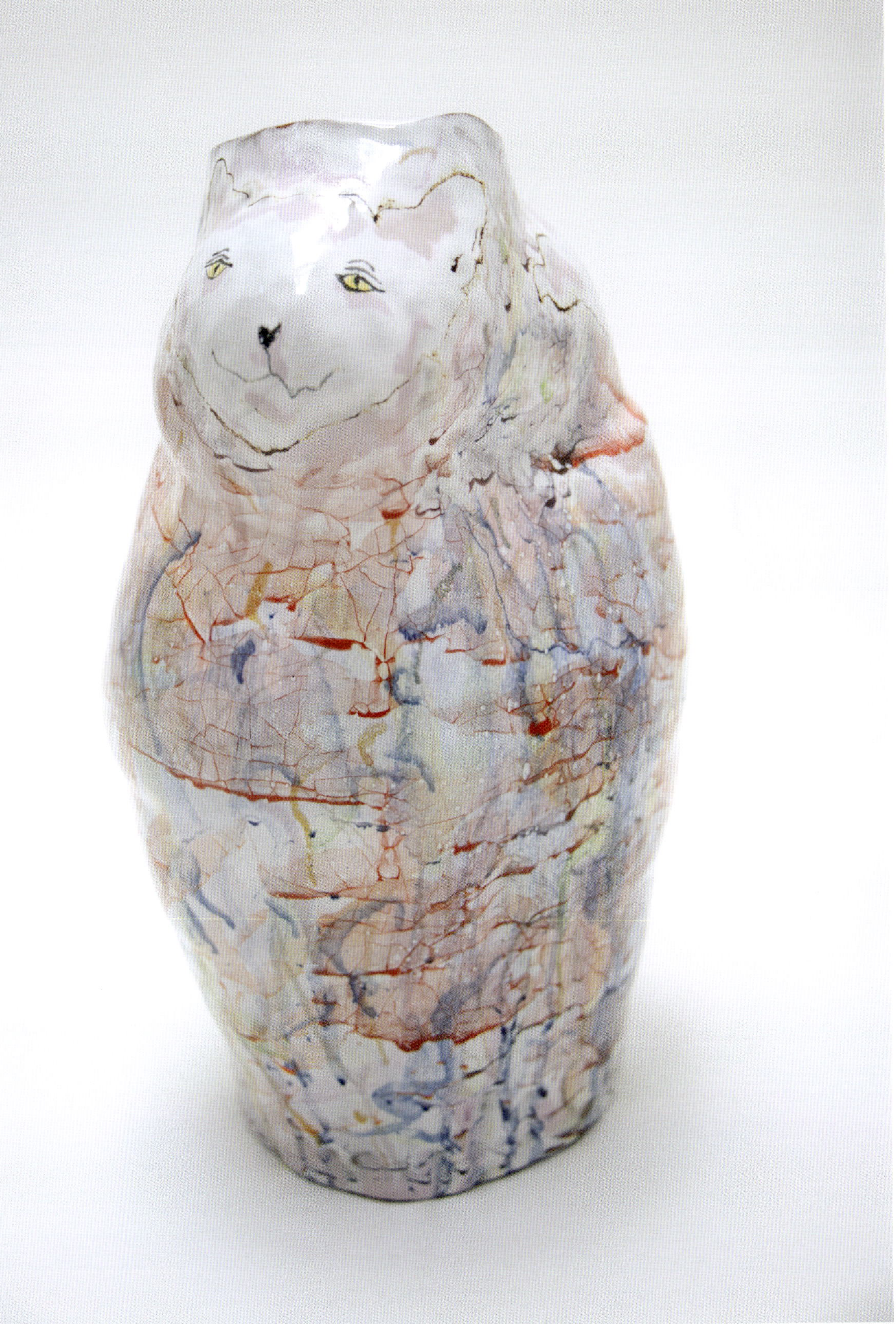

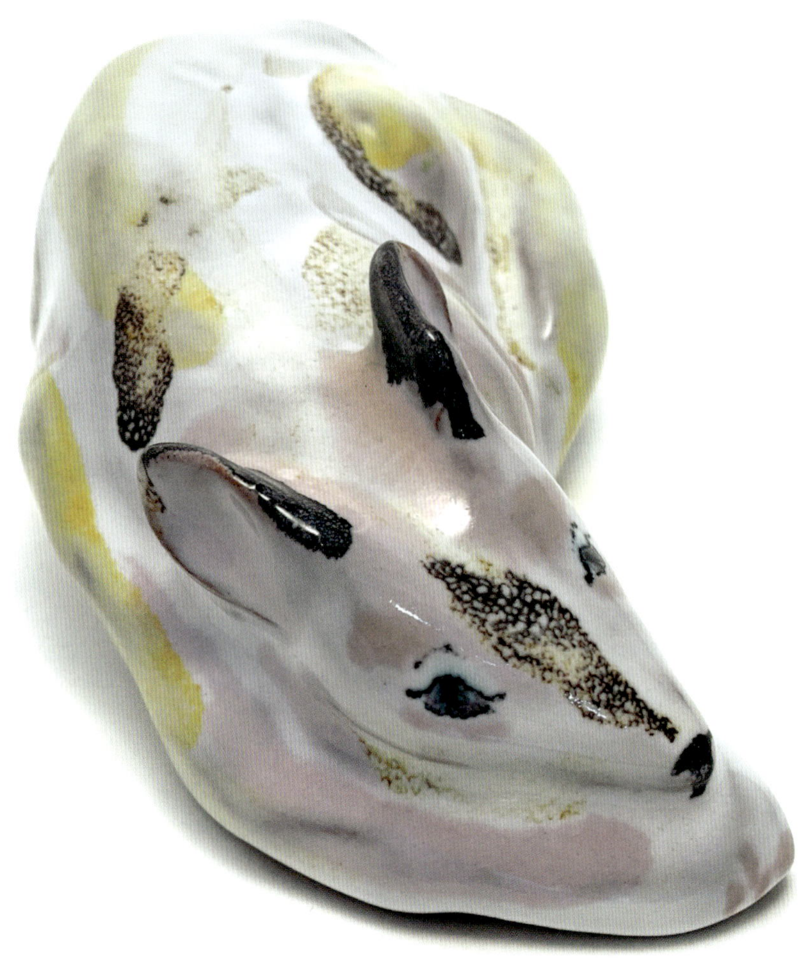

Vixen,
14 × 7 × 5 cm,
2021.

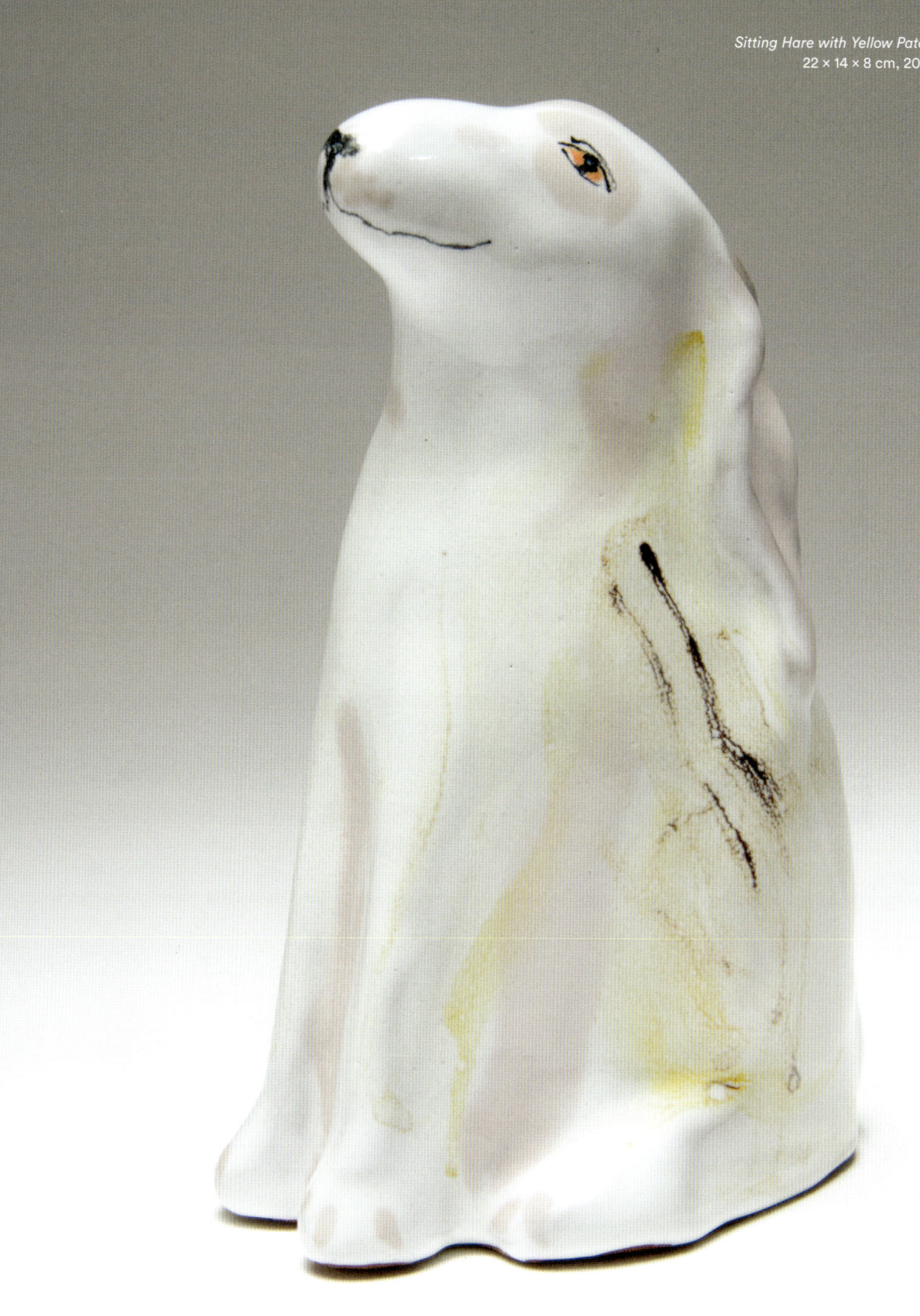

Sitting Hare with Yellow Patch,
22 × 14 × 8 cm, 2016.

Faces in a Crowd

Agalis Manessi

We are in Florence visiting the church of Santa Maria del Carmine.[10] I am in the Brancacci Chapel and I am looking at a crowded scene. The figures are close together, gazing at a miracle, Masaccio's *Resurrection of the Son of Theophilus*, and I return the gaze.

The colours are singing! There are crimson reds, oranges reminiscent of the colours of marigolds, salmon, flesh and rose pinks, Naples and crocus yellows, ultramarine, cerulean blue, emerald greens, some vivid, some soft pale washes. The expressions in their eyes are intense, the faces mostly serious; some look surprised, some have a tender smile. Some are exotically coiffeured, with curls framing their faces or peeping from under colourful hats, head coverings and turbans, their clothing indicating seniority and position within the Florentine community.

On the right-hand side of the chapel is another scene, another miracle, *The Healing of the Cripple*. This is taking place in a Florentine square; it is of St Peter healing a crippled man. Two figures stand out, alone in the centre of the scene, elegantly dressed, the one wearing an elaborately embroidered green gown, highly patterned in black and gold, the other in the palest of cyclamen pinks with a grey-green trim. Both are wearing wonderful turban hats.

Green Eyes from Brancacci, 20 × 17 cm, 2023.

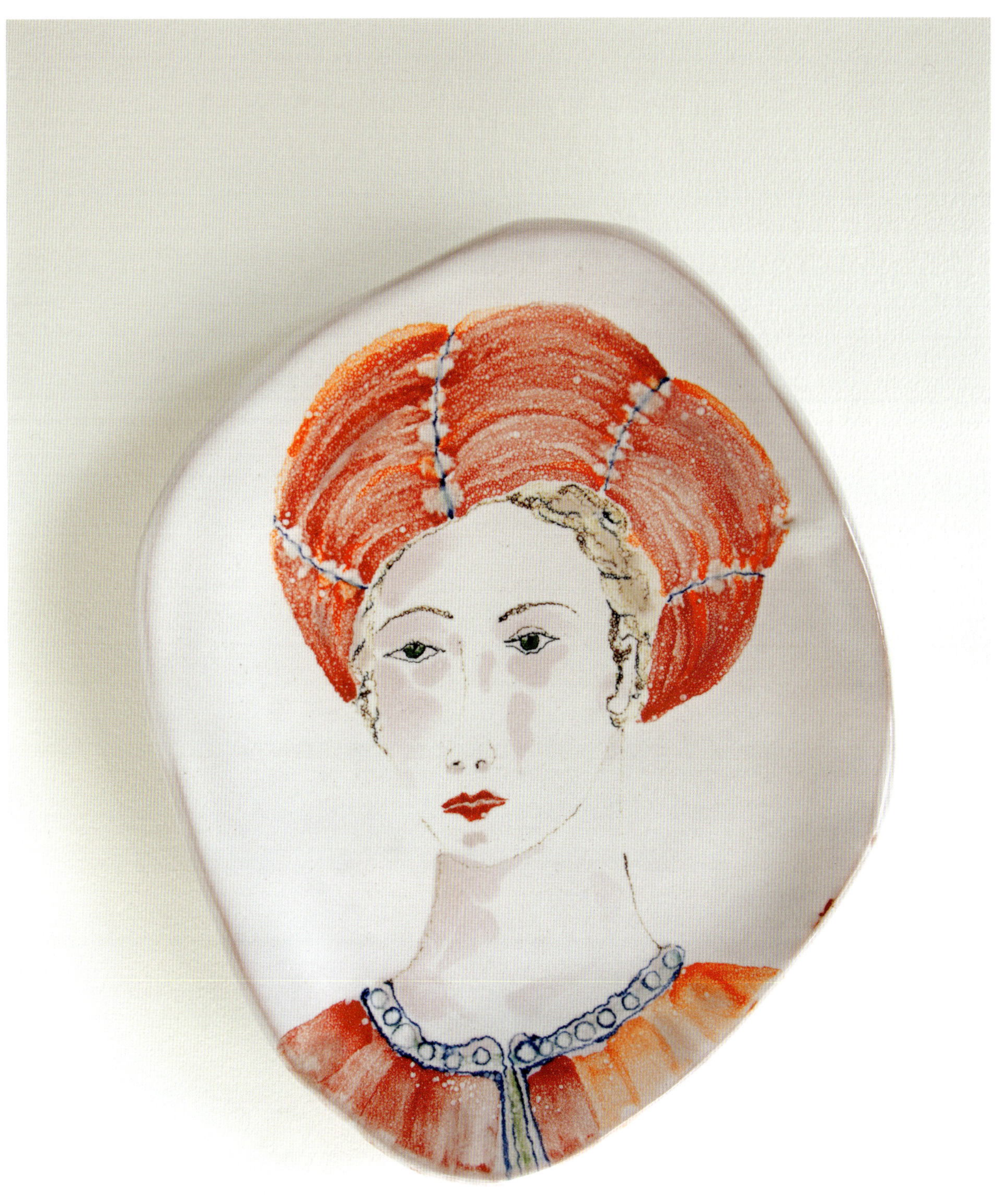

Looking at them, I can feel myself being drawn into their midst, and I am transported into their world. It is like time-travel. The more I gaze at them the more I think I hear the chatter and whisperings around them. There is warmth and sunshine emanating from the scene.

Framing these frescoes are medallions of women with pensive, angelic faces. Their looks, colours, expressions and elaborate hairdos stay in my mind, and I embark on putting them down on paper.

I love the medium of watercolour: it has an empathetic relationship to frescoes, and to maiolica, the technique I use in my ceramics. Watercolour paper, thick, grainy, highly absorbent, has qualities similar to the powdery, all-absorbent raw glaze coating my ceramic pieces and I imagine it is not unlike painting on the wet plaster. The final result, too, has a softness and similarity, and unlike any other medium it seems to capture light.

Brancacci Memory, 41 × 30 cm, 2019. Watercolour on paper

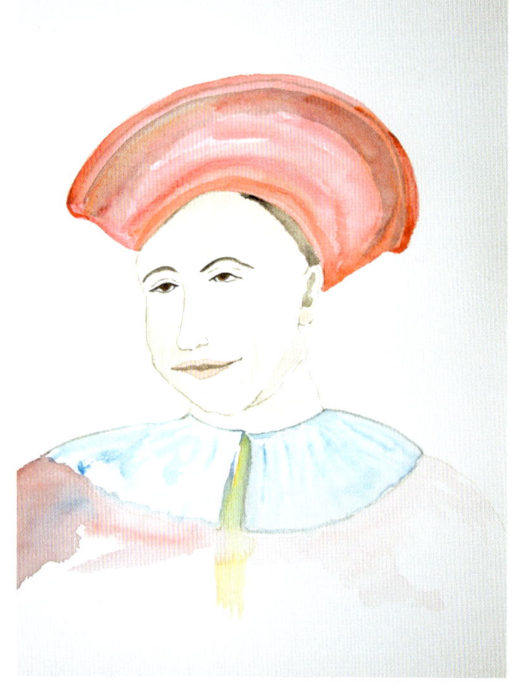

I enjoy the mixing of colours and I am enticed by a chromatic lexicon that speaks of distant lands: Alizarin Crimson and Cadmium Red for the hats and the lips; Prussian Blue, Ultramarine and Dioxazine Purple for collars, garments and more hats; Emerald, Viridian and Sap Green for trimmings and eyes; Earth colours, Yellow Ochre, Raw Umber, Burnt Sienna, Indian Red, Vandyke Brown, Sepia for hair, deep-set eyes and shadows.

From paper to ceramics is yet another journey. Plaquettes made from flat pieces of clay cut into almost ovoid shapes act as small canvases, quicker to make than the large, coiled dishes, and they become

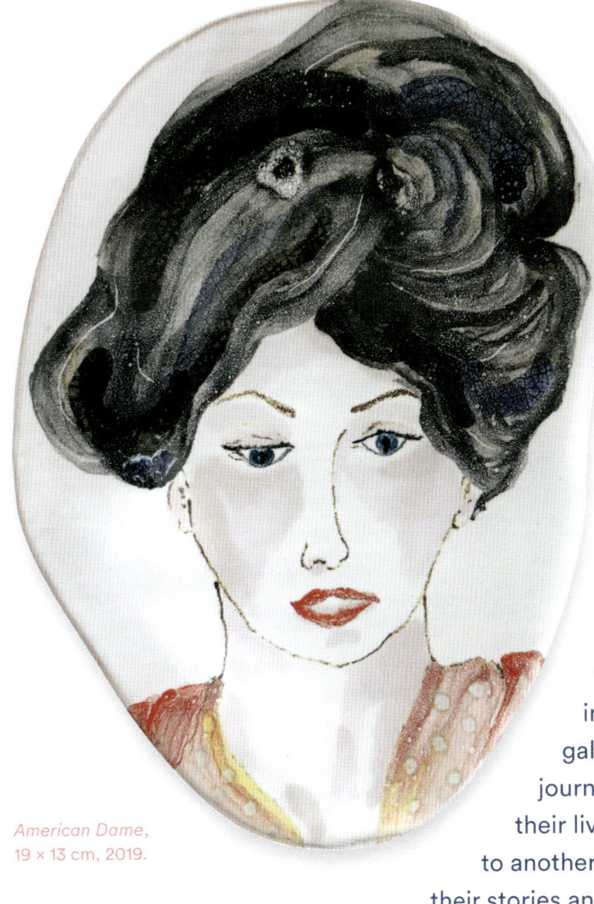

American Dame, 19 × 13 cm, 2019.

sketches of the many observed faces. They emerge from the frescoes but also from paintings and literature to create a different crowd. Spanning centuries, this is a crowd where Renaissance figures jostle side by side, keeping company with writers, painters and composers of the 19th, 20th and 21st centuries. Faces in magazines, faces on screen provide a gallery of protagonists which becomes a journey of discovery for me. The stories of their lives are enriching – one portrait leads to another. There are mythical protagonists with their stories and special attributes, heroines of the past and personalities of the now, the many who have contributed to our world in a positive way, the well-known and the forgotten.

Photographs and paintings of portraits are collected, filed for future reference, and revisited on many occasions. Trying to enter their worlds, to capture something of their story and personality, be it thoughtfulness, pleasure or melancholy, sparkle or beauty, challenges me. The crowd keeps growing as more and more faces beckon.

Watercolours were my first medium as a child. The small pressed-steel folding box that opened to reveal little pans of colour worn down by sable and water was a favourite possession. Portable, and with something reassuring about their immediacy and lack of preciousness, sketches can be set aside, and new iterations emerge with changing colour schemes and shifts in expression.

The technique of maiolica demands greater discipline. Colours are indicated by their names and through experience of how they perform in the kiln, as the metal oxides mixed with glaze do not show their true

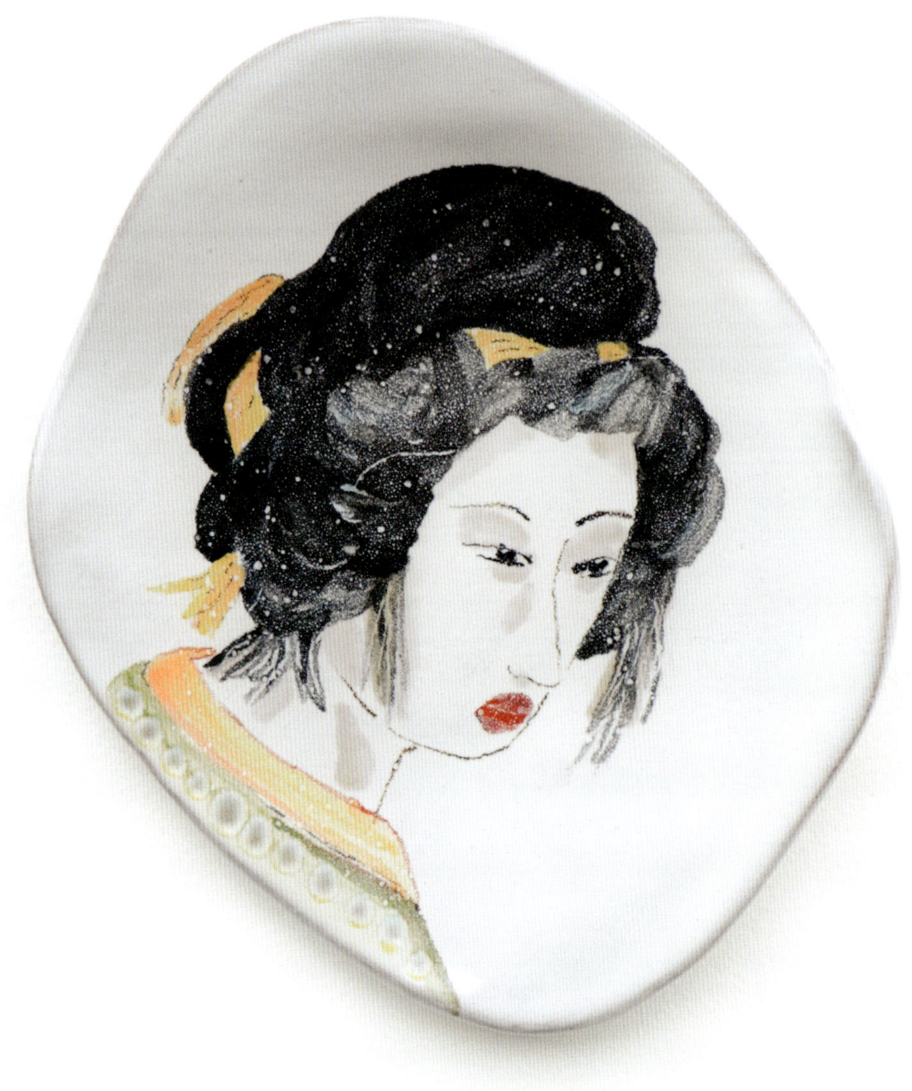

Lingering Spirit,
18 × 16, 2018.

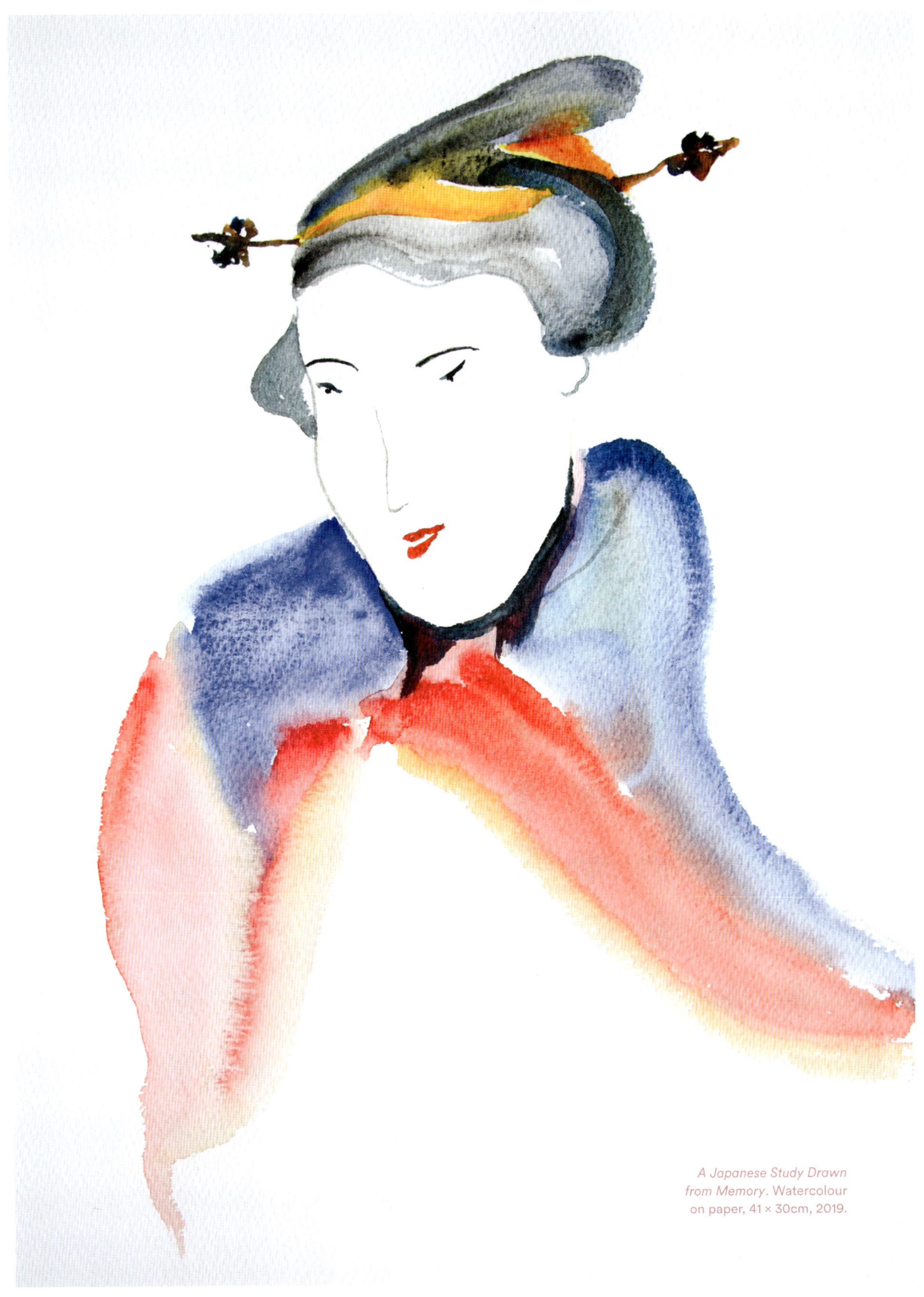

A Japanese Study Drawn from Memory. Watercolour on paper, 41 × 30cm, 2019.

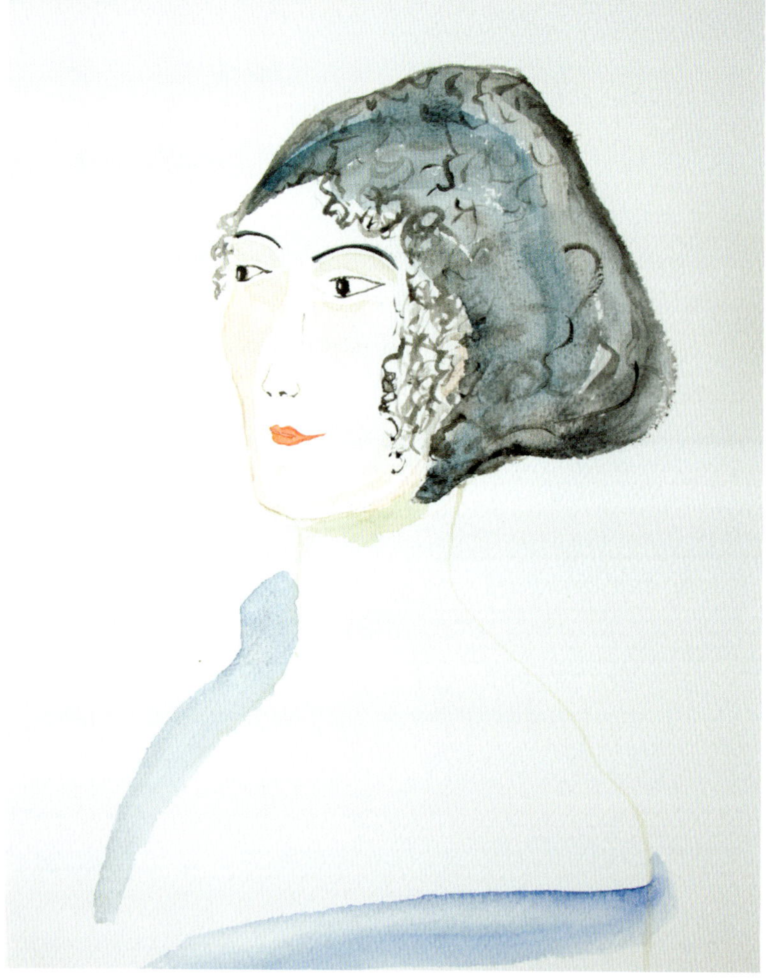

Study of an Infanta, 41 × 30 cm, 2019. Watercolour on paper.

colours in an unfired state. Certain oxides such as cobalt, copper and manganese, for example, appear as variants of black when painted, and their true colours – deep and lighter blues, silvery and turquoise greens, grainy browns – unveil themselves after the firing. They do not take kindly to being refired once the glaze has been transformed into a thin layer of glass. Striking a balance between controlled application and lightness of touch comes with experience and an acceptance that there is no going back. There is no formulaic recipe for the perfect result, there is always risk, but also the reward of capturing more than just a physiological likeness: a glance, an expression, the fold of a garment all coming together in a molten moment.

And so the cast of characters grows, fresh faces appear to grace another plaquette.

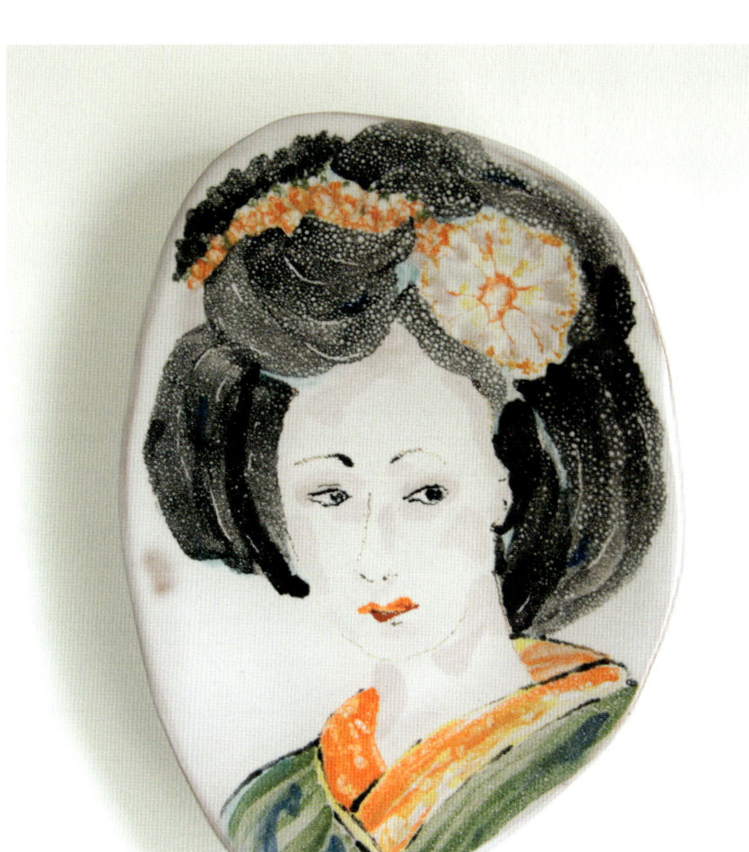

Little Flower,
17 × 13 cm, 2022.

For Piero,
23 × 22 cm, 2022.

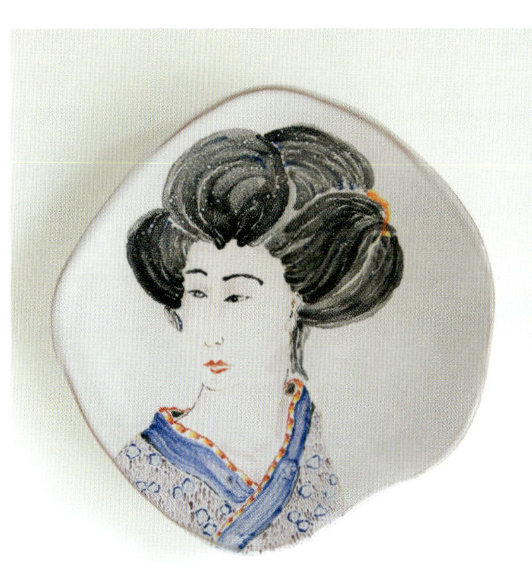

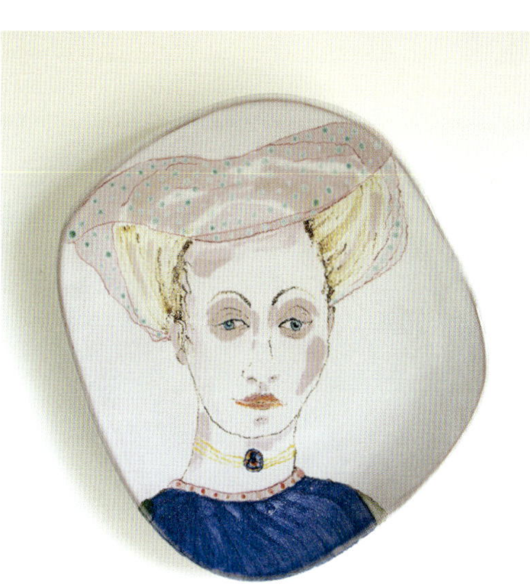

Kimono Girl,
19 × 18 cm, 2023.

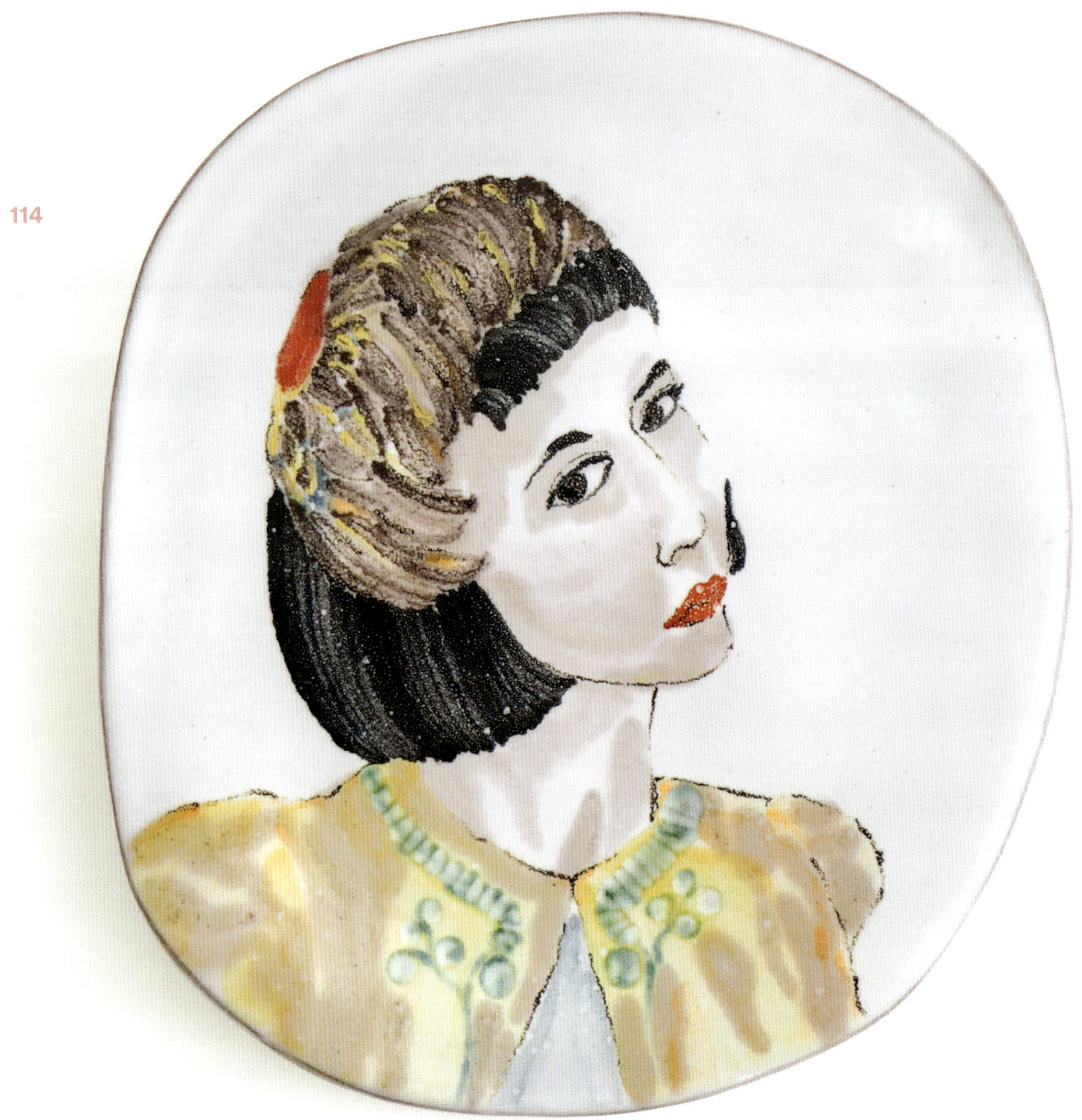

Californian Beauty,
19 × 19cm, 2020.

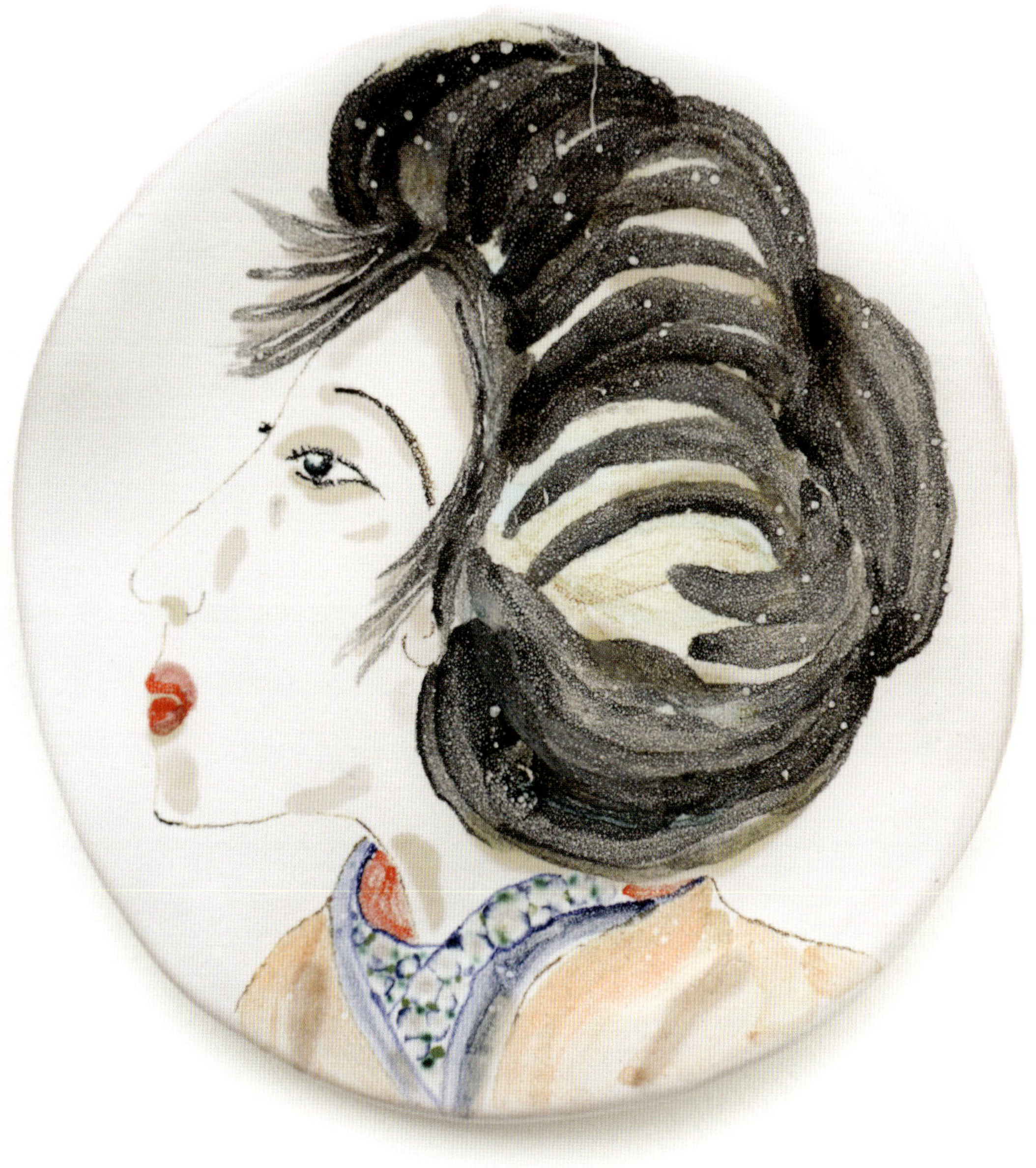

Looking at Birds,
17 × 18 cm, 2018.

Cargoes across Time

Agalis Manessi

Like the foreshore of the Thames near my studio, which is littered with ceramic sherds, the wrecks of ships scattered across the Mediterranean bear witness to the centuries of trade and their valuable cargoes of pottery that now lie strewn across the seabed. From Ancient Greece to Rome, pottery figured prominently in daily life, from the prized red and black Attic-ware vases to humble domestic pots. Occasionally friends returning from diving or fishing off Corfu would bring back found fragments as gifts, the neck of an amphora or a piece of Byzantine ware incised with cartoon-like drawings of animals and figures, loosely painted in copper greens and honey-coloured glazes. These barnacled treasures, softened by the action of sand and sea, speak of the fragility and permanence of ceramics and are a reminder of the pottery continuum in which I work.

Journeys may take us to unexpected places where responses beyond the habits of our usual practice are required. The Greek town of Aigio sits on the coast in the northern Peloponnese, a region where the grapes that become the famed Vostizza currants are cultivated. Historically the currants were loaded on to boats and exported across the Mediterranean to be unloaded in the ports

Byzantine Dog. Incised and glazed pottery dish with sgraffito drawing of a dog, c.14th century. Collection AM

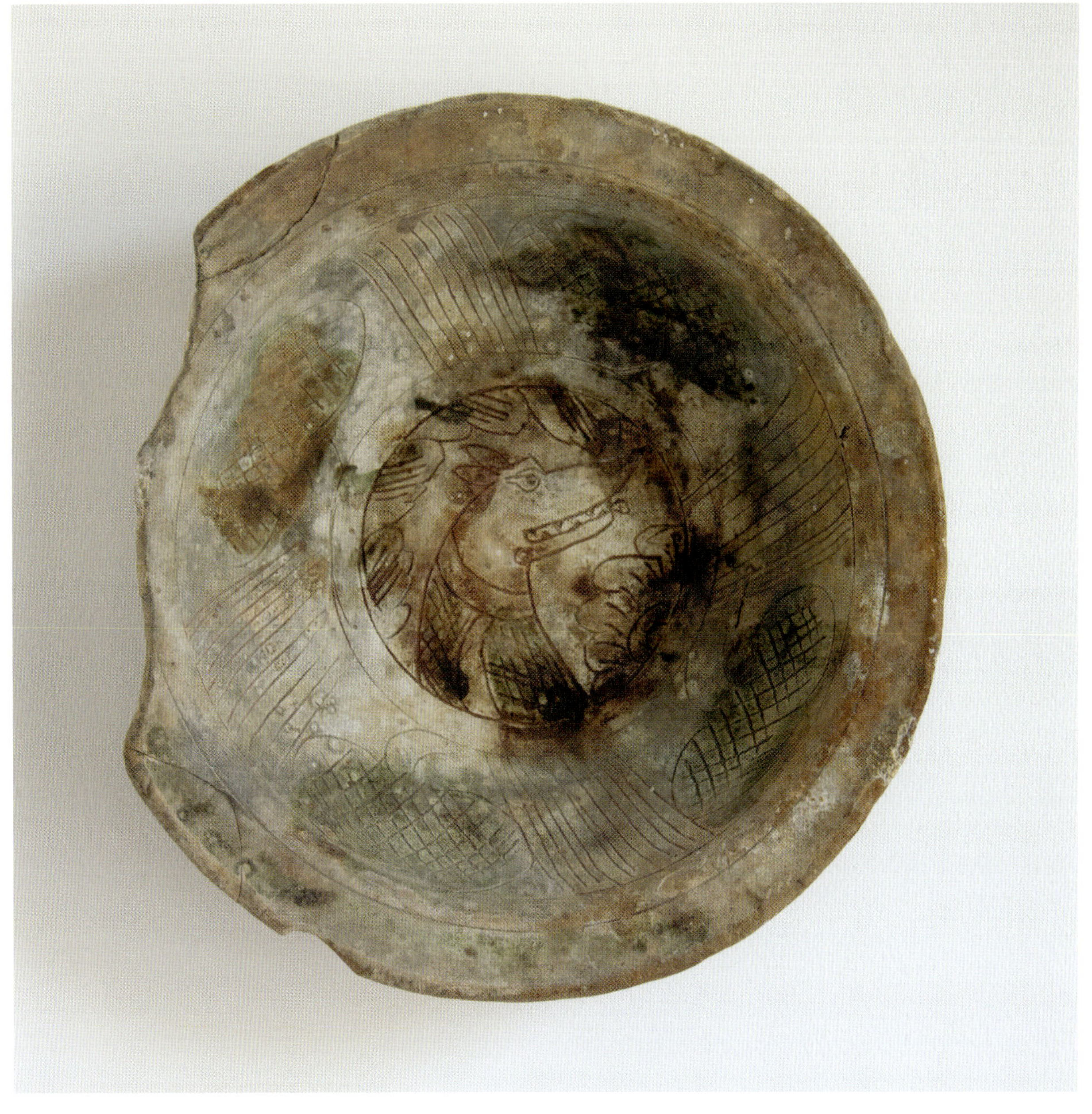

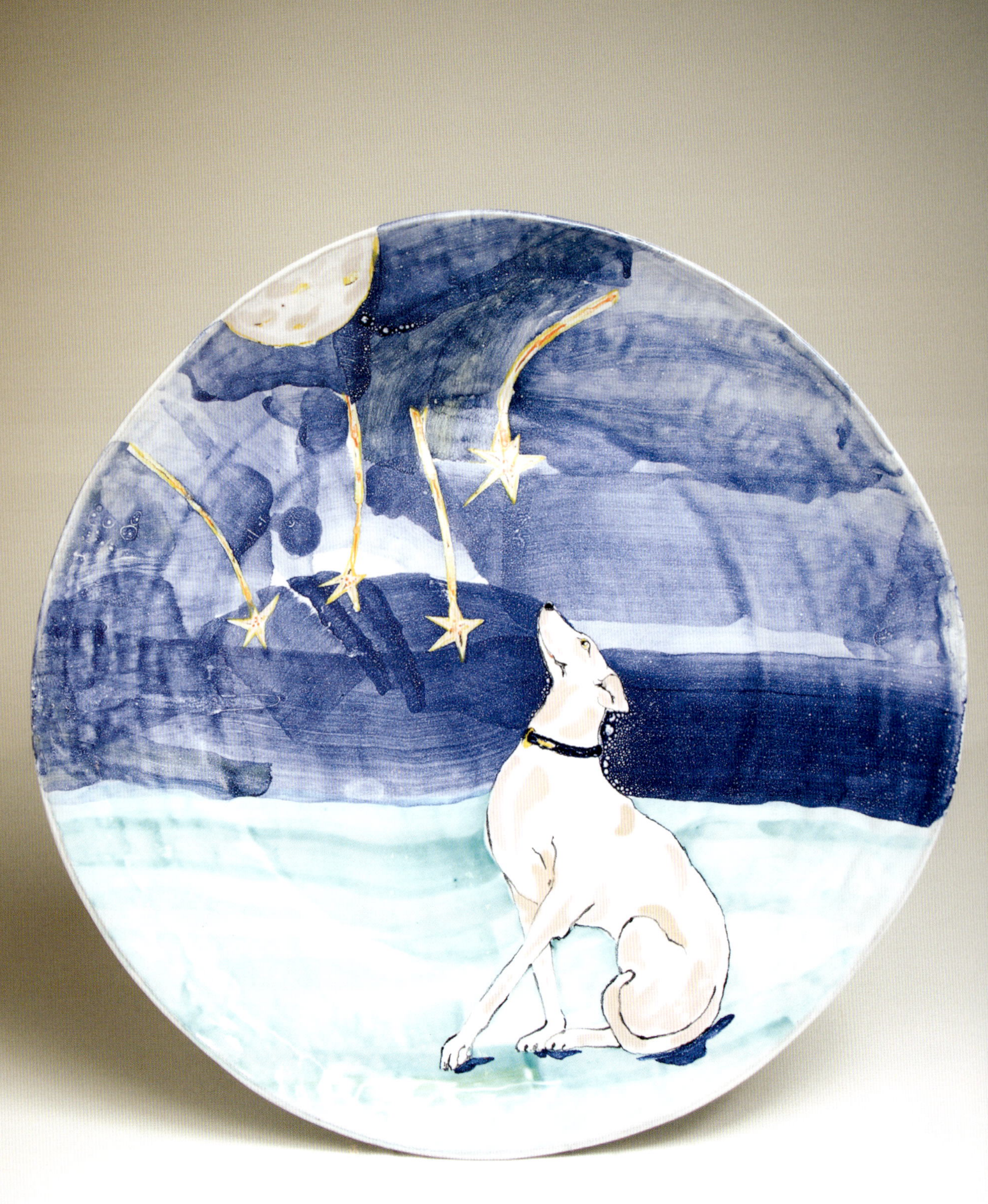

Star Gazer,
40 × 40 cm, 2015.

of London and Bristol before being packed and eventually sold in grocery stores all over the country. An invitation to make a piece of work for *Into my Garden Come*, as part of the Primarolia Festival in Aigio 2019 celebrating the historical trade in currants, was an opportunity to try something different.

The ancient word Φορτιο (cargo) implies a load, freight, burden or baggage; or, in the case of Primarolia, a precious cargo. As the currants travelled to distant parts, they carried the hopes of peoples emerging through times of hardship to a better and more prosperous future, earning the name 'black gold'. Clay too has been used since

Cargo, 2019. Installation view, Primarolia, Aigio, Greece. Terracotta, gold leaf, raisins, paper, leaf, wire, wood.

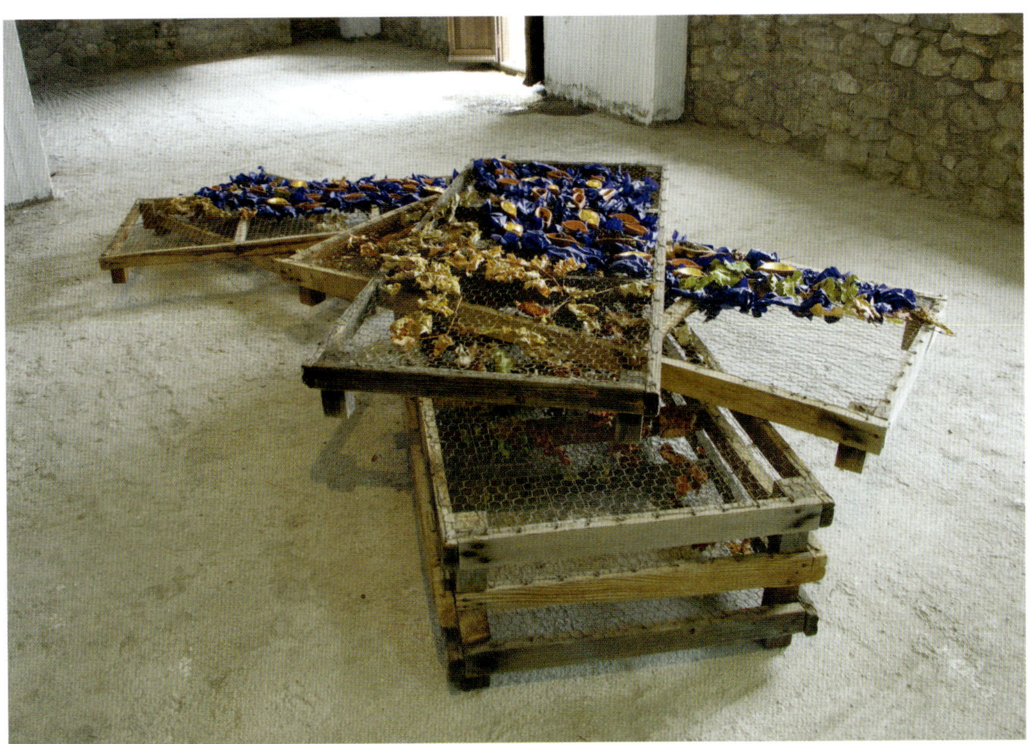

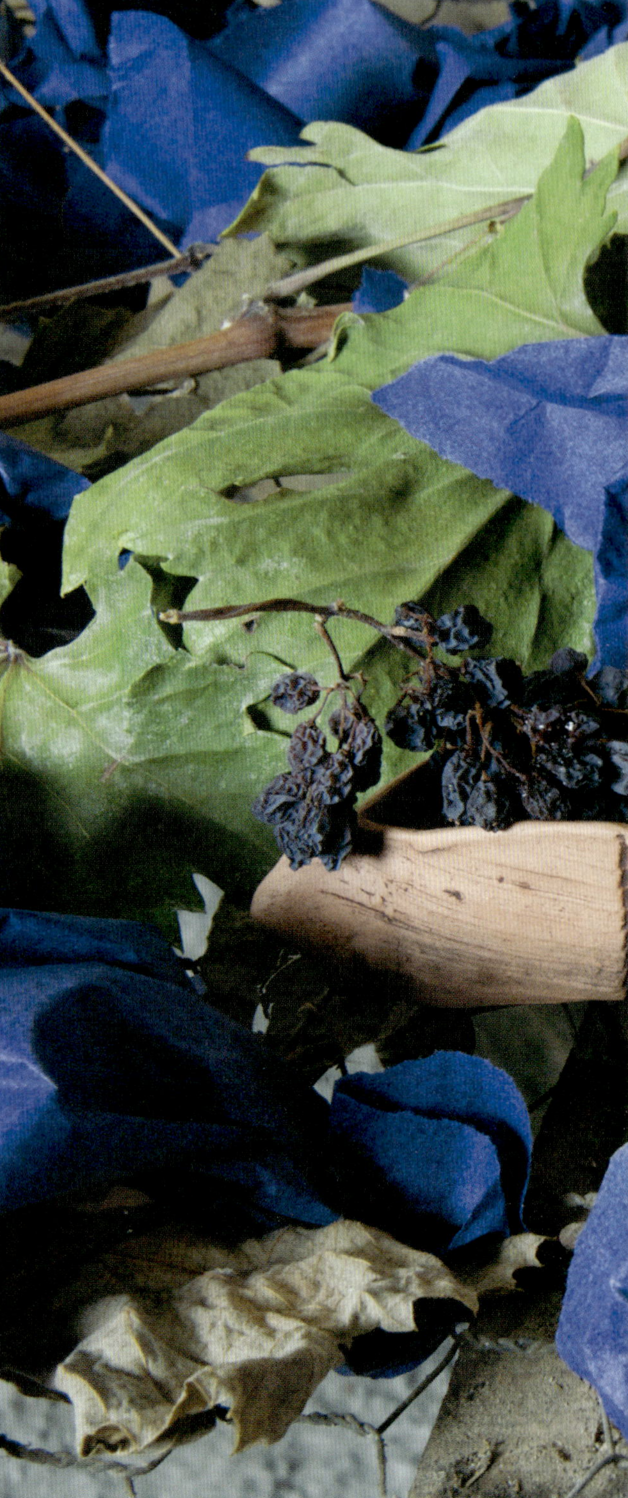
Cargo (detail), 2019.

antiquity to transport precious cargoes. Wine and oil were transported in clay *pithoi* and amphorae across the sea to distant lands. In the *Iliad* Homer refers to the sea as οίνοψ πόντος (8th century BC), or, in its poetic translation in English, the *wine-dark sea*. In the British Museum there are several ancient Greek clay vessels originally made to accompany the souls of the deceased on their journey through the underworld. Φορτιο creates a new fleet of clay boats floating in a wine-dark sea of black gold, poised for another journey.

For the exhibition, a collection of simple terracotta boat forms, some lined with gold leaf and filled with currants, were floated on a bed of dried vine leaves and sheets of crumpled blue paper retrieved from a derelict paper mill in the port. This turbulent tissue rested on old chicken wire frames normally used to dry the currants high up in the vineyards above the town. Stacked up, the frames floated like flotsam across the floor of the abandoned warehouse on the quayside.

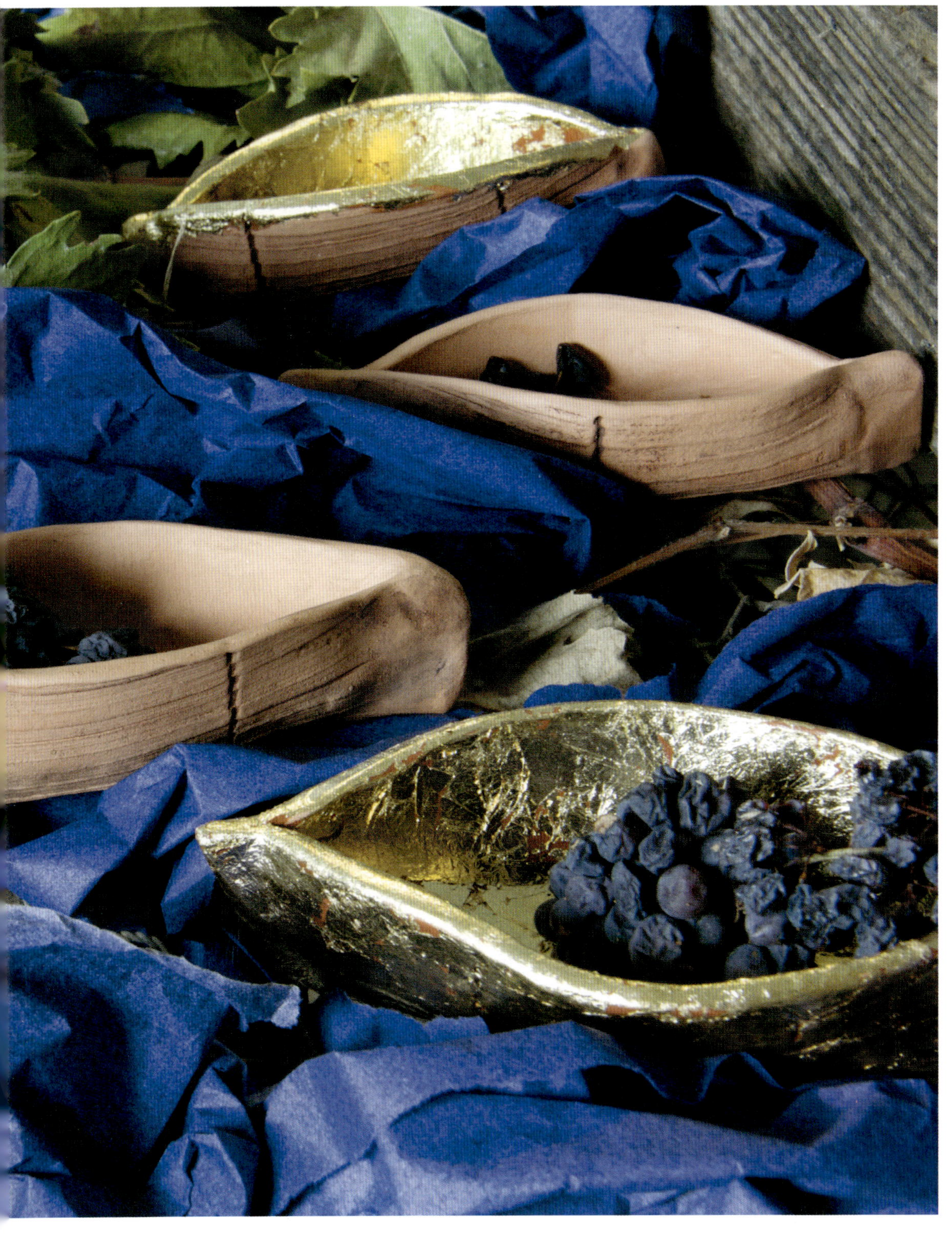

Crossing Continents

Marina Papasotiriou

From ancient cultures, across continents and civilisations, the art of clay has been practised throughout Greek culture for centuries, tracing a long and interesting course through antiquity to today. The first basic material of the potter's expression is clay in all its forms, with a huge diversity of properties. These present complex characteristics that enable the creation of an immense wealth of ceramic artefacts.

Since its earliest use there have evolved three distinct processes leading to the creation of the finished object. The first is that the wet clay is malleable: it can be formed, hardened and keeps its shape on drying. The second is that through firing, it is changed irreversibly into a ceramic object. The third is that with the addition of glass coatings the objects acquire new properties, enabling them to be employed for a greater variety of uses. These simple steps of creation, initially for function, evolved over a long period of time through the practical

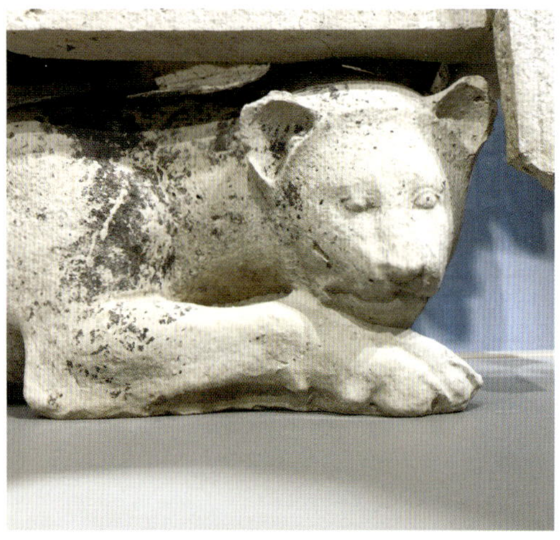

Detail of limestone pediment, (500 BC) from a temple to Dionysos, Archeologiocal Museum of Corfu.

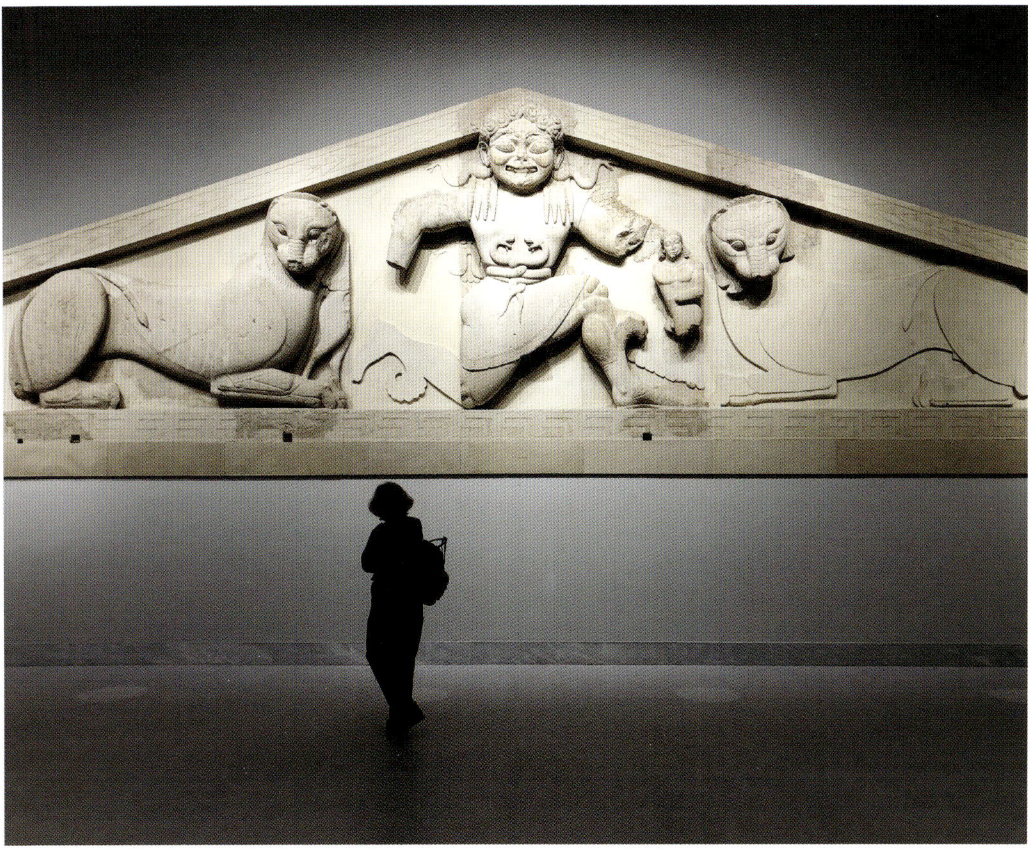

The Gorgon-Medusa pediment from the great temple of Artemis, 585 BC. Archeologiocal Museum of Corfu.

experiments of craftsmen and artists. These found expression through the development of form, volume, colour and other creative techniques.

One of these techniques is maiolica, practised since AD 900 in Mesopotamia and later from 1500 in Italy and Spain.

The ceramic technique of maiolica requires not only the deep, haptic knowledge of the ceramicist, but also the skilled application of colour and brushwork, on a 'canvas' in which the artist will draw upon their knowledge of the behaviour of oxides after firing. This is an artistry that rewards but does not allow for mistakes. It is a technique that transforms an unrefined object into a sophisticated creation where the result oscillates between a utilitarian object and one that could be defined as a work of art.

Agalis Manessi draws her inspiration from a lifelong journey through the world of ceramics and painting across time and place. During her long and productive career the artist brings with her a whole world, a plethora of visual and written sources on which she

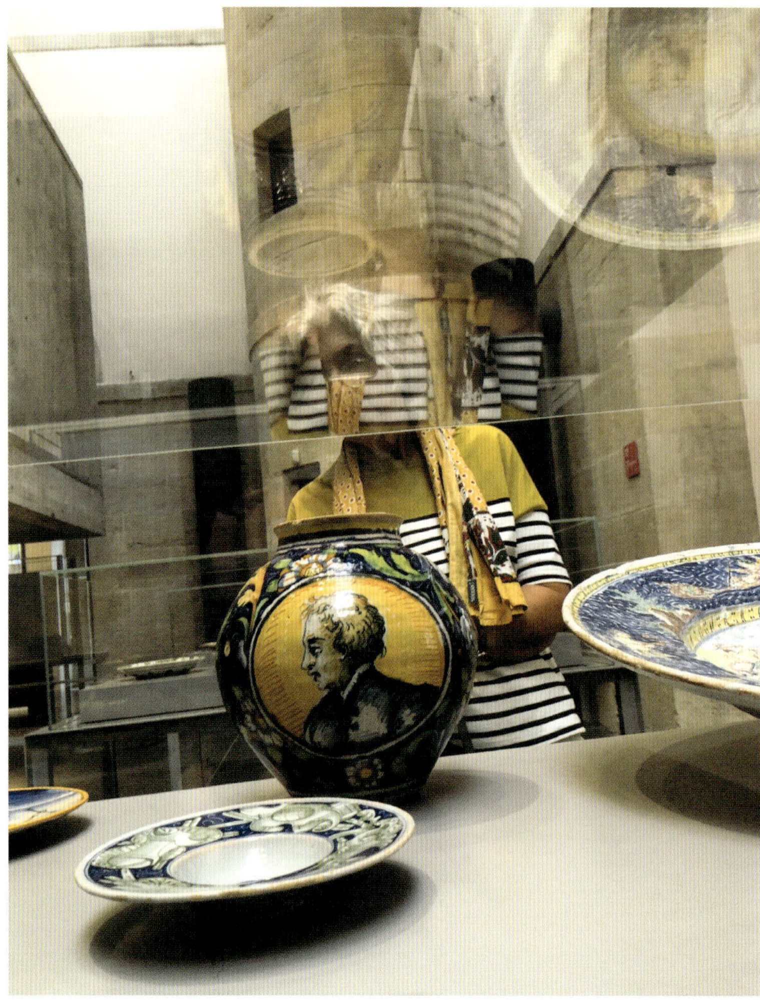

AM, research visit. Museum of Fine Arts and Archaeology of Besançon, France.

continues to work and translate into her own form of expression. Within this framework, on her annual pilgrimage between London and Corfu she visits museums and art spaces, cathedrals and ancient cities, studying particular artists and their works, which vary from the pastel-pigmented frescoes of Piero della Francesca to ancient Greek statues of magnificent lions. As she travels, she reads and informs herself, and is inspired by the past and the present, the remote and the everyday, the eternal and the ephemeral. The fresco faces and sculpted figures migrate on to her vessels and modelled objects, which reaffirm the possibility of ceramics to metamorphose through her ability to balance between ceramics and painting, substance and image, with an enigmatic frame of mind, a subtlety of humour, a tenderness and respect for the Great Masters of art.

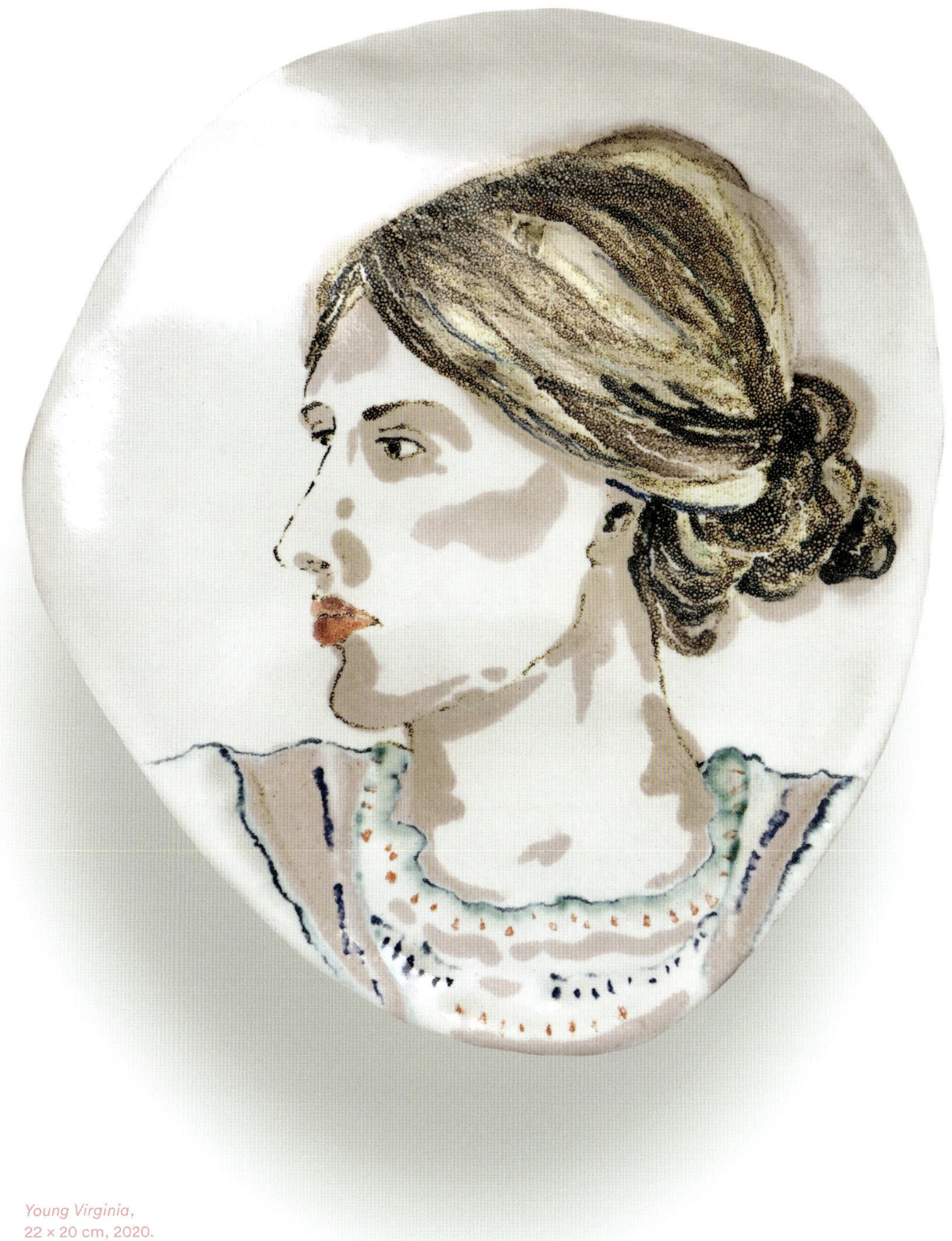

Young Virginia,
22 × 20 cm, 2020.

Acknowledgements

There are sincere thanks to be given to many for the existence of this book. I am grateful to all at Unicorn Press, especially to Ian Strathcarron for his enthusiastic response to my idea and for starting the ball rolling. I would also like to thank Lucy Duckworth, David Breuer and Lauren Tanner for their enthusiasm, hard work and positive attitude and to Elisabeth Ingles for her constructive editing of my essays and for advising on the texts. My thanks also go to Matthew Wilson for beautifully designing the book and bringing the work to life.

I am indebted to all my contributors, Jenni Lomax, Tanya Harrod, Mina Holland, Liz Rideal, Michael Petry, Megan Brooks, Marina Papasotiriou for giving their time so willingly and illuminating the work from their own perspective.

I am fortunate to have friends and family who have embraced the idea that a book was possible and have given enthusiastic support and encouragement, I would like to thank them all.
Alfred Chubb for believing in his godmother.
Marco and Meg, for building up my confidence and egging me on.
Above all to my partner in life Rob Kesseler,
For his enthusiasm, for believing in this project and in my work over the years,
For his critical eye and drawing attention to detail,
For spending long hours meticulously cleaning up images,
For enriching my process
For wise words
For always being there
For being my life-long companion.

I am grateful to the Craft Potters Charitable Trust for their generous award in supporting the publication.

And finally to my feline friends over the years, Rigas, Gillig, Rombilly, Kafka and Athos.

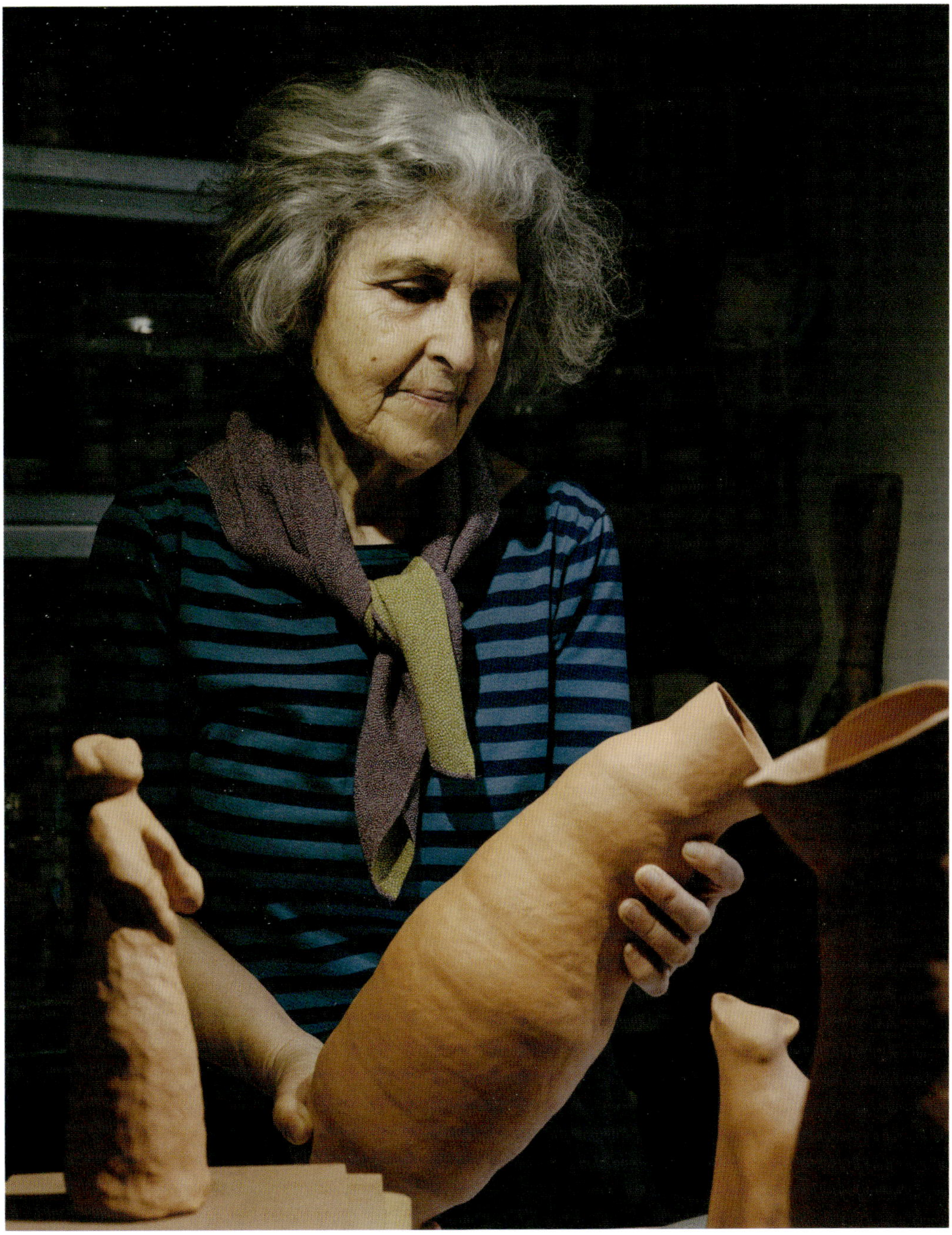

Endnotes

1 Sadly, like many of the small artisanal workshops and industries in Corfu town the pottery was subsequently demolished for new housing. However, as new younger generations return from education abroad and demand for better quality bespoke work is growing, new studios are starting to emerge, making contemporary work.

2 This was a time when evening classes were expanding into Adult Education and Further Education and ceramics courses were valued and extremely popular. Sadly, over time as local authority budgets diminished, courses were closed. After having given so much of my time to promoting the value of working with clay in the community, this was dispiriting. At this low ebb the vacuum became filled with a new generation of millennials seeking a release from spending hours in front of screens, who embraced the creative escape that working with clay gives. TV pottery programmes and the Grayson Perry factor have fuelled the appetite for all things clay.

3 Originally published in *TOAST* magazine. https://www.toa.st/blogs/magazine/agalis-manessi-toast-portraits

4 *A Picture of Dorian Gray*, Oscar Wilde (1854–1900)

5 c.1933. National Portrait Gallery 6375. The mask was in the artist's own collection and hung at first in her London showroom, and later in her studio.

6 Bowl with ideal profile of a woman, Castel Durante, Italy, c.1520–25. Tin-glazed earthenware. The Courtauld, London (Samuel Courtauld Trust) ©The Courtauld

7 Women decorating ceramics by hand in the Hanley Potteries were known as paintresses, and those who worked for Clarice Cliff (1899–1972) in the 1920s were also called 'Bizarre Girls' after her style of decorative ware.

8 Statement from the artist in personal correspondence, 23/6/21

9 A set of fifty Wedgwood plates painted in Charleston, Sussex by Vanessa Bell (1879–1961) and Duncan Grant (1885–1978) between 1932–4, Grant was the only man depicted in the set.

10 The '*we*', I refer to is Rob Kesseler, my partner and constant companion on the many journeys we have undertaken together.

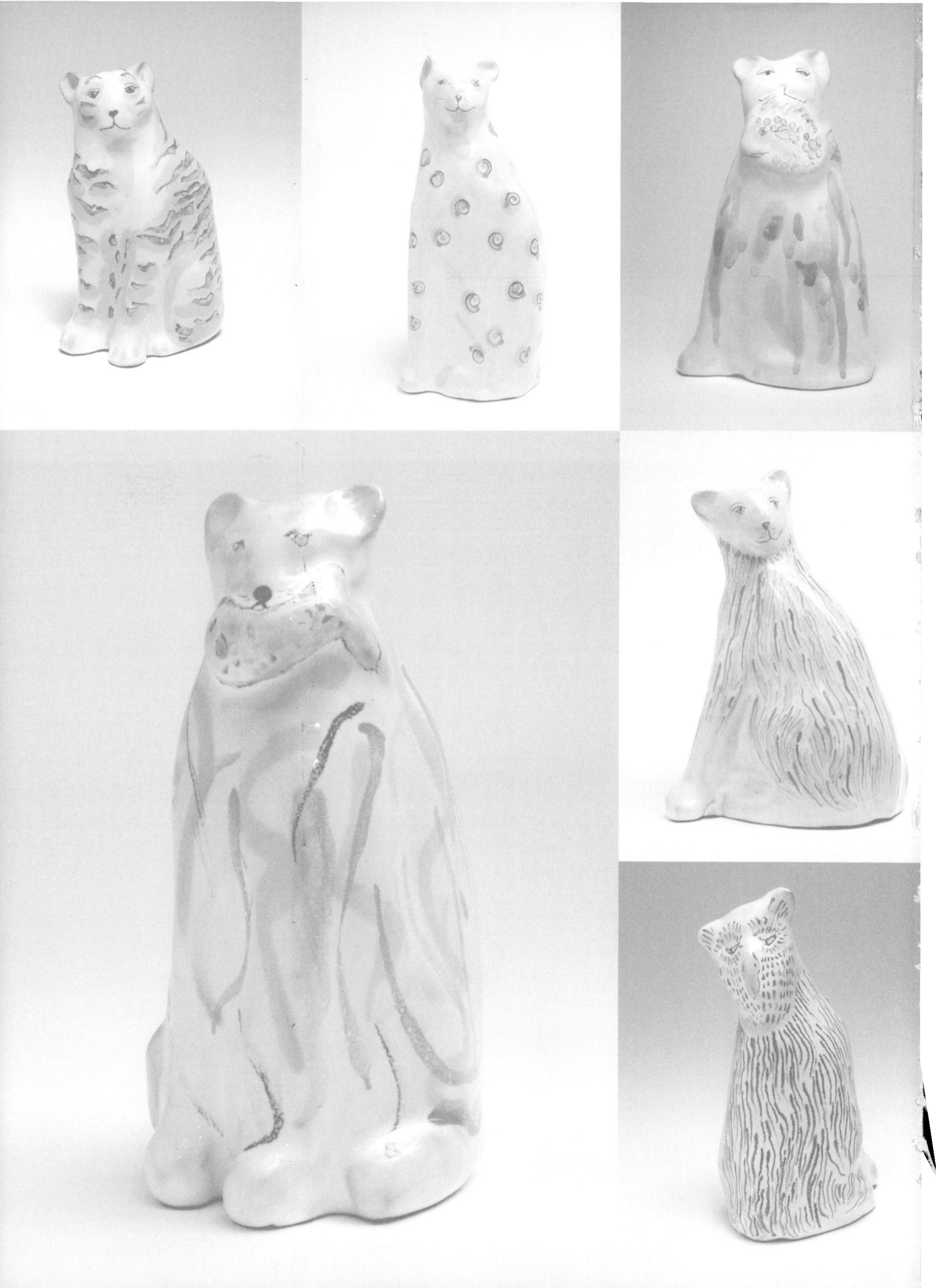